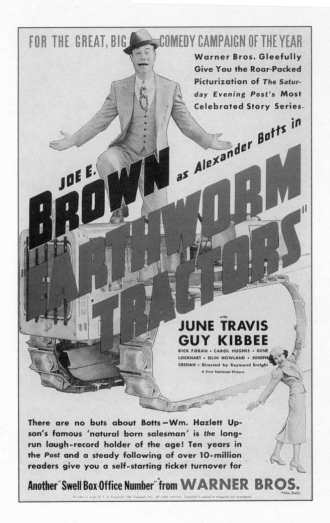

FOR THE GREAT, BIG COMEDY CAMPAIGN OF THE YEAR

Warner Bros. Gleefully Give You the Roar-Packed Picturization of *The Saturday Evening Post's* Most Celebrated Story Series—

JOE E. BROWN as Alexander Botts in

"EARTHWORM TRACTORS"

with **JUNE TRAVIS**
GUY KIBBEE

DICK FORAN • CAROL HUGHES • GENE LOCKHART • OLIN HOWLAND • JOSEPH CREHAN • Directed by Raymond Enright
A First National Picture

There are no buts about Botts—Wm. Hazlett Upson's famous 'natural born salesman' is *the* long-run laugh-record holder of the age! Ten years in the *Post* and a steady following of over 10-million readers give you a self-starting ticket turnover for

Another "Swell Box-Office Number" from **WARNER BROS.**

"Film Daily

The Fabulous Saga of

ALEXANDER
BOTTS
and the EARTHWORM TRACTOR

By William Hazlett Upson
VOYAGEUR PRESS

Edited by Margret Aldrich
Designed by Maria Friedrich
Printed in China

03   04   05   5   4   3   2

Library of Congress Cataloging-in-Publication Data

Upson, William Hazlett, 1891–1975
    The fabulous saga of Alexander Botts and the Earthworm tractor / William Hazlett Upson.
        p. cm.
    ISBN 0-89658-530-1 (alk. paper)
        1. Botts, Alexander (Fictitious character)—Fiction. 2. Tractor industry—Fiction. 3. Humorous stories, American. 4. Sales personnel—Fiction. 5. Tractors—Fiction. I. Title.

    PS3541.P74 A6 2001
    813'.52–dc21   2001023380

Distributed in Canada by Raincoast Books, 9050 Shaughnessy Street, Vancouver, B.C. V6P 6E5

Published by Voyageur Press, Inc.
123 North Second Street, P.O. Box 338, Stillwater, MN 55082 U.S.A.
651-430-2210, fax 651-430-2211
books@voyageurpress.com
www.voyageurpress.com

Educators, fundraisers, premium and gift buyers, publicists, and marketing managers: Looking for creative products and new sales ideas? Voyageur Press books are available at special discounts when purchased in quantities, and special editions can be created to your specifications. For details contact the marketing department at 800-888-9653.

Cover image: *"Alexander Botts" waves from atop an Earthworm tractor in this photograph from the 1936 film Earthworm Tractors, starring Joe E. Brown. (Wisconsin Center for Film and Theater Research)*

Frontispiece: *Always a showman, Alexander Botts, portrayed by Joe E. Brown, poses triumphantly atop a rugged Earthworm tractor on this movie poster. The poster urges its potential audience to come and see the "Roar-Packed Picturization of the Saturday Evening Post's Most Celebrated Story Series." (Wisconsin Center for Film and Theater Research)*

Acknowledgments

Voyageur Press would like to thank the following people for their generous help with this project: Dike Blair; Jeremy Brunner at Nostalgia Family Video; Connell B. Gallagher and Sylvia Bugbee at the University of Vermont Bailey/Howe Library; Dorinda Hartmann at the Wisconsin Center for Film and Theater Research; and Lisa Hinzman at the State Historical Society of Wisconsin Visual Materials Archive.

As this movie still from Earthworm Tractors *illustrates, Alexander Botts, portrayed here by Joe E. Brown, could be a very persuasive salesman. (Wisconsin Center for Film and Theater Research)*

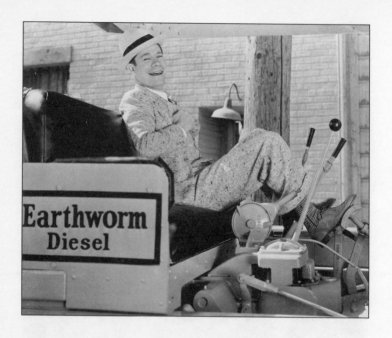

The role of Alexander Botts in the 1936 motion picture Earthworm Tractors *was perfect for rubber-faced comedic actor Joe E. Brown. With twinkling eyes and a winning smile, the actor looks as though he would have made a very convincing tractor salesman. (Wisconsin Center for Film and Theater Research)*

Contents

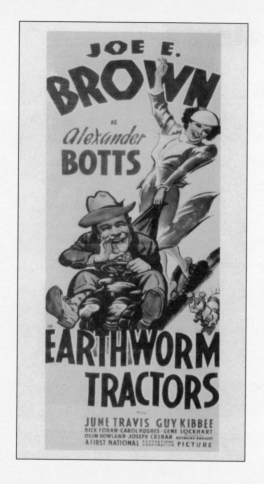

With adventures and mishaps galore, Alexander Botts was a natural for the big screen. This movie poster lists Joe E. Brown as Botts, June Travis as his love interest, and Guy Kibbee as the cantankerous sales prospect.

Introduction

Tractor salesman extraordinaire Alexander Botts was created by writer William Hazlett Upson for a story entitled "I'm a Natural-Born Salesman" that first appeared in the *Saturday Evening Post* on April 16, 1927. Botts sold the fictitious Earthworm crawler tractors, made by the Farmers' Friend Tractor Company of Earthworm City, Illinois. The Earthworm was based on Caterpillar's crawlers, but Botts was a true original.

Botts sprung from Upson's own experience working in the Holt Caterpillar Service Department from 1919 to 1924. "I spent a lot of time traveling around the country shooting trouble, repairing tractors, and instructing the operators," Upson wrote about his time with Holt. "My main job was to follow up the salesmen and try to make the tractors do what the salesmen had said they would. In this way I came to know more about salesmen than they know about themselves."

In the 1950s, Upson offered the following biography of his hero: "Alexander Botts was born in Smedleytown, Iowa, on March 15, 1892, the son of a prosperous farmer. He finished high school there; then embarked on a series of jobs—none of them quite worthy of his mettle. In these early days the largest piece of machinery he sold was the Excelsior Peerless Self-Adjusting Safety Razor Blade Sharpener. He became interested in heavy machinery in 1918 while serving in France as a cook with the motorized field artillery. In March, 1920, he was hired as a salesman by the Farmers' Friend Tractor Company, which later became the Earthworm Tractor Company.

"On April 12, 1926, he met Miss Mildred Deane, the attractive daughter of an Earthworm dealer in Mercedillo, California. Seven days later they were married. Mildred, later nicknamed Gadget, had attended the language schools at Middlebury College (Vermont) and acted as interpreter for her husband when he was sent to Europe in 1928 to open new tractor outlets there.

"Mr. and Mrs. Botts returned from Europe in early 1929 to await the birth of Alexander Botts, Jr., who arrived in February along with a twin sister, Little Gadget."

Upson's stories about Botts became so popular that he continued the series for decades, eventually penning 112 Botts tales for the *Saturday Evening Post* between 1927 and 1975. Battling mishaps and misadventures, a wary boss named Gilbert Henderson, and a slew of competing salesmen from the Steel Elephant, Behemoth, Goliath, Rough Rider, and Mammoth tractor companies, Alexander Botts and his Earthworms plowed through any obstacle with irrepressible ambition and perseverance.

Although much of Botts's success as a salesman seems to stem from a healthy dose of luck, and many of his sales strategies were questionable, Upson was quick to list several virtues held by Botts that made him a good salesman: "He is an extrovert. He likes people. He sincerely wants to help the customer. He never puts across a sale unless the customer will benefit. He has courage, resourcefulness. He never holds a grudge. He is, in short, a good egg."

The popularity of Upson's "good egg" spread from the *Saturday Evening Post* to other forms of media as well. Botts appeared in a comic strip called "Alexander the Great"; radio adaptations of his adverntures were broadcast; several anthologies of his stories were published; and in 1936, Hollywood immortalized the much-loved salesman in the movie *Earthworm Tractors* starring comedian actor Joe E. Brown as Botts, June Travis as his love interest, and Guy Kibbee as the stubborn sales prospect.

Joe E. Brown reportedly threw himself into the role of the determined salesman, using mud for his stage makeup, insisting on doing his own stunts (even though the antics of Alexander Botts were often dangerous), and learning how to operate the mightly crawlers on the movie set himself. Brown coined a new phrase, telling one reporter, "A guy that rides a mule is known as a muleskinner . . . I guess as long as I wrangle Caterpillars I must

Published in 1929, Alexander Botts: Earthworm Tractors *was the first book of Botts stories to be collected from the* Saturday Evening Post.

be a 'Catskinner.'" The movie crew took over the Caterpillar plant in Peoria, Illinois, for several weeks to make the film, and when the movie made its debut, it was first shown fittingly enough in the Peoria theater.

This collection of Upson's best Botts adventures is the first in print since the 1970s. It begins with Botts's first day on the job in "I'm a Natural-Born Salesman," has classics like "The Big Sales Talk" and "Tractors on Parade," includes "Botts and the Daredevil Driver," which does not appear in any other anthology, and features two never-before-published stories about Botts and his Earthworms: "Wrong Again, Henderson" and "Botts and the Fire Bug." The fabulous saga of our favorite salesman will entertain fans both old and new. So find a comfortable chair, sit back, and prepare to celebrate the triumphant return of Alexander Botts and his amazing Earthworm tractors.

ALEXANDER THE GREAT—A Soul Inspired

By WILLIAM HAZLETT UPSON

William Hazlett Upson converted his stories about Botts and the Earthworm tractor into a comic strip entitled "Alexander the Great," which appeared in newspapers from 1936 to 1938. (University of Vermont Bailey/Howe Library)

I'm a Natural-Born Salesman

STONEWALL JACKSON HOTEL
MEMPHIS, TENNESSEE

March 15, 1920.

The Farmers' Friend Tractor Company,
Earthworm City, Ill.

GENTLEMEN: I have decided you are the best tractor company in the country, and consequently I am giving you first chance to hire me as your salesman to sell tractors in this region.

I'm a natural-born salesman, have a very quick mind, am twenty-eight years old, am honest and reliable, and can give references if required. I have already had considerable experience as a machinery salesman, and I became familiar with your Earthworm tractors as a member of the motorized field artillery in France. I can demonstrate tractors as well as sell them.

When do I start work?

Very truly yours,
ALEXANDER BOTTS.

FARMERS' FRIEND TRACTOR COMPANY
MAKERS OF EARTHWORM TRACTORS
EARTHWORM CITY, ILLINOIS

March 17, 1920.

Mr. Alexander Botts,
Stonewall Jackson Hotel,
Memphis, Tenn.

DEAR MR. BOTTS: Your letter is received. We have no opening for a salesman at present, but we are badly in need of a service mechanic. As you say you are familiar with our tractors, we will try you out on this job, at $100 per month plus traveling expenses.

You will report at once to our Mr. George Healy, salesman for Tennessee and Mississippi, who is now at the Dartmouth Hotel, Memphis. You will go with him to Cyprus City, Mississippi, to demonstrate a ten ton Earthworm tractor for Mr. Jackson, a lumber operator of that place. Mr. Healy will tell you just what you are to do.

We enclose check for $100 advance expense money.

Very truly,

GILBERT HENDERSON,
Sales Manager.

STONEWALL JACKSON HOTEL
MEMPHIS, TENNESSEE

March 19, 1920.

The Farmers' Friend Tractor Company,
Earthworm City, Ill.

GENTLEMEN: As soon as your letter came, I went around to see Mr. Healy, and it is lucky for you that you hired me, because Mr. Healy has just been taken sick with appendicitis. They were getting ready to take him to the hospital, and he was pretty weak, but he managed to tell me that the tractor for the demonstration had already arrived at the freight station in Cyprus City.

He also explained that this Mr. Jackson down there owns about a million feet of cyprus timber which he wants to get out and sell right away before the present high price of lumber goes down. It seems the ground is so swampy and soft from the winter rains that with his present equipment of mules and wagons he won't be able to move any of his timber until summer.

But Mr. Healy was down there a couple of weeks ago, and he arranged to put on a demonstration to show Mr. Jackson that an Earthworm tractor can go into those swamps and drag out the timber right away. Mr. Jackson said he would buy the tractor if it did the work, and Mr. Healy was feeling very low because he was sick and couldn't go down to hold the demonstration.

"You can rest easy, Mr. Healy," I said. "When you look at me you're gazing on a natural-born salesman. I will go down there and do your work as well as mine. I will put on a swell demonstration, and then I will sell the goods."

As Mr. Healy did not seem to know just what to say to this, I gathered up all his order blanks, selling literature, price lists, etc., and also the bill of lading and the check to pay the freight on the tractor. Then I wished him good luck, and left.

From this you can see that I am quick to grasp an opportunity, and that you made no mistake in hiring me. I am leaving for Cyprus City tonight.

Cordially yours,
ALEXANDER BOTTS.

FARMERS' FRIEND TRACTOR COMPANY
SALESMAN'S DAILY REPORT
Date: March 20, 1920.
Written from: Delta Hotel, Cyprus City, Miss.
Written by: Alexander Botts, Service Mechanic and Pinch Hitter Salesman.

I found this pad of salesman's report blanks among the stuff I got from Mr. Healy. I see by the instructions on the cover that each salesman is supposed to send in a full and complete report of everything he does, so I will give you all the particulars of a very busy day.

I arrived at 7:51 this morning at Cyprus City—which turns out to be pretty much of a hick town in what they call the Yazoo Delta. The whole country here is nothing but a swamp, and the main street of the town ends in a high bank that they call a levee, on the other side of which is the Mississippi River flowing along about twenty feet higher than the town.

After alighting from the train, and after noting that it was a cloudy day and looked like rain, I engaged a room at the Delta Hotel. I then hurried over to the freight station where I found the big ten ton Earthworm tractor on the unloading platform. They had dragged it off the car with a block and tackle. And when I saw that beautiful machine standing there so big and powerful, with its fine wide tracks like an army tank, with its elegant new shiny paint, and with its stylish cab for the driver, I will admit that I felt a glow of pride to think that I was the salesman and service mechanic for such a splendid piece of machinery.

(NOTE: Of course, as I said in my letter, I am an old machinery salesman. But the largest thing I ever sold before was the Excelsior Peerless Self-adjusting Automatic Safety Razor Blade Sharpener. I did very well with this machine, but I could not take the pride in it that I feel I am going to have in this wonderful ten ton Earthworm tractor.)

After paying the freight, I hired several guys from the town garage to put gas and oil in the tractor, and then I started them bolting the little cleats onto the tracks. You see I am right tip on my toes all the time. I think of everything. And I figured that if we were going through the mud we would need these cleats to prevent slipping. While they were being put on, I stepped over to the office of Mr. Johnson, the lumber man.

(NOTE: This bird's name is Johnson—not Jackson, as you and Mr. Healy told me. Also it strikes me that Mr. Healy may have been fairly sick even as long as two weeks ago when he was down here. In addition to getting the name wrong, he did very poor work in preparing this prospect. He did not seem to be in a buying mood at all.)

As soon as I had explained my errand to this Mr. Johnson— who is a very large, hard-boiled bozo—he gave me what you might call a horse laugh. "You are wasting your time," he said. "I told that fool salesman who was here before that tractors would be no good to me. All my timber is four miles away on the other side of the Great Gumbo Swamp, which means that it would have to be brought through mud that is deeper and stickier than anything you ever seen, young feller."

"You would like to get it out, wouldn't you?" I asked.

"I sure would," he said, "but it's impossible. You don't understand conditions down here. Right on the roads the mules and horses sink in up to their bellies; and when you get off the roads, even ducks and turtles can hardly navigate."

"The Earthworm tractor," I said, "has more power than any duck or turtle. And if you'll come out with me, I'll show you that I can pull your logs through that swamp."

"I can't afford to waste my time with such crazy ideas," he said. "I've tried motor equipment. I have a motor truck now that is stuck three feet deep right on the main road at the edge of town."

"All right," I said, always quick to grasp an opportunity, "how about coming along with me while I pull out your truck?"

"Well," said Mr. Johnson, "I can spare about an hour this morning. If you'll go right now, I'll go with you—although I doubt if you can even pull out the truck. And even if you do, I won't buy your tractor."

"How about going this afternoon?" I asked.

"I'll be busy this afternoon. It's now or never."

"Come on!" I said.

We went over to the freight platform, and as the cleats were now all bolted on we both climbed into the cab.

(NOTE: I will explain that I was sorry that Mr. Johnson had been unable to wait until afternoon, as I had intended to use the morning in practicing up on driving the machine. It is true, as I said in my letter, that I became familiar with Earthworm tractors when I was a member of a motorized artillery outfit in France, but as my job in the artillery was that of cook, and as I had never before sat in the seat of one of these tractors, I was not as familiar with the details of driving as I might have wished. However, I was pleased to see that the tractor seemed to have a clutch and gear shift like the automobiles I have often driven, and a pair of handle bars for steering very much like those of a tricycle I had operated in my early boyhood.)

I sat down on the driver's seat with reasonable confidence; Mr. Johnson sat down beside me; and one of the garage men cranked up the motor. It started at once, and when I heard the splendid roar of the powerful exhaust, and saw that thirty or forty of the inhabitants, both white and otherwise, were standing around with wondering and admiring faces, I can tell you I felt proud of myself. I put the gear in low, opened the throttle, and let in the clutch.

(NOTE: I would suggest that you tell your chief engineer, or whoever it is that designs your tractors, that he ought to put in a standard gear shift. You can understand that it is very annoying— after you have pulled the gear shift lever to the left and then back—to find that instead of being low you are really in reverse.)

As I said, I opened the throttle, let in the clutch, and started forward. But I found that when I started forward, I was really— on account of the funny gear shift—moving backwards. And instead of going down the gentle slope of the ramp in front, the whole works backed off the rear edge of the platform, dropping at least four feet into a pile of crates with such a sickening crash that I thought the machine was wrecked and both of us killed.

But it soon appeared that, although we were both very much shaken up, we were still alive—especially Mr. Johnson, who began talking so loud and vigorously that I saw I need have no worry about his health. After I had got Mr. Johnson quieted down a bit; I inspected the machine and found that it was not hurt at all. As I am always alert to seize an opportunity, I told Mr. Johnson that I had run off the platform on purpose to show him how strongly built the tractor was. Then, after I had promised I would not make any more of these jumps, he consented to remain in the tractor, and we started off again.

(NOTE: Kindly tell your chief engineer that Alexander Botts congratulates him on producing a practically unbreakable tractor. But tell him that I wish he would design some thicker and softer seat cushions. If the base of the chief engineer's spine was as sore as mine still is, he would realize that there are times when good thick seat cushions are highly desirable.)

As we drove up the main street of Cyprus City, with a large

crowd of admiring natives following after, I seemed to smell something burning. At once I stopped, opened up the hood, and discovered that the paint on the cylinders was crackling and smoking like bacon in a frying pan.

"Perhaps," suggested Mr. Johnson, "there is no water in the radiator."

I promptly inspected the radiator, and, sure enough, that was the trouble.

(NOTE: I would suggest that if your chief engineer would design an air-cooled motor for the tractor, such incidents as the above would be avoided.)

I borrowed a pail from a store, and filled the radiator. Apparently, owing to my alertness in this emergency, no damage had been done.

When we started up again, we had not gone more than a few yards before I felt the tractor give a little lurch. After we had got a little farther along I looked back, and right at the side of the street I saw one of the biggest fountains I have ever seen in all my life. A solid column of water about eight inches thick was spouting high in the air, spreading out at the top like a mushroom, and raining down all around like Niagara Falls.

I heard somebody yell something about a fire plug; and, as I have a quick mind, I saw right away what had happened. The hood of the tractor is so big that it had prevented me from seeing a fire plug right in front of me. I had unfortunately run right into it, and as it was of very cheap, inferior construction, it had broken right off.

For a while there was great excitement, with people running here and there, hollering and yelling. The sheriff came up and took my name, as he seemed to think I was to blame—in spite of the fact that the fire plug was in such an exposed position. I was a bit worried at the way the water was accumulating in the street, and consequently I was much relieved when they finally got hold of the water works authorities and got the water turned off. You see the fire mains here are connected to the Mississippi River, and if they had not turned the water off the whole river would have flowed into the business district of Cyprus City.

(NOTE: I would suggest that your chief engineer design these tractor hoods a little lower so as to avoid such accidents in the future.)

After the water had been turned off, we got under way again, clanking along the main street in high gear, and then driving out of town to the eastward over one of the muddiest roads I ever saw. The tractor, on account of its wide tracks, stayed right up on top of the mud, and rolled along as easy and smooth as a Pullman car. Behind us a large crowd of local sightseers floundered along as best they could—some of them wading through the mud and slop, and others riding in buggies pulled by horses or mules.

Mr. Johnson acted as if he was pretty sore—and I did not blame him. Although the various mishaps and accidents we had been through were unavoidable and not my fault at all, I could understand that they might have been very annoying to my passenger. Perhaps that is one reason I am such a good salesman; I can always get the other fellow's point of view. I livened up the journey a bit by telling Mr. Johnson a number of Irish jokes, but I did not seem to get any laughs—possibly because the motor made so much noise Mr. Johnson couldn't hear me.

By this time I had got the hang of driving the machine very well, and I was going along like a veteran. When we reached Mr. Johnson's truck—which was deep in the mud at the side of the road about a half mile from town—I swung around and backed up in front of it in great style.

The road, as I have said, was soft and muddy enough; but off to the right was a low, flat stretch of swamp land that looked much muddier, and a whole lot softer. There were patches of standing water here and there, and most of it was covered with canebrake—which is a growth of tall canes that look like bamboo fishing poles.

Mr. Johnson pointed out over this mass of canebrake and mud. "That is an arm of the Great Gumbo Swamp," he yelled very loud so I could hear him above the noise of the motor. "Your machine may be able to navigate these roads, but it would never pull a load through a slough like that."

I rather doubted it myself, but I didn't admit it. "First of all," I said, "we'll pull out this truck."

We both got out of the tractor, and right away we sank up to our knees in the soft sticky mud. The truck was a big one, loaded with lumber, and it was mired down so deep that the wheels were practically out of sight, and the body seemed to be resting on the ground. Mr. Johnson didn't think the tractor could budge it, but I told him to get into the driver's seat of the truck so he could steer it when it got going.

By this time a gentle rain had started up, and Mr. Johnson told me to hurry up as the truck had no cab and he was getting wet. I grabbed a big chain out of the truck tool box, and told Mr. Johnson to get out his watch. He did so.

"In just thirty seconds," I said, "things are going to start moving around here."

I then rapidly hooked one end of the chain to the back of the tractor, fastened the other end to the truck, sprang into the tractor seat, and started the splendid machine moving forward. As the tractor rolled steadily and powerfully down the road, I could hear the shouting of the crowd even above the noise of the motor. Looking around, however, I saw that something was wrong. The truck—or rather, the major portion of it—was still in the same place, and I was pulling only the radiator. As I had a quick mind, I saw at once what had happened. Quite naturally, I had slung the chain around the handiest thing on the front of the truck—which happened to be the radiator cap. And as the truck was of a cheap make, with the radiator not properly anchored, if had come off.

I stopped at once, and then I had to spend about ten minutes calming down Mr. Johnson by assuring him that the Farmers' Friend Tractor Company would pay for a new radiator. I backed up to the truck again, and Mr. Johnson took the chain himself, and by burrowing down in the mud managed to get it fastened around the front axle. Then he climbed back into the seat of the truck and scowled at me very disagreeably. By this time the rain was falling fairly briskly, and this may have had something to do with his ill humor.

When I started up again, everything went well. The motor roared, the cleats on the tracks dug into the mud, and slowly and majestically the tractor moved down the road, dragging the heavy truck through the mud behind it.

At this point I stuck my head out of the tractor cab to acknowledge the cheers of the bystanders, and in so doing I unfortunately knocked off my hat, which was caught by the wind and blown some distance away. At once I jumped out and began chasing it through the mud. The crowd began to shout and yell, but I paid no attention to this noise until I had reached my hat and picked it up—which took me some time, as the hat had blown a good ways, and I could not make any speed through the mud. When at last I looked around, I saw that a very curious thing had happened.

In getting out of the tractor I had accidentally pulled on one of the handle bars enough to turn the tractor sidewise. And in my natural excitement—the hat having cost me $8.98 last week in Memphis—I had forgotten to pull out the clutch. So when I looked up, I saw that the tractor, with Mr. Johnson and his truck in tow, was headed right out into the Great Gumbo Swamp. It had already got a good start, and it was going strong. As Mr. Johnson seemed to be waving and yelling for help, I ran after him. But as soon as I got off the road the mud was so deep and soft that I could make no headway at all. Several of the bystanders also attempted to follow, but had to give it up as a bad job. There was nothing to do but let poor Mr. Johnson go dragging off through the swamp.

And, although I was really sorry to see Mr. Johnson going off all by himself this way, with no protection from the pouring rain, I could not help feeling a thrill of pride when I saw how the great ten ton Earthworm tractor was eating up that terrible soft mud. The wide tracks kept it from sinking in more than a few inches; the cleats gave it good traction; and the motor was so powerful that it pulled that big truck like it was a mere matchbox—and this in spite of the fact that the truck sank in so deep that it plowed a regular ditch as it went along.

As I am a natural-born salesman, and quick to grasp every

opportunity, I yelled a little sales talk after Mr. Johnson. "It's all right," I hollered; "I'm doing this on purpose to show you that the Earthworm can go through any swamp you got." But I doubt if he heard me; the roar of the tractor motor was too loud. And a moment later the tractor, the truck, and Mr. Johnson had disappeared in the canebrake.

While I was considering what to do next, a nice looking man in a corduroy suit came over to me from one of the groups of bystanders. "This is only an arm of the Great Gumbo Swamp," he said. "If that tractor doesn't mire down, and if it goes straight, it will come out on the levee on the other side about a mile from here."

"An Earthworm tractor never mires down," I said. "And as long as there is nobody there to pull on the handlebars, it can't help going straight."

"All right," said the man, "if you want to hop in my buggy, I'll drive you back to town and out the levee so we can meet it when it gets there."

"Fine!" I said. "Let's go." I have always been noted for my quick decisions, being similar to Napoleon in this particular. I at once climbed in the buggy with the man in the corduroy suit, and he drove the horse as fast as possible into town and then out the levee, with all the sightseers plowing along behind—both on foot and in buggies.

When we reached the place where the tractor ought to come out, we stopped and listened. Far out in the swamp we could hear the roar of the tractor motor. It got gradually louder and louder. We waited. It was still raining hard. Suddenly there was a shout from the crowd. The tractor came nosing out of the canebrake, and a moment later it had reached the bottom of the levee, with the big truck and Mr. Johnson dragging along behind. As the tractor was in low gear, I had no trouble in jumping aboard and stopping it—and it is just as well I was there to do this. If I had not stopped it, it would have shot right on over the levee and into the Mississippi River, probably drowning poor Mr. Johnson.

As it was, Mr. Johnson was as wet as a sponge, on account of the heavy rain, and because he had been too cheap to get himself a truck with a cab on it. But he was a long way from being drowned. In fact, he seemed very lively; and as I got down from the tractor he jumped out of the truck and came running at me, waving his arms around, and shouting and yelling, and with a very dirty look on his face. What he had to say to me would fill a small book; in fact, he said so much that I'm afraid I will have to put off telling you about it until my report tomorrow.

It is now midnight and I am very tired, so I will merely enclose my expense account for the day and wish you a pleasant good night. Kindly send check to cover expenses as soon as possible. As you will see, my $100 advance is already gone, and I have had to pay money out of my own pocket.

Cordially yours,
ALEXANDER BOTTS.

EXPENSE ACCOUNT

Railroad fare (Memphis to Cyprus City).	$6.10
Pullman ticket	3.20
Gas and oil for tractor	8.50
Labor (putting on cleats, etc.)	9.00
36 doz. eggs at 50 cents per doz	18.00

(NOTE: It seems the crates we landed on when we dropped off the freight platform were full of eggs.)

1 plate glass window	80.00

(NOTE: I forgot to say in my report that in the confusion following the breaking of the fire plug I accidentally side-swiped a drug store with the tractor.)

Radiator for truck, and labor to install	46.75
Cleaning hat and pressing trousers	3.50
TOTAL	$175.05

(NOTE: I will list the hotel bill, the bill for the fire plug, and other expenses when I pay them.)

FARMERS' FRIEND TRACTOR COMPANY
SALESMAN'S DAILY REPORT
Date: March 21, 1920.
Written from: Delta Hotel, Cyprus City, Miss.
Written by: Alexander Botts.

I will take up the report of my activities at the point where I stopped yesterday when Mr. Johnson had just gotten out of the truck and was coming in my direction. As I stated, he had a great deal to say. Instead of being grateful to me for having given him such a splendid demonstration of the ability of the Earthworm tractor to go through a swamp, and instead of thanking me for saving his life by stopping him just as he was about to shoot over the levee into the Mississippi River, he began using very abusive language which I will not repeat except to say that he told me he would not buy my tractor and that he never wanted to see me or my damn machinery again. He also said he was going to slam me down in the mud and jump on my face, and it took six of the bystanders to hold him and prevent him from doing this. And although there were six of them, they had a lot of trouble holding him, owing to the fact that he was so wet and slippery from the rain.

As I am a natural-born salesman, I saw right away that this was not an auspicious time to give Mr. Johnson any sales talk about tractors. I decided to wait until later, and I walked back to the tractor in a dignified manner, looking back over my shoulder, however, to make sure Mr. Johnson was not getting away from the guys that were holding him.

After they had led Mr. Johnson back to town, I made up my mind to be a good sport, and I hauled his truck into town and left it at the garage to be repaired. The rest of the day I spent settling up various expense items—which appeared on my yesterday's expense account—and in writing up my report. When I finally went to bed at midnight, it was with a glow of pride that I thought of the splendid work I had done on the first day of my employment with the great Farmers' Friend Tractor Company, Makers of Earthworm Tractors. Although I had not as yet made any sales, I could congratulate myself on having put on the best tractor demonstration ever seen in Cyprus City, Mississippi.

This morning, after breakfast, I had a visit from the nice-looking man in the corduroy suit who gave me the buggy ride yesterday.

"I am a lumber operator," he said, "and I have a lot of cyprus back in the swamps that I have been wanting to get out. I haven't been able to move it because the ground has been so soft. However, since I saw your tractor drag that big heavy truck through the swamp yesterday, I know that it is just what I want. I understand the price is $6000, and if you will let me have the machine right away I will take you over to the bank and give you a certified check for that amount."

"Well," I said, "I was supposed to sell this machine to Mr. Johnson, but as he has had a chance at it and hasn't taken it, I suppose I might as well let you have it."

"I don't see why you gave him first chance," said the man in the corduroy suit. "When your other salesman, Mr. Healy, was down here, I gave him more encouragement than anybody else he talked to. And he said he would ship a tractor down here and put on a demonstration for me."

"By the way," I said, "what is your name?"

"William Jackson," he said.

As I have a quick mind, I saw at once what had happened. This was the guy I had been supposed to give the demonstration for in the first place, but I had very naturally confused his name with that of Mr. Johnson. There ought to be a law against two men with such similar names being in the same kind of business in the same town.

However, it had come out all right. And, as I am a natural-born salesman, I decided that the thing to do was to take Mr. Jackson over to the bank right away—which I did. And now the tractor is his.

I enclose the certified check. And I have decided to remain in town several days more on the chance of selling some more machines.

Cordially yours,
ALEXANDER BOTTS.

TELEGRAM

EARTHWORM CITY ILLS 1015A MAR 22 1920

ALEXANDER BOTTS
DELTA HOTEL
CYPRUS CITY MISS
YOUR FIRST REPORT AND EXPENSE ACCOUNT RE-
CEIVED STOP YOU ARE FIRED STOP WILL DISCUSS
THAT EXPENSE ACCOUNT BY LETTER STOP IF YOU
SO MUCH AS TOUCH THAT TRACTOR AGAIN WE WILL
PROSECUTE YOU TO THE FULLEST EXTENT OF THE
LAW

    FARMERS FRIEND TRACTOR COMPANY
    GILBERT HENDERSON SALES MANAGER

NIGHT LETTER

CYPRUS CITY MISS 510P MAR 22 1920

FARMERS FRIEND TRACTOR CO
EARTHWORM CITY ILLS
YOUR TELEGRAM HERE STOP WAIT TILL YOU GET MY
SECOND REPORT STOP AND THAT IS NOT ALL STOP
THE WHOLE TOWN IS TALKING ABOUT MY WONDER-
FUL TRACTOR DEMONSTRATION STOP JOHNSON
HAS COME AROUND AND ORDERED TWO TRACTORS
STOP THE LEVEE CONSTRUCTION COMPANY OF THIS
PLACE HAS ORDERED ONE STOP NEXT WEEK IS TO
BE QUOTE USE MORE TRACTORS WEEK UNQUOTE

IN CYPRUS CITY STOP MASS MEETING MONDAY TO DECIDE HOW MANY EARTHWORMS THE CITY WILL BUY FOR GRADING ROADS STOP LUMBERMENS MASS MEETING TUESDAY AT WHICH I WILL URGE THEM TO BUY TRACTORS AND JACKSON AND JOHNSON WILL BACK ME UP STOP WEDNESDAY THURSDAY FRIDAY AND SATURDAY RESERVED FOR WRITING UP ORDERS FROM LUMBERMEN CON-TRACTORS AND OTHERS STOP TELL YOUR CHIEF ENGINEER TO GET READY TO INCREASE PRODUC-TION STOP YOU BETTER RECONSIDER YOUR WIRE OF THIS MORNING

 ALEXANDER BOTTS

TELEGRAM

EARTHWORM CITY ILLS 945A MAR 23 1920

ALEXANDER BOTTS

DELTA HOTEL

CYPRUS CITY MISS

OUR WIRE OF YESTERDAY STANDS STOP YOUR JOB AS SERVICE MECHANIC WITH THIS COMPANY IS GONE FOREVER STOP WE ARE PUTTING YOU ON PAY ROLL AS SALESMAN STOP TWO HUNDRED PER WEEK PLUS EXPENSES PLUS FIVE PER CENT COMMISSION ON ALL SALES

 FARMERS FRIEND TRACTOR COMPANY

 GILBERT HENDERSON SALES MANAGER

The Big Sales Talk

FARMERS' FRIEND TRACTOR COMPANY
MAKERS OF EARTHWORM TRACTORS
EARTHWORM CITY, ILLINOIS

November 30, 1921.

Mr. Alexander Botts,
McAlpin Hotel,
New York City.

DEAR MR. BOTTS: We want you to go to Chipman Falls, Vermont, to take charge of a demonstration which we have arranged to hold next Monday for Mr. Job Chipman, a big lumber operator of that place. Mr. Chipman is considering replacing most of his horses with tractors. He wants to use the machines in plowing out his wood roads following snow storms, and also in hauling sleds loaded with logs along these roads, after they have been sprinkled with water to give them an ice surface.

We have already shipped to Chipman Falls a ten ton Earthworm tractor equipped with snowplow, winter cab, and ice-spike grousers; and we are sending our service man, Mr. Samuel Simpson, to operate it.

You will have competition; we understand that the Mammoth Tractor Company will be on hand with one of their machines. But we have every confidence in your ability as a salesman, and we are relying on you to get Mr. Chipman's order for one or more Earthworms.

Very sincerely,
GILBERT HENDERSON,
Sales Manager.

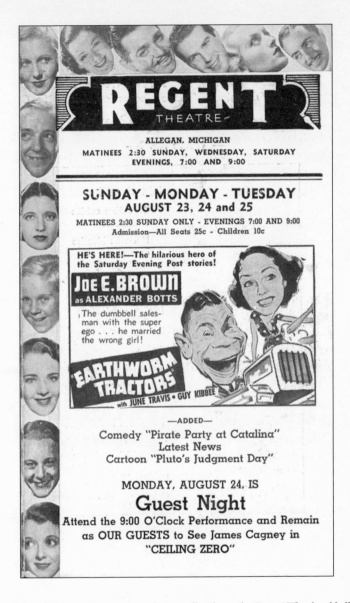

Although this movie promotional piece calls Alexander Botts "The dumbbell salesman with the super ego," the faithful Botts reader may deduce that there is a method to the salesman's madness.

FARMERS' FRIEND TRACTOR COMPANY
SALESMAN'S DAILY REPORT
Date: Saturday, December 4, 1921.
Written from: New York City.
Written by: Alexander Botts, Salesman.

It was indeed a pleasure to receive your letter of November 30; and you may be sure that you are making no mistake in sending me on this important mission.

As you know, I have always been one of the best natural talkers in your whole organization. But I am never satisfied; I am always trying to improve myself. And, realizing the fact that I had never had any experience in selling tractors to northern lumbermen, I have spent the past two days—ever since receiving your letter—at the New York Public Library studying up on all phases of lumber business as it is practised in the northern part of the country. It gives me great pleasure to inform you that I have now acquired all the information and knowledge that are necessary in order to adapt my already splendid sales arguments to the particular conditions which I shall meet with when I begin working on Mr. Job Chipman. It is not exaggerating to say that I will start on this selling campaign with a sales talk that is really BIG. I can hardly wait to get going.

I have engaged a berth on the sleeper leaving Grand Central tomorrow night and arriving at Chipman Falls early Monday morning. You may rest assured that by Monday night Mr. Chipman's order will be safely in the mails and on its way to your office.

Very sincerely yours,
ALEXANDER BOTTS.

FARMERS' FRIEND TRACTOR COMPANY
SALESMAN'S DAILY REPORT
Date: Monday, December 6, 1921.
Written from: Chipman Falls, Vermont.
Written by: Alexander Botts, Salesman.

Well, I have arrived, and I have put in a very busy day. But I may as well admit that things are not going as good as I had expected. In fact, I have run into a veritable nightmare of unexpected difficulties and misfortunes which are absolutely unparalleled in my experience as a salesman for the Farmers' Friend Tractor Company. I will relate exactly what has happened so you can see that I have done everything I could, but that fate has been against me.

When I first got off the train at seven o'clock this morning I had no hint of impending misfortune. The weather was dark and cloudy and very cold, but there was no sign of snow on the ground. I was sorry that we would be unable to show Mr. Chipman how well the Earthworm can travel through snow, but I was not worried. A demonstration is always a good thing, but the real heart and soul of any selling campaign is the sales talk, and I was confident in my knowledge that in this department of the game I was supreme.

As I walked up to the hotel I noted that the town of Chipman Falls is in a deep narrow valley in the Green Mountains, and that it consists of the railroad station, a small hotel, several dozen houses, and a large sawmill. The steep mountain slopes on both sides of the valley are covered with timber. The hotel clerk informed me that all this timber, as well as the sawmill, is the property of Mr. Job Chipman.

Leaving my baggage at the hotel, I walked over to the mill. Just outside the boiler house I found our ten ton demonstration Earthworm, equipped with its big snow plow, in charge of Mr. Samuel Simpson.

Sam reported that he had unloaded the machine the day before, and had kept it over night in the boiler house so that it was nice and warm and all ready to go. He had not seen Mr. Chipman, but the sawmill foreman had told him to be ready to put on a demonstration that morning.

"I understand," said Sam, "that Mr. Chipman wants a machine for snowplow work, and for hauling sleds on ice roads. As there is no snow, and consequently no ice roads, I don't see how we can put on much of a demonstration."

"Never mind about that," I said. "We will just run the machine around on the bare ground so the old man can see how it goes. Then I will give him such a vivid description of the way it rolls through the snow drifts that he will think he has actually seen it. Just wait till you hear me get going."

"Fine," said Sam. "In the grouser box here I have a set of the latest type ice-spike grousers, but as there is no snow or ice I don't suppose there is any use in putting them on."

"No use at all," I said.

At this point there was a sudden clanking and puffing, and out from the boiler house there came a big sixty horse power Mammoth tractor in charge of two mechanics and a salesman. I had never before seen this particular model of tractor. But when I looked it over and realized that it was actually attempting to compete with the Earthworm, I will admit that I had to laugh. For the Mammoth is undoubtedly the most outlandish engineering atrocity which has ever been thrown together and offered for sale to the long-suffering public. It is about ten years behind the times in design, and although it has about the same horse power as the ten ton Earthworm it weighs almost twice as much. It is at least twenty feet long, with two small wheels in front and two enormous bull wheels about nine feet in diameter in the rear. The motor consists of one big horizontal cylinder which works on a flywheel of monumental size and weight. All gears seem to be made of high grade stove iron. The whole works is heavy, slow, and clumsy, and it needs the proverbial ten acre lot to turn around. It is, in short, nothing but a mechanical joke when compared to the Earthworm with its modern four-cylinder motor, its small-sized steel gears, its light weight, its endless tracks, and its ease in steering and turning around.

After I had contemplated the Mammoth for some moments, the salesman in charge stepped up and introduced himself. It appears his name is Jones. As I looked him over I decided that I was not going to like the man. He had a coarse and rather stupid looking face. He was quite evidently lacking in both ideas and ideals. And he was, I decided, the type of person who makes up for his dearth of intelligence by developing a considerable degree of low cunning which is totally out of place, of course, in the noble profession of selling tractors.

As I say, I didn't like his looks. But, as I am always polite, I concealed my dislike.

"I suppose," I said affably, "that you have already seen Mr. Chipman and have given him a line of talk designed to prove that the Mammoth is a better machine than the Earthworm."

"I have seen Mr. Chipman," replied Mr. Jones, in a disagreeable, rasping voice, "but I have given him no line of talk. And what is more, I do not intend to."

"No?" I said, "what's the big idea?"

"I intend to put on a demonstration for him," said Mr. Jones. "When a man can give a real good demonstration, he does not need any sales talk."

"My boy," I said, "I can see you are new at this selling game; you are young, and you have much to learn. If you doubt the value of a good selling argument, you had better stick around when I start in on Mr. Chipman. You will see how a real salesman, by the skillful use of the English language, beats down and completely overcomes the sales resistance which is present in the mind of any prospect."

"Mr. Chipman is in his office now," said Mr. Jones. "Let's go in right away. Nothing would give me more pleasure than to see you doing your stuff."

"Very well," I said, "come on."

I have repeated my conversation with Mr. Jones so that you can see that I am, as always, frank, kindly, and helpful even to a competitor. When I relate what happened later you will see that Mr. Jones is quite the reverse, being one of the most underhanded, slimy, and dishonorable men who ever polluted the tractor business with their presence.

Mr. Jones and I entered the office together. Mr. Chipman turned out to be a tall, bony man, perhaps sixty years of age, with a pleasant, weather-beaten face. He had been sitting at a desk, but when we entered he arose and shook hands.

"Mr. Chipman," I said, "my name is Alexander Botts and I

represent the Farmers' Friend Tractor Company, makers of Earth-worm tractors, Earthworm City, Illinois. As you already know, we have one of our ten ton machines outside ready to give you a demonstration any time you want to see it. But before we start I would like to bring to your attention a few facts regarding the tractor and the company which makes it—facts which indicate conclusively that the Earthworm is the only feasible machine for a lumbering enterprise such as you conduct."

At this point I paused an instant, for I noticed that Mr. Chipman was pushing something across the table in my direction. Looking down I saw that it was a small slate, such as schoolboys used to use in former times. Attached to it by a short string was a slate pencil. Seeing that I was somewhat surprised and mystified by this procedure, Mr. Chipman opened his mouth, presumably to explain to me what it was all about. But as I had got started so good on my sales talk, I didn't wish to be switched off onto the subject of school slates. Consequently I continued talking as if there had been no interruption.

"When you first see this Earthworm tractor, Mr. Chipman," I said, "I wish you particularly to notice the method of propulsion. Instead of running on four wheels like a wagon or like certain other inferior tractors"—at this point I glanced meaningly at Mr. Jones—"the Earthworm goes along exactly like a war-time tank. It runs on two steel tracks, one on each side. Each track is like an endless belt or chain, composed of twenty-nine separate track shoes which are made of the highest grade of manganese steel, triple heat treated. The surfaces of these shoes are made perfectly flat, so as not to hurt the roads. These flat shoes will of course slip when the machine is used on snow or ice; consequently we sup-ply a set of sharp cleats or grousers, one of which is to be bolted on to each track shoe when the machine is to be used on snow or ice. Each of these grousers takes hold like the claw of a cat, giving the tractor a splendid grip and enabling it to pull tremendous loads through snow, ice, mud, rocks, sand, gravel, clay, or anything else in the world."

At this point I noticed that Mr. Chipman had picked up his

silly little schoolboy slate and was holding it out in my direction. As I paused momentarily he said:

"Kindly write what you have to say on this slate."

At first I failed to grasp the meaning of this procedure. Then I heard Mr. Jones, who stood behind me, chuckling in a very vulgar manner.

"You can save your lungs," remarked Mr. Jones, in a disrespectful tone. "The old bozo is stone deaf in one ear and can't hear anything out of the other."

At these words a sudden chill of horror settled down on my mind. I gave Mr. Chipman a quick, shrewd glance. He was pointing to the slate with one hand and to his ear with the other.

"I cannot hear as well as I used to," he was saying. "You will have to write down what you have to say."

As my perceptions are very quick and accurate, it was not long before I realized that Mr. Jones had in his untutored way spoken the exact truth. And like a flash my mind apprehended all the sickening implications of this discovery. I had come striding into this office with my usual masterful air, confident in the knowledge that I had the one essential, the *sine qua non,* of a successful sales campaign—a swell line of sales talk. And now, with a sickening shock I realized that it was all useless. For what good is a swell line of sales talk when it falls upon deaf ears? What can it accomplish when it is directed—as Mr. Jones phrased it—at one ear which is deaf and another which cannot be heard out of?

Behind me I could hear Mr. Jones—the big bum—still chuckling to himself.

And well he might. Considering his frog-like croak of a voice, his almost total lack of brains, and his undoubtedly feeble powers of expression, it was actually to his advantage to have Mr. Chipman deaf. But for me, with my pleasing and musical flow of language, with my wealth of imagination and ideas, and with my masterful command of the English language, it was as little short of calamity.

However, I am not the man to lie down and burst into tears when there is work to do. Grasping eagerly at the slate, I started to write. But almost at once I realized the futility of this procedure.

Using that stubby little pencil and that miserable scratchy slate, it would have taken me hours to put over even an abridged version of my splendid sales argument. Mr. Chipman would doubtless become bored and walk out before I had even half finished. And even if he were willing to wait and read the whole thing, it would be a tremendous letdown from what I had intended giving him. It would lack the breath of life, the musical tones that charm the ear, and the splendid ring of manly sincerity which has brought conviction to so many doubtful minds.

No, my wonderful sales talk was completely blowed up, knocked to pieces, and sunk without a trace. But I resolved to die fighting.

"My name is Alexander Botts," I wrote on the slate, in bold characters. "I have an Earthworm tractor outside. If you want to see something good, follow me."

Mr. Chipman read what I had written, and smiled cheerfully.

"Fine," he said, reaching for his coat and hat, which hung on a nail on the wall. "I will come right out, and you men can both do a little demonstrating."

As I helped Mr. Chipman on with his coat, I could not help feeling that he seemed to be a very decent sort of chap, bearing up very bravely under his infirmity, and I almost wept at the thought of the treat he was missing through not being able to hear my sales talk. As we walked out Mr. Jones gave an additional proof that his personality is most obnoxious and exactly the opposite of my own pleasant nature and that of Mr. Chipman.

"Thank you," said Mr. Jones, in his disagreeable voice. "You don't know how much I have appreciated observing the effect you made on Mr. Chipman with your wonderful sales ballyhoo. I am very much obliged."

"You can keep the change," I said with dignity. "If I cannot talk to this gentleman I can get along very well by putting on a demonstration for him."

"That's exactly what I said before we came in," said Mr. Jones. "If a man has a good demonstration he doesn't need any sales talk. I am glad to see that you are learning something from me."

To this wise crack I made no response. As soon as we reached the place where the two tractors were standing I turned to Mr. Chipman.

"I would suggest," I said, "that you take a little ride in our tractor. It is unfortunate that there is no snow and ice to give you a real demonstration, but if you will seat yourself on the comfortable cushion beside the driver and take a little ride you cannot fail to realize the superiority of the Earthworm tractor. I do not wish to knock any other machine, so I will let you see for yourself that the Earthworm has more flexibility, more speed, more power, and handles far more easily than any other machine in the world. It can go over the roughest sort of ground, and it is so light and compact that it steers as easily as a kiddy-car. It can turn right around in its own tracks. It is truly the latest word in engineering science."

"I am sorry," said Mr. Chipman politely, "but you will have to write that down."

He held out the little slate which he had brought with him and which he wore suspended by a string from a button of his overcoat. With a sinking heart I took the slate. It is impossible for me to describe how it cramps my style to express myself on a filthy square of slate which squeaks and scratches under the strokes of a stubby little pencil.

"Do you want a ride?" I wrote.

"Thank you," said Mr. Chipman, "it will give me the greatest pleasure." He climbed into the cab and sat down, and Sam gave him a swell little ride—up and down the road and out over a very rough field. Sam is certainly a peach of a driver. He handled the machine with real artistry; he changed gears with the greatest smoothness; he went over the bumps and depressions with no jar at all; and he turned and twisted the machine about so gracefully and beautifully that Mr. Chipman must have been very favorably impressed.

After this ride was over, Mr. Chipman took a short trip in the Mammoth tractor, which lumbered around over the ground in such a clumsy, slow, and awkward manner that I almost began to feel sorry for Mr. Jones. It seemed as if the Mammoth had no chance at all. But Mr. Chipman required further demonstration.

"I want you to bring your tractor down the road," he yelled to me. "We will lead the way in this tractor."

The Mammoth machine, carrying Mr. Chipman, Mr. Jones, and the two mechanics, started off. Sam and I followed in the Earthworm. About a quarter of a mile down the road we came to a medium sized pond which was frozen over tight. The Mammoth ran out over the ice to the center of the pond, with Sam and me in the Earthworm riding behind.

"Bring that machine over here," Mr. Chipman shouted to us.

Sam followed his directions, which were given with much shouting and waving of arms, and backed the Earthworm around until it stopped with its rear end almost touching the rear end of the Mammoth. At this point Mr. Chipman got off and proceeded to hitch the two machines together by means of a large chain which was carried on the draw-bar of the Mammoth. At once I began to feel that there might be trouble ahead.

"Here, here!" I shouted. "What are you trying to do?"

Mr. Chipman climbed up into the cab of the Earthworm and sat down between Sam and me.

"I need a tractor," he said, "that can pull sleds over ice. That is why I have brought you over onto this pond and hitched your two machines back to back. I want to see which one of you can pull the most on the ice. You can start any time you want."

"This won't be any test at all," I said. "You will have to give us time to bolt on our grousers. These smooth tracks are all right for pulling on dirt, but they don't have any more traction on ice than a couple of sled runners." I took a quick look at the Mammoth tractor. "Fortunately," I went on, "that other machine is in just as bad shape as we are. Mr. Jones will have to put on some cleats or grousers on those big, smooth drive wheels of his before he can do anything at all. You didn't tell us you were going to bring us out on the ice. But just give me time to put on the grousers, and I will enter any pulling contest with any machine in the world."

"Please write it down," said Mr. Chipman, holding out his slate. "I don't hear as well as I used to when I was younger."

"I grabbed the slate and was just beginning to write when there came a terrific jerk. The driver of the Mammoth had opened his throttle and thrown in the clutch. At once Sam, in self-defense, did the same thing. I looked around and saw that the chain between the two machines was stretched tight. The big bull drive-wheels of the Mammoth were turning round and round, and so were the tracks of the Earthworm. But both the wheels and the tracks were slipping on the ice so that neither of the machines was gaining anything on the other.

At first it looked like a draw. But then the driver of the Mammoth, acting under the orders of the obnoxious Mr. Jones who sat beside him, pulled one of the dirtiest tricks I have ever seen in all my experience in the tractor business. I saw him reach out beside his seat and pull a great big lever which was connected by long steel rods to a couple of sliding collars on the rear axle. The collars slid along the axle, causing a number of dogs or pawls to engage in some teeth cut in the hubs of the big drive wheels. As the drive wheels turned, the motion was carried through these pawls to a number of iron rods which in turn forced a lot of heavy iron spikes out through holes in the smooth iron tires of the big bull wheels. As soon as these spikes came out they bit into the ice. And all at once the Mammoth had splendid traction. I had never before seen an arrangement such as this, and I had to admit to myself that it was a rather clever scheme—in fact it is the only feature of the Mammoth tractor which is any good at all. But it was enough to put me in a very awkward position. The Mammoth at once started rolling off across the ice, dragging the Earthworm behind it. Sam was helpless. He could spin the tracks as much as he wanted, but they had absolutely no hold on the ice.

I at once began to protest, shouting and yelling and writing on the silly little slate as fast as I could. But nobody paid any attention. And I was treated to the heartrending experience of sitting in a perfectly good Earthworm tractor and being pulled backwards across the ice by that big overgrown bunch of stove iron known as the Mammoth. And that was not all. The mechanic who was driving the Mammoth actually had the discourtesy to go on a circular course, dragging the Earthworm—in spite of everything that poor Sam could do—three times around that pond. And all this time Mr. Jones kept waving and smiling at me in a most vulgar and insolent manner. When at last we stopped, and the motors of both machines had been shut off, I felt like going over and murdering the whole Mammoth crew; but with a great effort I held onto myself.

"Mr. Chipman," I said, with dignity and restraint, "this is an outrage. This demonstration means nothing at all. You didn't give us time to put on our grousers. It's a dirty trick."

"Write it down," said Mr. Chipman, politely pointing to the slate. As everything I had written during the ride appeared to be illegible, I rubbed the slate clean and started again.

"This demonstration is unfair," I wrote. "You should have given us time to put on the grousers."

"What are grousers?" asked Mr. Chipman.

"Points," I wrote, "like those things on the wheels of the other tractor."

Mr. Chipman looked at the Mammoth, and then he looked at the tracks of the Earthworm. His face lit up as if he understood, and I began to think I was making some impression on him. But I was wrong.

"I see what you mean," he said. "But you had just as much time as the other fellow. If he can put points on his machine in two seconds, and you cannot, that just shows that his machine is more convenient than yours, as well as being able to pull better."

As soon as I heard this crazy line of reasoning, I rubbed out everything on the slate and started to write a full explanation of the true state of affairs. But I had hardly started before Mr. Chipman looked at his watch, and then started climbing down out of the tractor.

"I am very sorry," he said, "but I have an engagement to go down the valley to one of my other sawmills. And I will have to get started right away."

"Wait a minute, wait a minute!" I yelled. And then I wrote on the slate: "When will you be back?"

"Late tonight," said Mr. Chipman.

"How about another demonstration tomorrow?" I wrote.

"It is hardly worth while," said Mr. Chipman. "The Mammoth seems to be the best machine. But I will not sign any orders until tomorrow night, and if you care to do any more driving I will be glad to watch you."

With these words he nodded a cheerful good-bye and hurried back to the sawmill. A few minutes later I saw him driving away in his car.

While Sam and I were unhooking our Earthworm from the Mammoth, Mr. Jones stood around with the most insulting look I have ever seen on the face of a human being.

"Well, Mr. Botts," he said, with a coarse laugh, "it appears that I was right. If a man can put on a real good demonstration, he doesn't need any sales talk."

As Sam and I are both gentlemen, we paid absolutely no attention to this clumsy and useless attempt at humor, but cranked up the Earthworm and drove back to the boiler house. Here I left Sam to put on the grousers in readiness for tomorrow's demonstration while I came over to the hotel where I borrowed a typewriter from the manager and spent the balance of the morning and all the afternoon in writing up the sales talk which I had hoped to give orally. Since supper I have spent my time on this report.

In summing up the day's events, I will not conceal from you the fact that I am a disappointed man, and that things look very black indeed. But if I fail in this enterprise, you may be sure that I am going down fighting, with all flags flying. Although I am at my best as a talker and orator, I am not entirely helpless—as you no doubt realize from reading my reports—when it comes to slinging the ink.

The little sales talk which I have prepared for Mr. Chipman consists of thirty-one and a half pages of typewritten material, couched in the choicest English, taking up all points regarding the superiority of the Earthworm tractor, and explaining clearly and logically all the reasons why today's so-called demonstration was absolutely and completely worthless as a basis for comparing the two machines. It is perfectly obvious, of course, that there can be no scientific value in any demonstration which seems to show that the Earthworm is inferior to any other machine.

I will now retire to bed so that I will be fit for whatever work is necessary tomorrow. I wish, however, to report one hopeful event. Early this afternoon it started snowing. And now, at ten P.M., it is still coming down hard, and there are already several inches of snow on the ground. It is obvious that the more snow we have the harder the traveling will be and the greater will be the superiority of the Earthworm over the heavy Mammoth.

In conclusion I wish to impress upon you that none of today's misfortunes should be blamed on Mr. Sam Simpson. I consider Sam one of the best mechanics in the employ of the company; he has done everything he could; and if any blame is to be attached to anyone it should be upon the shoulders of

Your unfortunate salesman,
ALEXANDER BOTTS.

FARMERS' FRIEND TRACTOR COMPANY
SALESMAN'S DAILY REPORT
Date: Tuesday, December 7, 1921.
Written from: Chipman Falls, Vermont.
Written by: Alexander Botts, Salesman.

Never in all my experience as a salesman have I run into so much hard luck concentrated into a single selling campaign. My plans have once more been frustrated by an unexpected and crushing blow—which I will describe later on. This blow was doubly discouraging in view of the fact that it came at a time when I had every reason to suppose that matters were in a slightly more hopeful condition.

When I got up this morning I observed that the snowstorm was over. The weather was clear and cold, and there seemed to be about two feet of snow on the ground. There had been practically no wind and so the snow was level. I had hoped for a regular blizzard with big drifts. Such a condition would have been a wonderful thing for us because the Earthworm, of course, can go through the deepest snow there is, whereas I knew that the big, clumsy Mammoth was sure to get stuck in the first big drift it came to.

Although two feet of snow is not enough to stop the Mammoth, I knew it would be slowed up a good bit and that we could therefore make a slightly better showing with the Earthworm.

This slightly better showing, of course, would not be sufficient to overcome the bad impression caused by yesterday's so-called demonstration, so I was relying particularly upon my masterful sales argument in thirty-one and a half typewritten pages, which I had produced at such great labor yesterday. With my precious document buttoned safely into the inside pocket of my overcoat, I sallied forth with Sam immediately after breakfast.

We ran the Earthworm, fully equipped with its grousers and its snowplow, out of the boiler house where it had spent the night. Mr. Jones and his mechanics brought out the Mammoth immediately afterward. On the front of their machine they had adjusted a snowplow, somewhat similar to ours.

A few minutes later Mr. Chipman appeared and explained what he wanted us to do. He pointed out a road which led from the sawmill up the wooded mountain slope on the west side of the valley.

"That is my principal logging road," said Mr. Chipman "About half a mile up the slope it divides into two roads. You can see the north fork running straight along the face of the mountain yonder." He pointed. "And you can see the south fork zig-zagging up around that shoulder. Beyond the shoulder the road is hidden in that little side valley, but you can see it coming into view several miles further on and zig-zagging across the slope of South Mountain, quite high up and a long way off."

We all looked. And, sure enough, we could see the faint traces of the two roads as they zig-zagged along through the woods on the steep mountain side.

"I want to see," he continued, "how well you people can plow snow. You can start any time you want. One of you can take the north fork and the other the south. You can plow out three or four miles apiece and then come back. Set your snowplows fairly high and leave about a foot of snow so we will have a good basis for an ice surface when we get out the water wagons and begin sprinkling. You can start any time you want."

"Fine," said Sam, "I am on my way right now."

"Wait a minute," I said, and then turned to Mr. Chipman.

"Would you like to ride along in our machine?" I asked.

"You will have to write it down," said Mr. Chipman. I wrote it on the slate.

"No, thank you," said Mr. Chipman.

"All right, Sam," I said, "you can go. I will stay here with Mr. Chipman."

As Sam drove off up the road through the snow, I reached into my pocket and brought out the precious paper. I handed it to Mr. Chipman.

"What is this?" he asked.

In reply I pointed to the title at the top of the first page: "One Hundred and One Reasons Why The Earthworm Is The Tractor For You."

As I looked at the title of the work upon which I had spent so much careful thought and hard labor the day before, I felt within myself a pardonable glow of pride. But this glow was short-lived. Because at this moment there descended the unexpected and crushing blow which I mentioned at the beginning of this report.

Instead of starting to read, Mr. Chipman handed the paper back to me. "I am sorry," he said, "but I broke my reading glasses yesterday and they won't be fixed for several days."

To this remark I made no reply. For once in my life I was speechless—which perhaps was just as well, as Mr. Chipman couldn't have heard anything anyway.

"Of course," he continued, "I can read to some extent even without my glasses, but if I tried to go through as much fine print as this it would be too much of a strain on my eyes. Besides, I am more interested in seeing the tractors work than I am in reading about them. And I have promised Mr. Jones I would ride along in his machine this morning."

With these words he climbed aboard the Mammoth tractor, which immediately started off up the road, carrying with it—in addition to Mr. Chipman—the two mechanics and Mr. Jones.

And there was I, left standing in the snow with my carefully worked out sales argument in my hand. Never in my life have I been so humiliated.

The worst of it was there was nothing that I could do but stand around and wait. And I have been waiting a couple of hours. I watched Sam as he took the north fork and went plowing along across the face of the mountain. And I watched the Mammoth take the south fork and go zig-zagging up through the woods and finally disappear around the shoulder into the little side valley. I regret to state that the snow is not deep enough to stop the Mammoth tractor.

Of course we are putting on a better demonstration; Sam is making three miles an hour, while the clumsy Mammoth is making hardly more than a mile and a half. But I doubt if that will do us any good. I must be getting old; I am getting pessimistic. But what hat sense is there, I ask you, in wearing yourself out on an old bozo like Job Chipman who is deaf and half-blind and—I am beginning to think—hopelessly feeble-minded?

However, while there is even a spark of hope, Alexander Botts is not the man to lay down on any job. I have come back to the hotel, and in between periods of watching the distant tractors on the mountain side, I have been improving my time in writing this report. And in addition, as a last desperate hope, I have prepared an abridged one-page edition of my sales talk. The old idiot ought to be able to read at least that much. It is a mere pitiful skeleton of the splendid thirty-one and a half page sales argument, but at least it is something.

When Mr. Chipman gets back I will hand it to him, and if he will read it he may get a faint idea of what he will be missing in case he fails to buy the Earthworm.

It is now ten o'clock, and I can see from my window that Sam has finished plowing out his road and is on his way back. Accordingly I will go down to the sawmill and talk things over with him when he arrives.

Later. 2 P.M.

Since writing the above words a most unusual and extraordinary series of events has taken place. But before relating these happenings I wish to remind you of a remark I made in a previous report to the effect that I considered Mr. Sam Simpson one of the best mechanics in the employ of the company. It now appears that I was right as usual. As a judge of men I am practically perfect. For Sam is not only one of the best mechanics in the country but he is also not so terribly bad as a salesman.

When I left the hotel, after writing the first part of this report, I walked down to the sawmill to wait for Sam. But I was somewhat surprised to see that when Sam reached the fork in the roads he did not return to the mill. Instead, he swung up the south fork, following the path which had been taken by the Mammoth tractor. As the road had already been plowed he was able to go along at full speed and before long he had disappeared—as the Mammoth tractor had done before him—around the shoulder of the mountain. This procedure on Sam's part puzzled me somewhat, but as I have every confidence in his judgment I assumed that he had some reason for this action. And it turned out that this was the case.

For two hours nothing happened. And then, a little after noon, the Earthworm appeared once more, coming back down the south fork road. It rolled merrily along and before many minutes it arrived at the sawmill. The door of the cab opened and out stepped Sam and Mr. Chipman. Mr. Chipman walked right over to me.

"Let's go down to your room at the hotel," he said. "I want to talk to you."

As we walked along I noticed that Sam's honest face was lit up by a smile of perfect peace and happiness.

"It worked!" he said. "It worked!"

"What worked?" I asked.

"A little plan I had," said Sam. "I didn't tell you about it before because I wasn't sure it would succeed, and I didn't want to raise your hopes too high."

"What happened?" I asked.

"After I finished putting on the grousers yesterday afternoon," Sam explained, "I got to talking with one of the mill hands about those roads. He told me that Mr. Chipman would probably have us plow them out. He said the north road is about four miles long and ends in a nice flat open space where it is easy to turn around. But the south road is twenty miles long and you have to go clear to the end before you find any real good place to turn. So that was why I hurried off so fast this morning. I wanted to get to the fork first and take the north road that had the good turning-around place."

"You didn't need to do that," I said. "The Earthworm can swing right around anywhere in its own tracks."

"Exactly so," said Sam, "but the Mammoth can't, and I had a feeling that if I could once get old Jones started up that south fork he would be a blowed-up sucker. And I was right."

"Go on," I said.

"After I had finished plowing my road," said Sam, "I chased up the south fork and caught up with the Mammoth about five miles out. I found Mr. Chipman hollering and yelling that it was time to turn around and go home—that he had to get back so he could make an early start on a trip he was going to take down the valley—and that it was a hell of a fine tractor that could only go in one direction. And all the time Mr. Jones was writing on the silly little slate, trying to smooth him down by explaining that the road was too narrow and that they would turn around just as soon as they got to a good place."

"So what did you do then?"

"Nothing much," said Sam, "except give them a little demonstration. I ran up and down the road four or five times and let them see how easy I turned around at the end of each little trip. As soon as Mr. Jones saw how nice the Earthworm did it, he took a terrible chance an tried to turn around with the Mammoth."

"Did he make it?"

"No," said Sam, "he did not. He picked a place where they had made the road extra wide to let the log sleds pass, and he started to swing around very slow and cautious, but all he did was get his big clumsy machine stuck deep down in the ditch beside the road."

"Is he still stuck?" I asked.

"No," said Sam. "We hooked on to him with the Earthworm and yanked him out—all of which gave Mr. Chipman a swell demonstration of how well the Earthworm can pull. So the Mammoth is not stuck any more; but it is still headed in the wrong direction, and it still has about fifteen miles to go before it can turn around. After I had pulled the Mammoth out, I took Mr. Chipman aboard and brought him back here."

By this time we had reached my room in the hotel. Looking out the window we could see a little speck moving slowly along far away on the side of South Mountain. It was the great Mammoth tractor—with a long trip still ahead of it. But Sam said it had plenty of gasoline and ought to get back some time tonight.

As we turned away from the window, I decided that the time was ripe for action. I handed out my little one-page abridged sales talk. But I was doomed to one last bitter disappointment. Mr. Chipman shoved it to one side, saying he was not interested in such things.

He went on to say, however, that he had seen such a good demonstration that he wanted to keep the Earthworm and order three more just like it. So, with deep humility—realizing that all my frenzied activity of the past two days had made absolutely no impression on anybody, and that the success of the sale was due entirely to Sam—I signed up Mr. Chipman for four ten ton Earthworms.

Sam and I are leaving on the afternoon train. And, in a very humble spirit, I am writing a polite little note to be given to Mr. Jones when he gets back to the hotel. This note ought to cheer him up a great deal because it informs him that he is a wise egg and that he was absolutely right when he said that if a man can put on a real good demonstration he doesn't have to have any sales talk.

Very sincerely,
ALEXANDER BOTTS.

Botts steers a wary sales prospect astray in this movie still from the motion picture, Earthworm Tractors. *(Wisconsin Center for Film and Theater Research)*

The Old Home Town

FARMERS' FRIEND TRACTOR COMPANY
EARTHWORM CITY, ILLINOIS
JANUARY 5, 1925.

Mr. Alexander Botts,
LaSalle Hotel, Chicago, Illinois.

DEAR MR. BOTTS: We have been informed that the road commissioners of Smedley County, Iowa, are holding a special meeting on January ninth at the county seat, Smedleytown, to consider the purchase of equipment to remove the snow from the county highways, which have been completely blocked by recent heavy snowstorms.

We have shipped to Smedleytown one ten ton Earthworm Tractor equipped with the new Wahoo Improved High-power Double-Rotary Snowplow. We want you to go there at once to demonstrate this machine and, if possible, sell it to the commissioners. We are sending on our service man, Mr. Samuel Simpson, to handle the mechanical end of the demonstration.

Very sincerely,

GILBERT HENDERSON,

Sales Manager.

FARMERS' FRIEND TRACTOR COMPANY
SALESMAN'S DAILY REPORT
Date: January 8, 1925.
Written from: Smedleytown, Iowa.
Written by: Alexander Botts, Salesman.
Subject: Smedleytown Snowplow Demonstration.

As soon as I received your letter I started for Smedleytown, arriving here early this morning. And I want to say that I would rather put on a demonstration in this town than in any other place in the country. Very possibly you do not know it, but Smedleytown, Iowa, is the birthplace and early boyhood home of Alexander Botts. This is the first time I have been back to the old home town since I left it at the age of eighteen. All my folks have moved away, but I still have a great many old friends and former schoolmates living here. And it will give me the greatest satisfaction to put on a swell demonstration, and let them see how good I am, and sell them some of the finest snow-removal machinery in the world.

There will be competition. I hear that the Steel Elephant Tractor salesman is in town. But he has no machine here, so he can't put on any demonstration, and I am not afraid of those Steel Elephant people anyway.

The Earthworm tractor and the plow arrived last night. Sam Simpson got in this morning. He at once unloaded the machinery, and he has been spending the rest of the day checking it over and getting it ready.

We ought to make a big sensation in this town. Neither Sam nor myself ever operated one of these powerful new rotary snowplows. In fact, we never even saw one before. But Sam has been studying the plow that you sent on, and he is sure he can drive it through any drift in the country. Fortunately, there is lots of snow around here. The streets in town have been partly broken out, but most of the country roads are still blocked. So we have a chance to put on a wonderful demonstration tomorrow.

The County Road Commission meets at nine A.M., and I expect to attend the meeting. While I am giving a preliminary address to the commissioners, I have instructed Sam to drive the plow straight down the main street of the town and on out into the country. An hour or so later the commissioners and myself will follow him in automobiles. And as soon as they see what wonderful work the machine does, they will want to buy it right away.

Although the heavy work will not come until tomorrow, I have not been idle today. I have been getting myself in strong with various citizens of the town. This morning I called on Lemuel Sanders, one of the road commissioners, who used to be my Sunday-school teacher. I have changed so much that at first he did not recognize me. But when I told him who I was, he gave me a smile that pretty near split his face.

"Alexander," he said, "I am delighted to see you. And I trust that you are still going to church regularly."

"You bet I am," I replied. I go twice every Sunday, and I am almost always on hand for Thursday evening prayer meeting."

"Splendid!" he said.

(NOTE: I will have to admit that my statement to Mr. Sanders was slightly exaggerated. But he is such a nice old bird that I just did not have the heart to disappoint him in any way. Furthermore, as he is one of the county commissioners, it is just as well for me to humor him as much as possible.)

I also called on a couple of my old high-school teachers, who were most cordial. My marks in school were never any too good, but they probably realize that this was due to my original and independent way of thinking, rather than to lack of ability.

Old Doctor Merton, formerly our family physician, welcomed me very warmly. He at once demanded whether I had had my appendix removed yet; and if not, why not. I was deeply touched to see the loving way in which he remembered the symptoms of long ago. I had to admit that I still suffered from occasional mild attacks, but I let him know very positively that I did not intend to have an operation until I had to.

Besides these people, I called on a number of other prominent citizens of the town, including Arthur Myers, who used to be in my class in school and is now a reporter on the Smedleytown Evening Times-Courier. I gave him a swell interview, which came out in the evening paper. I am enclosing a copy. You will note that I have very slightly exaggerated my position with the company. And I wish to explain that this is not due to vanity on my part.

But it seemed to me that I would make a better impression, and that I would, therefore, be much more apt to sell a tractor, if I let them think that I was a person of even more importance than I actually am.

Very sincerely,
ALEXANDER BOTTS.

CLIPPING FROM THE SMEDLEYTOWN EVENING TIMES-COURIER:

ALEXANDER BOTTS VISITS SMEDLEYTOWN FORMER RESIDENT NOW CAPTAIN OF INDUSTRY WILL SELL TRACTORS TO COUNTY COMMISSIONERS

Alexander Botts, Vice President in Charge of Sales for the Farmers' Friend Tractor Company, manufacturers of Earthworm Tractors, arrived in town this morning and is staying at the Smedleytown Hotel. Older residents will recall that Mr. Botts was born and raised here, and Smedleytown may well be proud of this local boy who has made good in a big way in the world of finance and industry. Mr. Botts, in addition to holding a high executive position with the tractor company, is a director of more than a dozen banks and trust companies. He is in town for the purpose of negotiating a large sale of snow-removal machinery to the county road commissioners.

When Mr. Botts was asked to what he attributed his phenomenal success, he replied, "You can tell the young men of this town that the first rule is hard work, the second is hard work, and all the other rules are the same. My own phenomenal rise has been due to the fact that I have never been a clock watcher. I have always tried to give my employers a little more than they expected."

FARMERS' FRIEND TRACTOR COMPANY
SALESMAN'S DAILY REPORT
Date: January 9, 1925. 10 A.M.
Written from: Smedleytown, Iowa.
Written by: Alexander Botts.
Subject: Snowplow Demonstration.

This is just a short note to let you know everything is going fine. At nine o'clock I left Sam Simpson all ready to start out with the big snowplow. For the past hour I have been giving one of my best sales talks to the county commissioners. They are now listening to the Steel Elephant man, but his arguments are so weak that I am really sorry for the poor fellow.

I will now slip down to the Post Office and mail this. Then I will come back and take the commissioners to see the work that Sammy has been doing. And this evening I confidently expect to report that I have closed the sale.

Yours,

ALEXANDER BOTTS.

FARMERS' FRIEND TRACTOR COMPANY
SALESMAN'S DAILY REPORT
Date: January 9, 1925. 4 P.M.
Written from: Smedleytown Hospital, Smedleytown, Iowa.
Written by: Alexander Botts.
Subject: Unfortunate Incident Prevents Complete Success of Snowplow Demonstration at Smedleytown.

I regret to inform you that since my last report the situation has changed. And though I never like to give up hope, I will have to admit that our chances of selling a tractor in this town do not seem quite so good as they did early this morning. In order that you may appreciate the difficulties I have run into, and in order that you may understand exactly why I happen to be in the hospital, I will relate as clearly as I can everything that has happened.

I finished my last report at about ten o'clock this morning. After placing it in the envelope and addressing, stamping, and sealing it, I started out from the Court House—where the meeting of the road commissioners was being held—with the intention of going down to the Post Office, mailing the report, and then coming back to join the commissioners and take them out to admire the work of the snowplow.

That was my intention, but my plans went astray. I got down to the Post Office all right, and I mailed the report, but I never got back to the county commissioners.

When I left the Court House—which is in a small park at one end of town—I had no premonition of disaster. As I walked through the park I noted that it was a beautiful day—clear and cold, with blue sky overhead, and the white snow sparkling all around in the brilliant sunshine. My heart was gay and untroubled.

But as I left the park and turned into the main street of the town I was startled to observe that the entire business section was in a state of the wildest excitement. Dozens of people were running back and forth across the street, others were gathering in groups as if to discuss something, and from the upper windows of the houses many heads were thrust forth to see what was the matter.

And there was plenty the matter. The building on the corner housed a drug store—or rather, what had once been a drug store. But now the big plate-glass window in front was completely smashed in. And inside there seemed to be hundreds of broken bottles and all manner of other material such as is commonly sold in drug stores—magazines, boxes of writing paper, rubber goods, typewriters, picture postal cards, boxes of candy, toilet articles, and so on. Everything was busted up and thrown around in a way that was horrible to see, and mixed in with the débris were great quantities of snow and ice.

The sidewalk, which an hour before had been shoveled clean, was now covered with snow. But the center of the street, which had held at least a foot of densely packed snow, was now almost completely clean. Across the street was a men's furnishing store.

Its front was also broken, and inside were great piles of snow, mingled with a mass of neckties, shirts, pajamas, and I don't know what all.

Stepping out into the center of the street, where the walking was good, I continued on my way. I proceeded for two blocks—as far as the Post Office—and all the windows of all the stores on both sides of the street were smashed in. People were running hither and thither. Others were at work inside the stores, picking up and arranging the scattered stock, and shoveling out into the street great quantities of snow. For once in my life I was completely bewildered. Never had I seen a more curious, a more extraordinary sight.

After mailing my letter I engaged one of the bystanders in conversation.

"What has happened?" I asked. "What is the cause of this holocaust? Was it an explosion or an earthquake? Or was it a tornado?"

"Tornado nothing!" said the bystander. "Didn't you see it?"

"See what?"

"That damn tractor snowplow," said the bystander.

At these words I will have to admit that a faint feeling of dizziness came over me.

"Tell me about it," I said. "What happened?"

"You certainly missed it if you wasn't here," said my informant. "I was standing in front of Polsky's Hardware Store when I heard a roaring like an airplane motor. And I looked up and I saw this big machine turning the corner onto Main Street."

"Yes," I said. "Go on."

"It was the damnedest-looking machine I ever saw. It had a snowplow with two big paddle wheels, one on each side. As soon as the guy driving it got well around the corner he threw those paddles into gear some way and they began whirling around something terrible, digging up the snow from the street and throwing it off to each side so hard that it sent it right through every window in sight."

"Holy Moses!" I said. "And he drove right along the whole street?"

"He did. I never seen anything like it—big solid chunks of snow and ice crashing and banging through the windows, and the fine dust making such a fog in the air that you could hardly see anything, and people dodging into alleys, and women screaming, and children crying, and that great big motor roaring. And crash after crash, as them plate-glass windows was knocked in. I tell you, it's something I'll never forget as long as I live."

"But the man must have been crazy," I said. "Why didn't he stop? Couldn't he see what he was doing?"

"I don't know," said the man. "That fine snow dust made such a fog that maybe he couldn't see anything."

"Why didn't somebody stop him?" I asked.

"I guess everybody was too busy running away from all that flying snow and ice. You see, the snow on this street was packed down pretty hard, and the machine chewed it out in big, solid hunks which went flying through the air like regular young cannon balls. But the sheriff and a lot of deputies are after this man now, and I guess they'll get him before long."

"Where did he go?" I asked.

"He went right down Main Street and on out into the country." The man pointed down the street in the opposite direction from the Court House. "Who are you?" he asked. "Are you a stranger in town?"

"Yes," I said, "I'm just visiting here for a short time. Yes, probably a very short time."

"You're lucky, then," said the man. "All this is going to make it pretty hard for the merchants, and for the whole town. But, of course, it doesn't make any difference to a guy like you."

"Oh, no, of course not," I said. "This won't affect me at all—not at all."

I continued my walk down the street in the direction away from the Court House. Pretty soon I was stopped by an old gentleman with a beard. He wore large smoked glasses; apparently to protect his eyes from the glare of the sun on the snow.

"Have they got 'em?" asked the old gentleman. "Have you heard whether they've arrested them yet?"

"I don't know," I replied politely.

"Well," the old gentleman went on, "if they haven't got 'em yet, they will soon. And I hope they send both of them to state's prison for good long terms."

"What do you mean—both of them?" I asked. "I thought there was only one man driving the tractor."

"There was. He is the mechanic, and they're going to stick him in jail just as soon as they catch him. But the main guy they are after is the salesman that was in charge of the machine. It was him that ordered this mechanic to drive it right through the center of town this way."

"You don't know how you interest me," I said. "So they really think the salesman is to blame too?"

"Of course he is. I'd certainly hate to be in his shoes. But if the sheriff finds him first and gets him locked up, he'll be safe enough. It's a good strong jail."

"What do you mean—he'll be safe enough?" I asked.

"I mean, if they once land him inside the jail there won't be much danger of his getting lynched."

"You don't mean they're talking of lynching him?"

"I'll say they are," said the old gentleman. "Most of the men in this town are so mad they'd kill that tractor man as quick as they would a rabbit. But we got a good sheriff; he would die fighting before he'd let any mob take a prisoner away from him."

"Well," I said, "that's a comforting thought, anyway."

"Yes," said the old gentleman, "it always gives a town a bad name to have a lynching."

"I agree with you absolutely," I said, "and I certainly hope that nobody will do anything to sully the fair name of Smedleytown."

With these words I took leave of the old gentleman. And as I said good-by to him I looked with a certain amount of envy upon his copious white beard and smoked glasses. It occurred to me that similar accessories might be very advantageous to a tractor salesman whose popularity was so decidedly on the wane as mine seemed to be. Unfortunately, I could not hope to grow an adequate beard quick enough to help me in the present crisis. Furthermore, I have had no experience in stage make-up; and false whiskers, unless they are very cleverly devised, are worse than useless. I decided, therefore, to give up the idea of hiding behind a bush.

But smoked glasses seemed entirely practicable. And they would not seem unusual, as many people use them on bright, sunny days. After a few minutes' search I located the pitiful ruins of an optician's shop. The proprietor was busy cleaning the snow out of a broken showcase full of glass eyes, but he stopped long enough to sell me the largest pair of smoked glasses that had survived the wreck.

Then, with my hat pulled down over my forehead, with the glasses covering most of my face between the eyebrows and the mouth, and with my coat collar turned up so that it concealed my chin, I sallied forth once more. I was rather pleased with my ingenuity in working out this disguise so quickly. I felt quite sure that even the county commissioners, whom I had just talked to for an hour, would not recognize me. For the time being, at least, I was safe.

But I will have to admit that I was not in what might be called a buoyant or jovial state of mind. Here I had come back to my boyhood home, full of enthusiasm, and prepared to make a splendid and magnificent impression upon my former friends and neighbors. It seemed that I was making an impression all right, but not in exactly the way I had hoped.

A short distance down the street I found a group of several men who were discussing the amount of the damage. It seemed to be the general consensus of opinion that the repair bills would amount to something between two and three hundred thousand dollars.

"Of course," said one of the men, "the company that makes the tractor will have to pay all the repair bills."

These words fell upon my ear in a most unpleasant way. My mind is still in something of a daze, and I have no idea how all this will come out. But I believe I am correct in assuming that the executives of the Farmers' Friend Tractor Company will be distinctly annoyed if they have to pay two or three hundred thousand dollars expenses for a single demonstration; especially in view of the fact that this demonstration may not result in any sale.

I left the group that were discussing this unpleasant subject of damages, and soon met a man who gave me the latest news from the sheriff's posse.

"They found the tractor," he said. "It was stuck in a snowdrift about a mile outside of town. But the driver had skipped. I guess he knew they were after him, and he decided to do a fade-away while there was still time. But they're sure to catch him later."

"How so?" I asked.

"The country roads are blocked with snow," said the man, "so he'll have to sneak back here. They've got men all over town—at the hotel, and at the railroad station, and everywhere. It won't be long before they have the driver and that salesman both locked up in jail, where they belong."

"Probably you're right," I said.

As I moved on, my thoughts became gloomier than ever. As you know, I am by nature an optimistic soul. I always look on the bright side of things. But the present grim and stunning disaster did not seem to have any bright side. I could not then, and I cannot now, explain why Sammy Simpson wrecked this town the way he did. I have never been the kind of a man who tries to pass the buck; and I will admit that I myself directed Sammy to run the machine through the center of town. But that was because I had never seen one of these high-powered rotary snowplows in action. I thought that the paddle wheels rotated in a reasonable and civilized manner, lifting the snow gently out to the sides of the road. I never supposed that the thing was a combination of a Swiss avalanche and a volcanic eruption on wheels. But Sammy Simpson has always been one of the best men we have. Why didn't he use a little judgment? Why didn't he look around? Why didn't he see what he was doing, and stop before he ruined the whole region? And when he got stuck out in the country, why did he run away and leave the whole mess on my hands?

If we ever find Sammy, we may get the answers to these questions. But in the meantime, everything is a puzzle to me. The only thing I'm sure of is that Smedleytown, Iowa, today looks very much like Soissons, France, in 1918.

I walked the whole length of the business section—more than half a mile—and every single store on both sides of the street was smashed up in a way that was sickening to see. When I had passed the last wrecked store, I turned up a quiet residence street and strolled slowly along, trying to collect my thoughts and decide on some plan of action. But I could not think of anything.

Before long I found myself in front of a large brick building set back among a lot of trees. As I was vaguely wondering what this building could be, an automobile drew up at the curb beside me. A man started to get out. I paid no attention to him and walked on, but he came running after me and laid a heavy hand on my shoulder. "Those glasses pretty near fooled me," he said, "but I know you just the same, Alexander Botts."

A feeling of black despair settled upon me. Apparently my disguise wasn't so good after all.

And at this point I will have to stop, as the hospital nurse won't let me write any more. She will see that this report is mailed to you tonight. And in a few days, if I am able, I will write you again and let you know more about this most distressing affair.

Yours,

ALEXANDER BOTTS.

FARMERS' FRIEND TRACTOR COMPANY
SALESMAN'S DAILY REPORT
Date: January 14, 1925.
Written from: Smedleytown Hospital, Smedleytown, Iowa.
Written by: Alexander Botts.
Subject: Final Report on Smedleytown Snowplow Demonstration

It gives me great pleasure to report that I am now sitting up and taking nourishment. For the first time in several days I am strong enough to write; so I will give you the additional facts, as far as I know them, regarding this interesting and curious snowplow business.

In my last report I think I told you of my walk through the

main street of Smedleytown, and of my bewildered surprise when I found the whole place looking like The Last Days of Pompeii. I think I also told you how I walked up a side street, and how a man got out of an automobile and called me by name. At first I was sure it was the sheriff. But my fears were groundless. For when I turned around I saw that it was none other than my old friend Doctor Merton, former physician to the Botts family.

"Take off those glasses," he said. "I want to look at you." I took off the glasses. "Alexander," he said, "you look sick."

"As a matter of fact," I replied, "I feel sick."

"And I know what's the matter with you."

"So you have just come from downtown, too?"

"No," said the doctor, "I have just been making some calls out in the north end of town."

"So you haven't been down on Main Street for quite a while?" I asked.

"Not since early this morning."

"Then very likely you don't know what makes me feel sick."

"I do," said the doctor. "It's that appendix. When you left here several years ago you had a very well-developed case of chronic, low-grade appendicitis. And you admitted yourself yesterday that it had been bothering you off and on ever since."

"That's right," I said.

"All this time," the doctor went on, "it has been filling your system with poison. You're a sick man."

"Yes," I said, "I feel bad all over."

"You ought to have that appendix out right away," the, doctor said. "This is one of the best hospitals in the state." He pointed to the brick building in front of which we were standing. "I'll get you a room here any time you want. It's a simple operation, and in a couple of weeks you'll be out again and feeling fine. What do you say?"

Rapidly I considered the situation. There were several courses open to me. I could try to sneak out of town, in spite of all the deputy sheriffs that were looking for me. But I have never been a quitter, and I felt that it was my duty to stick around and do everything I could to smooth out this horrible mess.

I could go back downtown. But I had a distinct feeling that for several days at least the county and town authorities would not be in any mood to listen sympathetically to what I had to say—assuming that I could think of anything to say. It appeared certain that for the present I would accomplish nothing except getting myself locked up in jail, or even lynched.

But here was another possibility. I could enter this excellent hospital, where I could rest my weary body, and where my troubled spirit would find refuge from the turmoil of the wicked world.

Somehow it seemed to me that there was something very attractive in the idea of a pleasant bed, a quiet room, and a gentle, sympathetic nurse to look after me. And I was reasonably sure that if I were a sick man in a hospital the deputies and others would not bother me. And they might even feel sorry for me, so that they would be easier to talk to when I got out again.

"All right, doctor," I said, "let's go."

At first he wanted to delay the operation until the next morning, but I told him it would have to be that afternoon or never. And after he had learned that I had eaten no luncheon, and that I had had only a very light breakfast, he consented. He had several other operations to perform that afternoon, and he saved me until the last, so I had time to write up my daily report. It is now four days later. The first couple of days I was a pretty sick pup, but it seems that the operation was very simple and entirely successful, and now I am feeling fairly good again.

This morning they told me I could have visitors. And a few minutes later in walked Sammy Simpson. I was not pleased to see him.

"You don't belong here," I said. "You're supposed to be in jail."

"Why?" he asked pleasantly.

"You know why," I said. "Why did you do it? After you got started, you should have seen that a high-powered rotary plow is no machine to take through the business section of town that way.

"Exactly so," said Sam. "I tested that plow down by the freight station, and as soon as I saw how it threw the snow around I decided not to go up Main Street after all. I drove right out into the country and spent the whole day plowing the main highways. And the machine worked so well and cleaned up so many miles of road that the county commissioners have bought it. They gave me a check in full payment and I have mailed it in to the company."

"Then you didn't smash up the town after all?"

"I certainly did not."

"Sam," I said, "this ether must have affected my brain more than I thought. Because I seem to have a very distinct memory of walking up Main Street and noticing that every single plate-glass window was smashed into very small fragments. Everything seemed so clear and distinct that I could have sworn that it was real. And now it turns out that it was nothing but a dream—just a bad dream."

"Dream nothing," said Sam. "That part of it was real enough. After I got back from plowing the roads I found that a demonstration Steel Elephant tractor and plow had come in on the morning freight a few minutes after I had left. The Steel Elephant operator had been on some sort of a party the night before, and he was still so lubricated that I guess he didn't know just what he was doing. He went down and unloaded the machine, and you saw what he did with it. He certainly did plenty. They caught him that night, trying to hop a freight out of town. He's still in jail. They arrested the Steel Elephant salesman and let him out later. But I hear they're bringing suit against the Steel Elephant Company for two hundred and sixty-seven thousand dollars."

So that is all I have to report at present. The nurse says I have to stop writing and get a little rest. But I will be all right soon. And now that my appendix is gone I have a feeling that in the future I am going to be a greater and finer salesman than ever before.

Yours,

ALEXANDER BOTTS.

"Thar's Gold in Them Thar Mountains"

ALEXANDER BOTTS
SALES PROMOTION REPRESENTATIVE
EARTHWORM TRACTOR COMPANY
DOW'S GULF, VERMONT

Monday evening, June 6, 1932.

Mr. Gilbert Henderson,
Sales Manager,
Earthworm Tractor Company,
Earthworm City, Illinois.

DEAR HENDERSON: It gives me great pleasure to report that I have started my activities in this town with even more than my usual energy. Although I arrived only this morning, I have already become deeply involved in the promotion of a gold mine.

In case you should wonder why a man who was sent out primarily to infuse new life and selling enthusiasm in the Earthworm-tractor dealers of the country should turn to mining, I will explain that this new activity is necessary in order to stimulate and revivify Mr. George Dow, who is our dealer in this territory, and also one of the laziest yokels I have ever run across.

Honestly, Henderson, he is as sleepy, as dumb and as contented as a superannuated Holstein cow. When I called on him this morning at his office, he languidly invited me to take a chair and then sat down himself, arranged his long, skinny legs on the desk, stuck an old pipe in his mouth, and settled himself as if he was going to take a nap. He was too lazy even to light the pipe.

"How's business?" I asked.

"Can't complain," he said.

"Selling any tractors?"

"No."

"Got any on hand?"

"Yes. I got two sixty-horse-power models in the warehouse."

"How long since you've sold a tractor?"

"I don't know. I guess the last sale I made was about a year ago—maybe a year and a half."

"That's terrible," I said. "I had no idea things were so bad up in this country. But you can cheer up, Mr. Dow, for the Earthworm Tractor Company has sent me out to help you dealers. I am ready to assist you in any way I can; and if we get together and attack this situation with energy and enthusiasm, I feel sure we can achieve some real results."

At this, Mr. Dow smiled in what might be described as an amused and tolerant manner. He was a rather likable old bozo, maybe sixty years old, and he had a lot of pleasant-looking little wrinkles around his eyes.

"Well, well," he said, "it does beat all how you young chaps are always rushing around, full of energy and excitement. But when you're as old as I am, my boy, you will learn to take things more calmly."

"Possibly," I said, "you are taking things too calmly. If you don't get out and buzz about a bit, how can you expect to pull yourself out of this depression?"

"But there isn't any depression here," he said. "In Vermont we don't have these crazy booms that you have in the big cities, and we don't have big depressions either. We just live along quiet and sensible. At the moment it is true that business is rotten and times are rather hard. But it doesn't bother me at all."

"What?" I asked. "Business is rotten, and it doesn't bother you?"

"Certainly not. I've got everything I need. I have a nice house at the edge of town here, a splendid vegetable garden, a couple of cows, a fine flock of hens, a little orchard, and a woodpile big enough to last all next winter. I have about five thousand dollars in the bank—and I intend to keep it there. Most of my neighbors are fixed the same way, so we none of us have to worry very much about hard times. Of course, there are a few people who are out of luck and have nothing at all, but we have them with us even when times are supposed to be good. In some ways I am better off than the average."

"I thought you just said you hadn't sold a single tractor for over a year."

"Yes, but I have a little garage and filling station that I run in connection with my tractor agency, and this business is still going on—after a fashion."

"Is it making any money?"

"No, but it's not losing any, either. And I'm paying the help enough to live on. Another fortunate thing is that my son, who has been taking a course in mining engineering down at Columbia, has just graduated, so I won't have any more expense for his college course. He hasn't been able to get a job, so I have told him to come home and stay with his father and mother, where the cost of living is almost nothing. He will be here in a day or two. There are plenty of good chairs in the office here, and room enough for another pair of feet on the desk, so he and I can just sit around and discuss the weather and politics and so on, and thumb our noses at this much-advertised business depression."

Having finished these remarks, Mr. Dow stretched himself contentedly and settled down even deeper into his comfortable swivel chair. It seemed to be up to me to make some adequate reply. And this was difficult, because, although Mr. Dow's line of argument was completely cockeyed, it nevertheless had a certain plausibility about it. If he actually had everything he needed already, and was completely satisfied, possibly there was no logical reason why he should start tearing around and trying to rake in more cash. For a moment he almost had me converted to his point of view. But, naturally, a high-powered salesman like myself, whose whole business is to inspire pep and energy, cannot afford to listen to any such insidious propaganda as Mr. Dow was putting out.

"Your whole point of view is wrong," I said. "To hear you talk, anybody would think you had given up even trying to sell tractors."

"Of course I have," he said. "Why should I waste my time trying to sell tractors when there isn't anybody around here at the present time that needs any such thing?"

"But there must be a few possible customers. How about the farmers?"

"They are all feeling too poor."

"Any lumbering going on in these mountains?"

"There used to be, but there isn't any more."

"Any industries that could use tractors?"

"No. We used to have a pulp mill and several sawmills. And a long time ago we even had a gold mine. But they all shut down."

"You say there used to be a gold mine? I didn't know they had such things in Vermont."

"Oh, yes," said Mr. Dow. "There has always been a certain amount of mining in the Green Mountains—iron, copper, gold, silver, and so on. But they're not doing anything these days—can't compete with the big Western production. This particular gold mine belongs to me."

"It does?"

"Yes, I inherited it from my father. He opened it up back in the 70's, and sank about all the money he had in it. If you look out the window there, you'll see a little tumble-down shed up on the side of the mountain. That shed is at the mouth of the mine."

"I see it," I said. "Is there really any gold there?"

"Oh, yes. There's a little. But not enough so my father could make it pay. He went completely busted."

"And you've never tried to work it yourself?"

"Absolutely not. I don't know anything about mining, and I don't want to. As I told you before, I'm perfectly happy and contented, and I intend to remain so. I'm not going to risk any of my money in any speculative enterprise, whether it's gold mining or high-powered tractor-selling campaigns, or anything else."

"Well," I said, "maybe you're right. But don't get the idea that a tractor-selling campaign necessarily takes a lot of money. The important thing is plenty of energy and persistence. There must be some place around here where we can sell tractors. Is there any road building going on?"

"Yes, the local road commissioner is putting in several miles of driveway through a tract of woods that has been bequeathed to the town as a park. It's quite a big job. There's a lot of grading and cut-and-fill work. The commissioner is spending about fifteen thousand dollars—which was left for this purpose by the man who bequeathed the park."

"Is the commissioner using tractors?"

"No."

"All right. We'll sell him a few."

"We can't. He's doing the whole thing by hand labor—picks and shovels and wheelbarrows."

"I'll soon argue him out of that idea," I said. "Just wait till I show him how much labor he'll save by getting rid of his medieval implements and doing the job as the Lord intended—with Earthworm tractors."

"But he doesn't want to save labor."

"Why not? Is he crazy?"

"No. He's just trying to be public-spirited. He is building the road without machinery so as to provide work for all of the town's unemployed who want it—which means about twenty men. Besides helping these people, the commissioner feels he is benefiting the whole town by keeping all the money right here."

"A swell benefit that is to the town as a whole," I said. "All that guy is doing is subsidizing inefficiency. He may be handing out a little temporary relief to a few unfortunates, but he is cheating all the rest of the town by giving them only about a quarter as much road as they are entitled to from the money he is spending."

"Maybe you're right," said Mr. Dow, "but you'll never make the road commissioner see it that way. He has made up his mind that he is the guardian angel of the unemployed, and nobody can tell him any different. He's just as stubborn as I am."

"In that case," I said, "he must be a tough customer. But there must be some way to get to him."

"I'm afraid not," said Mr. Dow. "He'll never buy a tractor as long as there are men in this town who want work and can't get it."

At this point I suddenly got one of those keen and practical ideas which so often come to me in difficult situations. "I know how we can handle this thing," I said. "It is very simple. All we have to do is get rid of the unemployed."

"Drown them in the river or something?"

"No. Give them jobs."

"Doing what?"

"Anything. You might, for instance, open up your gold mine and hire all these men away from the road commissioner. Then he would have to buy a tractor."

"Maybe so. But where would I come out? I'd be paying wages to twenty men and nothing to show for it."

"You would have a lot to show for it," I said. "You would sell a four-thousand-dollar tractor, on which your commission would be eight hundred dollars. That would carry your pay roll for a week and still show you a handsome profit. At the end of the week—after you had sold the tractor—you could shut down."

"And turn all those men loose again without any jobs?"

"Oh, they would be all right," I said. "The road commissioner would probably hire them back. He has enough money to buy a tractor and hire these men besides. But you might find you could make enough out of the mine to keep running for quite a while."

"And eventually go busted like my father did."

"No," I said. "If you were a deep student of political economy, such as I am, you would know that this is a peculiarly auspicious time to run a gold mine."

"In spite of the depression?"

"Because of the depression," I said. "Production costs—labor and supplies and everything—are low. And the product, gold, automatically sells at par. You would have a much better chance than your father had."

"Well, I don't know," said Mr. Dow. "I'm not a student of political economy, like you, but I do know that in the 70's, when my father was working this mine, prices were even lower than they are today. And gold was selling at a premium, because all the money was paper, which was not redeemable in specie. It looks like my father had a better chance than I would have."

"At first sight," I admitted, "it might look that way. And as you are not a student of political economy, I can't go into the matter deeply enough to show you where you are wrong. But, regardless of theoretical considerations, I am convinced that it would be of tremendous practical benefit both to yourself and to the tractor business if you would take a chance on this gold-mining proposition."

"I wouldn't even consider it," said Mr. Dow. "I've told you before that I don't know anything about gold mining—and I don't want to know anything about it."

"You said your son has just graduated in mining engineering, and has no job. Why not let him run this mine?"

"And bankrupt the whole family? I should say not."

"Your son will be home in a day or so, won't he?"

"Yes."

"It wouldn't hurt anything to talk the thing over with him?"

"No, I suppose not."

"All right then," I said, "I won't bother you any more about it right now, but when your son arrives we will get together and decide what to do."

"It don't sound good to me," said Mr. Dow.

"Perhaps you will change your mind later," I said. "And now I think I'll be getting back to the hotel for lunch. I'll see you again this afternoon or tomorrow. Good-by."

I left the old guy sprawled out languidly in his office chair with his feet in the same position on top of the desk. As I walked along toward the hotel I kept turning this gold-mine idea over and over in my mind, and the more I thought about it the better it seemed. By the time I reached the hotel, I had made up my mind to make a little private investigation of the mine as soon as possible. As I am fairly ignorant about such matters, I decided I would need expert advice. On the chance that I might possibly run across something, I asked the hotel clerk whether there was such a thing as a mining engineer in town, and if not, where would be the nearest place I could find one.

The clerk did not even seem to know what a mining engineer was. He doubted if any such thing could be found in town, or even in Rutland or Burlington. He said, however, he would make inquiries. After thanking him I went in to lunch.

Half an hour later, when I came out of the dining room, the clerk called me and introduced a very courteous and pleasant-spoken gentleman by the name of Mr. Bailey Bryant. It appeared that Mr. Bryant was from New York, and had arrived at the hotel two or three days before to take advantage of the excellent fishing in the mountain streams of the neighborhood. He had heard the hotel clerk inquiring for a mining engineer, and as that was his profession he had stepped forward to offer his services.

This was indeed a piece of splendid good luck, and a striking example of how fortune seems to favor a man like myself who is always on the alert and ready to grasp any opportunity that presents itself.

At once I took Mr. Bryant aside, explained the whole situation completely and frankly, much as I have set it forth in this letter, and asked him if he would look over the mine and give me his opinion on it. He replied that he would be delighted, and we started to walk up the mountain to the little shed which Mr. Dow had pointed out to me.

On the way Mr. Bryant gave me a number of fascinating reminiscences of his gold-mining experiences in South Africa, in California and in Alaska. Seldom have I met a more brilliant conversationalist. As I am a very good judge of men, it did not take me long to realize that in spite of his modest manner Mr. Bryant possessed an unusually powerful intellect and was a real authority in his field.

When we reached the mine we discovered that it was a small tunnel, perhaps six feet in diameter, cut horizontally into the solid rock of the mountain. Mr. Bryant, with admirable foresight, had brought an electric flash light. Although the tunnel was partially obstructed by fallen rocks and rubbish, we had no trouble in penetrating to its end, which was perhaps a hundred yards from the opening.

My companion subjected the rock walls to the most minute and painstaking examination, while I stood by in a state of suppressed excitement—eager to ask questions, but holding on to myself so as not to interrupt the train of his thought. From time to time he loosened small fragments of stone, examined them with a lens and put them in his pocket. He seemed particularly interested in the rock at the end of the tunnel, and here he took three or four samples. After perhaps half an hour, we returned to the opening.

"This is most interesting," he said. "As a careful scientist, I naturally hesitate to commit myself absolutely, but I do not mind telling you that every indication points to the fact that the work on this mine was stopped at the very moment when the richest ore was about to be uncovered."

"You really think so?" I asked.

"That is my opinion," he said. "Look. Here is a specimen from about the middle of the tunnel. Ordinary Barre granite with a trace of mica. Possibly a little gold in it, but obviously not much."

"It certainly is not much to look at," I said.

"No," he agreed, "but now cast your eye on this, which came from the end of the tunnel." He held up a piece of whitish stone. "Pure quartz, and in a formation completely analogous to that of the great Comstock lode in Nevada. It is most interesting."

"Then you really think it would pay to work this mine?"

"Before giving you a definite answer, I should have to make a more complete survey. It will be necessary for me to blast off a little more rock at the end of the tunnel, so as to uncover the richer ore which I hope to find just back of the present face. Then, after making a chemical and microscopic examination of the ore, I would be in a position to give you a very definite opinion based upon solid scientific facts."

"Would you be willing," I asked, "to make this examination for me?"

"Certainly," he replied. "You understand, of course, that I will have to charge you for it. I have been glad to give you my unofficial opinion free, but for a regular professional report I would have to ask my regular professional fee, which is a hundred dollars."

"Holy Moses!" I said. "A hundred dollars?"

"That," he said, "is my regular fee."

"Well," I said, "I guess that's perfectly reasonable for expert advice from an important guy like you, but I don't know just how I am going to pay it. I can't afford the expense myself. And I'm afraid the company wouldn't let me get away with it on the expense account. Mr. Dow really ought to pay it himself. But he's so tight with his money that I don't believe we could talk it out of him—unless, of course, it turned out that the mine was a real bonanza like you think it is. And listen. That gives me an idea. How would you like to gamble on this—double or quits?"

"What do you mean?" he asked.

"If it turns out that this thing is a big money maker, I'll guarantee you two hundred dollars—double your fee. In that case I'm practically sure I can get that much out of old man Dow. Almost anybody would pay two hundred dollars for a real gold mine. So I'm willing to take a chance, and, if he won't pay you, I will. On the other hand, if we don't find this rich ore you're looking for, we'll call it quits and you get nothing. How about it?"

"Fair enough," said Mr. Bryant. "Every mining engineer is a gambler at heart, and I'm no exception."

We shook hands on the bargain and returned to the town, where Mr. Bryant left me. He said he would get the supplies he needed and return to the mine to make his investigations, and he courteously declined my offer of assistance, saying that he could work better and concentrate more effectively when he was alone.

I spent the remainder of the afternoon seeing if I could discover any further opportunities for possible tractor sales. I ran into nothing, however, that looked in any way promising.

This evening I have been writing this report. I have just seen Mr. Bryant in the lobby. He reports that his investigations have proceeded very satisfactorily, and he wishes me to bring Mr. Dow up to the mine tomorrow morning so that we can all look over the ground together. When I asked him whether his report would be as favorable as he had hoped, he merely smiled and said that he would prefer to say nothing until tomorrow.

I have just called up Mr. Dow and arranged to go with him to the mine in the morning. So the stage is all set, and I have high hopes.

I have given you this very full account of my activities, so that you can see I am pulling off a very remarkable and brainy piece of work here, and so that there will be no question about allowing the two hundred dollars in case I should have to put it in my expense account.

Very sincerely,

ALEXANDER BOTTS.

ALEXANDER BOTTS
SALES PROMOTION REPRESENTATIVE
EARTHWORM TRACTOR COMPANY
DOW'S GULF, VERMONT

Tuesday, June 7, 1932.

Mr. Gilbert Henderson,
Sales Manager,
Earthworm Tractor Company,
Earthworm City, Illinois.

DEAR HENDERSON: What a day this has been—what a day! When I wrote you yesterday, I was expecting something pretty good, but never in my wildest dreams had I anticipated anything so sensational and so glorious as what has actually come to pass. But I must try to begin at the beginning and relate my wonderful news in an orderly manner.

This morning Mr. Bryant, Mr. Dow and I walked up to the mine. Mr. Bryant maintained his quiet and sophisticated reserve, but there was about him a subtle air of optimism which both stimulated me and aroused my curiosity. Mr. Dow was good-natured, but inclined to scoff at the whole expedition. I had told him that my friend was a mining engineer who had kindly consented to look over his mine and give him an opinion as to its value. As for myself, I was in such a flutter of anxiety and suspense that I could hardly wait to hear Mr. Bryant's verdict.

When we reached the mouth of the tunnel, Mr. Bryant gave us a brief description of the geological formation in which the mine was located, and then explained the various factors which had caused him to believe that there might be a very rich vein of what he called auriferous quartz immediately beyond the end of the tunnel. This explanation was couched in scientific language—which I will not repeat, partly because I can't remember it, and partly because you guys at the tractor factory couldn't understand it anyway. After giving us the low-down on these theoretical matters, Mr. Bryant told us what he had done the previous afternoon.

"I got some tools and a couple of sticks of dynamite at the hardware store," he said. "Then I came up here, drilled a hole into the rock face at the end of the tunnel, and set off a small charge. The results"—and here he smiled in a mysterious and highly dramatic manner—"were so favorable that I think they can be appreciated by almost anyone. If you will step this way I will show you something that you will have no trouble in comprehending, no matter whether you have any technical training or not."

Snapping on his electric flash light, he led us through the tunnel to its extreme end. At once I noticed that the blast he had spoken of had exposed a fresh surface of rock. It was white quartz.

"Look at it a little closer," said Mr. Bryant.

Mr. Dow and I did so. And what I saw made my heart start beating and pounding in a way that it has not done for years. All over the surface of the rock, embedded in the seams and crevices, were thousands of glittering, shining yellow particles. Some were as small as grains of the finest powder. Others were the size of peas, and a few were actually as large as small acorns. It was some minutes before I could speak.

"Is it," I asked—"is it really gold?"

"Yes," said Mr. Bryant, "it is gold—and as remarkable a vein as I've seen for years." He turned to Mr. Dow. "Permit me to congratulate you," he said. "You are many times a millionaire."

It was quite evident from Mr. Dow's expression that this great discovery had knocked his intellect into a confused and dizzy whirl. He leaped forward and began clawing little chunks of the beautiful yellow metal out of the rock and turning them over and over in his hands. His naturally cautious nature prevented him from completely accepting the obvious facts, but, at the same time, he was rapidly becoming drunk at the sight and the feel of the gold, and at the thought of the incredible riches that now were his.

"I can hardly believe it," he kept saying. "I can hardly believe it. Is it really true that I am a millionaire?"

"Well," said Mr. Bryant, "the great Comstock Lode yielded something over three hundred million dollars."

"Three hundred millions dollars!" gasped Mr. Dow.

"Three hundred million dollars," repeated Mr. Bryant. "And the geologic formation here is strikingly similar to the Comstock formation—which is a fact of great scientific interest. Of course, I do not claim that this vein will turn out as well. It might yield much more, but, on the other hand, it might not run more than fifty or a hundred million."

"Well," said Mr. Dow, "even if it was only one million dollars, that would be quite a bit of money." He continued clawing out little pieces of the metal. Apparently he couldn't wait even a moment, and he wanted to get the stuff into his hands as fast as possible.

I began to get the fever myself, and it occurred to me that possibly I had handled this thing wrong. The investigation of the mine had been my idea in the first place, and with a little more forethought I might have managed so that I would have owned a substantial share.

Mr. Bryant, the engineer, was the only one of us who maintained a normal calmness. "I would suggest," he said to Mr. Dow, "that you say nothing about this to anyone until you have checked over your title to the land and made absolutely sure that no one else has even a shadow of a claim on it. Furthermore, you may want to buy additional land, in case investigation should indicate that you do not own the entire deposit."

"That certainly is a good idea," said Mr. Dow. "You have a real head on you, Mr. Bryant. How would you advise me to go about working this mine?"

"That," said Mr. Bryant, "will have to be decided after a thorough investigation of all the factors involved. Unfortunately, I won't be able to stay long enough to see the mine put on a permanent operating basis. I'm up here only for a short vacation, and pressing business will make it necessary for me to return to New York very soon. But, if you wish, I can stay around for three or four days to advise you and get you started right."

"That would be fine," said Mr. Dow. "That would be wonderful. You don't know how I appreciate this, Mr. Bryant. How can I ever repay you for what you have done ?"

"Well," said Mr. Bryant, "my fee for this preliminary examination, as agreed upon by Mr. Botts and myself, is two hundred dollars. That will include my time for yesterday and today. For each additional day, starting tomorrow, I will charge you my usual rate of one hundred dollars a day."

The mention of this rate of payment served to arouse momentarily Mr. Dow's deeply ingrained New England thrift. "A hundred dollars a day is a lot of money," he said.

"Yes," agreed Mr. Bryant pleasantly, "but not a great deal in comparison to a three-hundred-million-dollar gold mine."

"You're right," said Mr. Dow, "and you will have to excuse me for seeming so small-minded. As a matter of fact, I guess your charges are pretty small, and I will be delighted to pay them. They will be a mere drop in the bucket as compared to the gold in this mine. But I was just wondering—have you really analyzed this stuff in here? Are you absolutely sure it's actually gold, and not just copper or something? Wouldn't it, perhaps, be a good idea to get some real chemist to analyze it for us, so we'd be certain? I have a cousin that teaches in the chemistry department of

Middlebury College, which is only about thirty miles away across these mountains. I could take a sample over and he could tell me all about it."

"If you ask me," I said, "I would say that you would just be wasting your time. Mr. Bryant is a professional mining engineer. He has worked in mines all over the world. And he knows his gold, and his silver, and his copper, and his tin, and everything else. If he says it's gold, that's what it is. What more could you learn from a fool college professor?"

At this point Mr. Bryant spoke up and showed what a truly broad-minded man he is. "Mr. Dow is perfectly right," he said. "To a man of my experience, it is evident that this material is gold. It is my business to know about such things, and I do know. I am certain. But it is perfectly natural for a man like Mr. Dow to have his doubts. And it is reasonable, in a matter of so much importance, that he should check the facts carefully. I should very much prefer that he get an independent opinion. In fact, I was going to suggest it myself. Here, take this."

He reached into his pocket, drew out a small pasteboard box and handed it to Mr. Dow.

"What's this for?" asked Mr. Dow.

"It is something to carry the gold which you have been pulling out of that rock."

By this time Mr. Dow had a whole handful of small nuggets. He put them in the pasteboard box. Mr. Bryant snapped a rubber band around it and handed it back.

"There you are," he said. "My advice would be that you step into your car, drive over to Middlebury and get your cousin to analyze that gold right away. While you are gone I will start an examination of this entire mountainside with a view to determining the possible extent of this deposit of auriferous quartz."

"It's a good idea," said Mr. Dow. "I'll start right away."

"And remember," cautioned Mr. Bryant, "don't breathe a word of this to anyone. Don't tell your cousin any more than you have to, and impress it upon him that the matter is to be kept secret."

"You can trust me," said Mr. Dow.

We all returned to the town, and Mr. Dow drove away in his

car. Mr. Bryant invited me to accompany him on his geologic expedition, explaining laughingly that he was afraid to leave me sitting around the hotel lobby, for fear I might be tempted to spread the great news. We had a very interesting day, tramping about the mountains. As I have said before, Mr. Bryant is one of the most charming conversationalists I have ever met. And the information which he gave me about the various rock formations was not only educational but highly interesting and enjoyable.

We got back to the hotel late in the afternoon, and soon afterward Mr. Dow arrived from Middlebury. He seemed even more agitated than in the morning, and as soon as the three of us were alone in my room he actually began dancing around the floor, gibbering at us like an idiot.

"It's all true!" he said. "My cousin analyzed it, and it's gold! Think of it! Real gold! And there's millions of dollars' worth in that mountain! And it all belongs to me! It all belongs to me!"

The old guy raved along, gloating over his good fortune in such a disgusting manner that I could not help being slightly annoyed—especially as I was to have no share in all this money that he was yawping about so loudly. At the same time I could get a little cynical amusement out of the change that had taken place in Mr. Dow's character. He had completely lost that quiet, philosophical manner, that quiet contentment with the simple life, which had been so evident at our first meeting. The sudden appearance of this vast amount of filthy gold had turned him into as greedy and material-minded a man as I had ever met. Ah, well, I thought to myself, all these things are no direct concern of mine. I came here for the purpose of promoting a few tractor sales, and it looked as if I were going to do it.

After a short conference we decided upon a definite plan of action for the next few days. Mr. Bryant is going to write to various firms in different parts of the country, asking their prices on machinery to be used in working the mine. The ore is so rich that the mine could be run at a profit with the crudest possible equipment, but Mr. Bryant pointed out that the greatest profits could only be realized through the use of the most up-to-date machinery. While waiting to hear from the manufacturers, Mr. Bryant will continue his geologic investigations.

Mr. Dow is going over tomorrow morning to hire away practically all the road commissioner's workmen. With these men and one of the two tractors which he has on hand, he is going to start building a road to the mine so that the heavy ore-crushing machinery, when it arrives, may be moved up without delay. He will tell his men that the road is to be used for getting out logs, and will carefully guard the secret of the great gold strike. As for myself, I will take the second of the two tractors which Mr. Dow has on hand, and start giving a demonstration to the road commissioner.

Thus you see that everything promises to work out splendidly. I am still somewhat confused by the magnitude of the events which have been transpiring, but I trust I have given you a reasonably clear account of them. Kindly keep all this news about the gold mine strictly confidential. We do not wish the discovery to leak out at this time.

Very sincerely,
ALEXANDER BOTTS.

ALEXANDER BOTTS
SALES PROMOTION REPRESENTATIVE
EARTHWORM TRACTOR COMPANY
DOW'S GULF, VERMONT

Thursday night, June 9, 1932.

Mr. Gilbert Henderson,
Sales Manager,
Earthworm Tractor Company,
Earthworm City, Illinois.

DEAR HENDERSON: Two days have passed since my last letter and there is nothing much to report except that everything is going along as planned. The great gold discovery is still a secret. Mr. Bryant is continuing his geologic researches. Mr. Dow is hard at work on his new road. He has two lawyers searching the titles of his land. And he is so smug and self-satisfied that he is positively obnoxious.

As for myself, I have been spending the last two days demonstrating the tractor to the road commissioner. This gentleman is a little sore at the high-handed way in which Mr. Dow has hired most of his men away from him. But he is a reasonable guy, holds no grudge against me, and is so favorably impressed with the tractor that I think he will decide to buy it in a day or so.

No more at present.

Very truly,
ALEXANDER BOTTS.

ALEXANDER BOTTS
SALES PROMOTION REPRESENTATIVE
EARTHWORM TRACTOR COMPANY
DOW'S GULF, VERMONT

Friday, June 10, 1932.

Mr. Gilbert Henderson,
Sales Manager,
Earthworm Tractor Company,
Earthworm City, Illinois.

DEAR HENDERSON: I regret to report that affairs here are not progressing in exactly the way I had expected. In fact, it now appears that in certain important matters I was so completely and absolutely mistaken that it is most embarrassing for me to explain what has occurred. However, it is always my policy to be perfectly frank. So in this case I will go ahead, following my usual custom, and tell you the whole distressing truth.

I spent this morning and most of this afternoon uneventfully enough, demonstrating the tractor on the road commissioner's cut-and-fill job. The commissioner himself was not present, being in town on some other business, but I went ahead just the same. At five o'clock I returned to town and stopped in at the post office to buy some stamps.

And here, without any warning whatsoever, I received what I can only describe as a very severe shock. As I turned away from the stamp window my eye was suddenly attracted to a picture which was posted on the bulletin board. This picture was a printed reproduction of a photograph, and it showed with great clearness the handsome and distinguished features of Mr. Bailey Bryant, the mining engineer from New York.

Above the picture were the words, "Wanted, For Grand Larceny, Uttering Counterfeit Notes, Using the Mails to Defraud, Obtaining Money Under False Pretenses, and Forgery." Beneath was a long list of names: "John Bailey, alias John Bryant, alias Bailey Spencer, alias Spencer the Spieler, alias Peter Livingston, alias Pete the Prestidigitator." After a full physical description, there followed further information: "This man is well educated, is a good talker on almost all subjects, has a most pleasing personality, and is remarkable for his versatility and for the variety of his swindles. Is an accomplished amateur magician and has, on several occasions, robbed jewelers by substituting an empty box for one containing valuable gems. Has posed at various times as physician, clergyman, Army officer and college president." The notice ended with a request that anyone apprehending this person should place him under arrest and communicate with a gentleman called Mulrooney down in New York.

You can well imagine the astonishment and consternation which filled my mind. At once I removed the notice from the bulletin board, folded it up, put it in my pocket and hurried over to Mr. Dow's office. Mr. Dow greeted me and introduced me to his son, who had arrived the day before from Columbia.

"Mr. Dow," I said, "I have very grave news for you. I have just discovered certain facts which lead me to believe that our friend, Mr. Bailey Bryant, is not the sort of man we think he is. In fact, I'm beginning to suspect that there may be something faintly cockeyed about this whole gold-mining enterprise."

"Yes," said Mr. Dow, "the same thought occurred to my son and myself this morning."

"This morning?" I asked.

"Well, my son began to be suspicious as long ago as yesterday afternoon. As soon as he got home I told him the great news, but he was not so enthusiastic as I had expected. It seems that last fall, without telling me anything about it, he had examined the mine, gathered up a few samples of the ore, and taken them to New York with him to be analyzed. The analysis showed a certain amount of gold, but there was nothing to indicate even the possibility of any such rich deposits as we had run across. So yesterday day my son went up to the mine, collected a few of those little golden nuggets and made some tests on them. They turned out to be nothing but brass."

"This is terrible," I said. "Did you tell Mr. Bryant about it?"

"At that time," said Mr. Dow, "Mr. Bryant was up in the mountains somewhere on one of his geological expeditions. In his absence we made a few inquiries around town."

"And what did you find?"

"We found that he had bought some brass pipe and a cheap shotgun at one of the hardware stores. Then he had visited a blacksmith and had him melt up the brass pipe and pour it out so that it formed a lot of small, irregular globules. He had also paid a visit to a dentist."

"You mean he was having trouble with his teeth?"

"No, he bought five dollars' worth of gold, and had the dentist melt it up and pour it out in little chunks very similar to the brass which the blacksmith had worked on. All this we found out yesterday. This morning we got Mr. Bryant in the office here and told him that we had the goods on him, and his game was up."

"What did he say?" I asked.

"At first he was very smooth, and pretended he didn't know what we were talking about. But when he saw that we had him right and proper, he owned up."

"He explained everything to you?"

"Yes," said Mr. Dow. "And some of it was pretty good. Especially what he had to say about you."

"Good Lord," I said, "what did he say about me?"

"He said that up to the time he met you he hadn't intended to pull anything crooked in this town at all. He was here partly for some fishing and a little vacation, and partly to get away from what he described as a rather unfortunate situation down in New York. But when he saw you he said you were such a perfect example of a born easy mark that he couldn't resist taking you for a ride."

"Well," I said sadly, "he certainly succeeded. He took me on a whole cruise. And I'm not sure that I understand even yet just how he managed everything."

"He told us," said Mr. Dow, "that he was going to be paid only in case the mine turned out to be worth something. That is why he arranged such a spectacular set-up. He wanted to make the mine look as good as possible. After he had uncovered a new face of rock with dynamite, he shot all that brass into it with his shotgun."

"But what about that sample that your cousin analyzed?"

"Apparently Mr. Bryant's hand is quicker than my eye. While he was putting a rubber band around the box I had filled with brass, he slipped it up his sleeve or something, and then handed me back another box with the dentist's gold in it."

"And to think," I said, "that I actually believed that guy, and swallowed everything he told me. I certainly owe you my most abject apologies. I thought I was helping you, and all I have done is to put you to a lot of trouble and expense over a mine that isn't worth a nickel."

"It isn't as bad as that," said Mr. Dow's son. "The mine is no such bonanza as you thought. But the analysis of the ore, which I made in New York last winter, shows that there actually is a small amount of gold present. In my grandfather's day the mine was a failure. But now, by putting in a little modern machinery and using the cyanide process, I'm certain that we can work it with a small but steady profit. I had intended to ask my father to finance the thing and let me run it, but he is so cautious that he never would have consented unless you and Mr. Bryant had got him started. As it is, he has to go on. He can't back out now."

"Why not?" I asked.

"He has already built a road halfway up to the mine. And he

promised all those men he hired from the road commissioner that he would give them work for the rest of the year. So he has to go on—and it's a very good thing."

I looked at Mr. Dow, Senior, to see what he thought of this. He was all stretched out in his office chair with his feet up on the desk, and his whole attitude expressed the same languid contentment which had been so noticeable on the day I first met him.

"Yes," he said, "the whole business suits me fine. For a while you had me all excited and het up over the idea of being a millionaire. And that is all wrong for a man of my age who has always been used to peace and quiet. If the excitement had kept up much longer I would have just naturally worn myself out and come to an unfortunate and premature end. As it is, I can sit around as usual with nothing in the world to worry me. On the other hand, I'm grateful to you because—"

"Why should you be grateful to me?" I asked.

"Because I had perhaps been getting a little too quiet and contented, and you have shaken me up enough to get me started on this gold mine. It will make a very nice little business for my son. It has already provided employment for a number of people here in town. And besides that, it has been of some assistance to the tractor business. I saw the road commissioner this afternoon and he told me he wants to buy the machine which you have been demonstrating. So everything is fine, and my thanks are due to both yourself and Mr. Bryant."

"By the way," I said, "what did you do with that guy? You didn't pay him anything, did you?"

"No. He agreed with us that, under the circumstances, we owed him nothing."

"But I suppose you know he's wanted down in New York." I showed him the notice I had brought from the post office.

"Well, well," said Mr. Dow. "My son and I had not seen this. If we had known about it, I suppose it would have been our duty to turn him over to the police. But as it was, we had no grudge against him and we let him go. He took the noon train for Canada. And on the whole, I'm glad he got away. It was a lucky thing for us he came to town. And I can say the same thing regarding you, Mr. Botts."

"I hope," I said, "that you're not classing me with Mr. Bryant. Certainly, you don't believe that I'm a crook?"

"Oh, no, indeed," said Mr. Dow. "Anybody as slow-witted as you couldn't be a crook. We realize perfectly that you are completely honest and that you meant well. And as a matter of fact you have, in your awkward way, helped us and our business a great deal. So we thank you from the bottom of our hearts."

As I could not think of any good answer to these various cracks of Mr. Dow's, I wished him and his son good afternoon as politely as I could and returned to the hotel. I am leaving tomorrow for the next job.

As ever,

ALEXANDER BOTTS.

The Depression Is Over

OFFICE OF THE SALES MANAGER
EARTHWORM TRACTOR COMPANY
EARTHWORM CITY, ILLINOIS

Thursday, July 12, 1934.

Mr. Olaf Andersen,
Manager Earthworm Tractor Exhibit,
Century of Progress Exposition,
Chicago, Illinois.

DEAR MR. ANDERSEN: We are shipping you today by express one special high-speed rotary water pump designed to be attached to the rear end of the transmission case of our new one-hundred-horse-power Earthworm Tractor.

This pump is a new model and will not be in regular production until the middle of next month. In order that you may have a sample of the pump to exhibit at the fair, we have assembled one out of such parts as are at present available. It is complete in every way except for the two steel gears in the case behind the pump chamber. As production on these gears has been delayed, we have had our pattern shop turn out two mahogany gears which have been installed in place of the steel ones. The mahogany gears have been coated with aluminum paint, so they look just like steel. And they are so accurately made that they operate with complete smoothness.

If you will remove the cover plates from the pump and gear case, you can give prospective customers a very effective demonstration by turning the gears by hand. Be sure that nobody tries to use the pump. I have attached a tag reading: "For exhibition purposes only. Not to be sold or attached to any tractor," and I would suggest that you leave this tag in place. But you had better not tell anyone that the gears are fakes. We do not want to advertise the fact that we are behind in our production. If anybody wants to buy a pump, you will order it through the factory, and shipment will be made as soon as possible.

I am inclosing a letter for Mr. Alexander Botts, our traveling representative. Mr. Botts has been in the East, and expects to arrive in Chicago and call on you within the next few days.

Very truly,

GILBERT HENDERSON,

Sales Manager.

OFFICE OF THE SALES MANAGER
EARTHWORM TRACTOR COMPANY
EARTHWORM CITY, ILLINOIS

Thursday, July 12, 1934.

Mr. Alexander Botts,
Care Mr. Olaf Andersen,
Earthworm Tractor Exhibit,
Century of Progress Exposition,
Chicago, Illinois.

DEAR BOTTS: Our business has recently been increasing to such an extent that we are planning a reorganization in the sales department, as well as in certain other parts of the company. As this may affect your position, we want you to come down to Earthworm City at once, so that we may talk matters over with you.

Very sincerely,

GILBERT HENDERSON,

Sales Manager.

ALEXANDER BOTTS
SALES PROMOTION REPRESENTATIVE
EARTHWORM TRACTOR COMPANY
CHICAGO, ILLINOIS

Monday, July 16, 1934.

Mr. Gilbert Henderson,
Sales Manager,
Earthworm Tractor Company,
Earthworm City, Illinois.

DEAR HENDERSON: I arrived in Chicago this morning. I am certainly glad to hear, from your letter, that the business of the Earthworm Company is increasing. It begins to look as if the depression is very definitely a thing of the past. Here at the World's Fair, everything seems to be booming. The whole place swarms with people, and most of them look as if they had money and wanted to spend it. Our Earthworm tractor exhibit is crowded all the time, and a whole lot of the visitors are big contractors who are real sure-enough hot prospects.

As a matter of fact, business is so active that I will not be able, at the present time, to come down to Earthworm City as suggested in your letter. I am leaving for Cold River, Wisconsin, instead, for the purpose of selling one or more of our machines to a big contractor by the name of Duffield Watt. Mr. Watt stopped in at our exhibit at the fair soon after I arrived this morning. I discovered he was interested in buying some extra machinery for a large sewer-ditch-digging job which he is starting at the town of Cold River, Wisconsin. He had talked with our dealer at Cold River. And this dealer had apparently been so ineffective in his sales arguments that Mr. Watt had failed to buy, and had come down here to the fair in order to look over our exhibit and also the exhibits of our competitors.

As soon as Mr. Watt told me this, I decided that I would have to get busy. If the Earthworm dealer at Cold River is such a sap that he weakly permits a live prospect to get out of his clutches and go wandering about the country investigating competing machines, it is high time for somebody like myself to step in and take charge of affairs.

Mr. Watt is returning to Cold River tomorrow morning. I am going along with him, and I will camp right on his trail until he buys at least one Earthworm tractor. You may address me in care of the Earthworm dealer at Cold River, Wisconsin.

Very sincerely,

ALEXANDER BOTTS.

TELEGRAM

EARTHWORM CITY ILL JULY 17 1934

ALEXANDER BOTTS
CARE EARTHWORM TRACTOR DEALER
COLD RIVER WIS
COME TO EARTHWORM CITY AT ONCE AS RE-
QUESTED IN MY LETTER STOP LET LOCAL DEALER
HANDLE SALE TO DUFFIELD WATT
GILBERT HENDERSON

NIGHT LETTER

COLD RIVER WIS JULY 18 1934

GILBERT HENDERSON
EARTHWORM TRACTOR COMPANY
EARTHWORM CITY ILL
LOCAL DEALER IS A MERE SPINELESS OYSTER INCA-
PABLE OF HANDLING THIS IMPORTANT DEAL STOP I
HAVE INVESTIGATED MR WATTS DITCH DIGGING JOB
AND FIND HE IS HAVING TROUBLE WITH WATER SEEP-
ING INTO DITCH AND NEEDS TO PURCHASE PUMP-
ING EQUIPMENT STOP I AM SURE I CAN SELL HIM
ONE OF THE TRACTORS IN DEALERS STOCK HERE IF

IT IS EQUIPPED WITH PUMP STOP AND IF THIS WORKS
WELL HE MAY BUY SEVERAL MORE OUTFITS STOP
PLEASE SHIP EXPRESS DOUBLE RUSH ONE SPECIAL
HIGHSPEED ROTARY WATER PUMP FOR ONE HUN-
DRED HORSE POWER EARTHWORM TRACTOR JUST
LIKE THE ONE ON EXHIBITION AT FAIR IN CHICAGO
    ALEXANDER BOTTS

––––––––––––––––

TELEGRAM
EARTHWORM CITY ILL JULY 19 1934

ALEXANDER BOTTS
CARE EARTHWORM TRACTOR DEALER
COLD RIVER WIS
WATER PUMP AS ORDERED IN YOUR WIRE IS NEW
MODEL NOT YET AVAILABLE STOP WILL SHIP AS SOON
AS POSSIBLE PROBABLY ABOUT THREE WEEKS STOP
IMPERATIVE THAT YOU COME TO EARTHWORM CITY
AT ONCE
    GILBERT HENDERSON

––––––––––––––––

TELEGRAM
COLD RIVER WIS JULY 19 1934

GILBERT HENDERSON
EARTHWORM TRACTOR COMPANY
EARTHWORM CITY ILL
CANT WAIT THREE WEEKS STOP YOU WILL HAVE TO
SHIP ME THE PUMP ON EXHIBIT AT CHICAGO STOP
PLEASE SEND BY EXPRESS RUSH
    ALEXANDER BOTTS

TELEGRAM
EARTHWORM CITY ILL JULY 19 1934

ALEXANDER BOTTS
CARE EARTHWORM TRACTOR DEALER
COLD RIVER WIS
CANNOT SHIP PUMP FROM FAIR AS IT IS FOR EXHI-
BITION PURPOSES ONLY AND NOT FOR SALE STOP
COME TO EARTHWORM CITY AT ONCE STOP YOU
MUST BE HERE IN TIME FOR SPECIAL MEETING OF
OFFICERS AND DIRECTORS AT TEN OCLOCK SATUR-
DAY MORNING JULY TWENTY FIRST
    GILBERT HENDERSON

ALEXANDER BOTTS
SALES PROMOTION REPRESENTATIVE
EARTHWORM TRACTOR COMPANY
COLD RIVER, WISCONSIN

Saturday evening, July 21, 1934.

Mr. Gilbert Henderson,
Sales Manager,
Earthworm Tractor Company,
Earthworm City, Illinois.

DEAR HENDERSON: I have very good news for you.

Your wire refusing to ship the pump from Chicago arrived yesterday morning—Friday. As soon as I had read it, I realized that you had no real comprehension of the urgency of the situation up here, and I therefore decided that I would have to get busy and go ahead on my own initiative.

Accordingly, I took the first train to Chicago. I arrived there late yesterday afternoon and went at once to our exhibit at the fair, where I informed Mr. Olaf Andersen that I had come to take away the water pump. I had anticipated no great trouble in talk-

95

ing him out of this piece of machinery, but, unfortunately, he seems to be as dumb and stubborn an old fellow as I have ever run across. All my arguments made no impression on him.

He first of all told me that he could not let me take the pump, and then he showed me a silly tag which some boob had fastened onto it. The tag read as follows: "For exhibition purposes only. Not to be sold or attached to any tractor." When I explained to him that my need for this pump was far more important than any mere exhibit, and asked him if there was any real reason why he could not let me have it, he merely became evasive and said that he did not care to discuss the matter. Somehow, I don't like that guy—which is natural enough, because his failure to cooperate caused me a most annoying delay.

As a matter of fact, I had to wait until five o'clock the next morning—today—at which time I went out to the fair grounds and carted away the pump in a little pick-up truck, which I had rented for this purpose. I had an awful time talking my way past the guards at the gate and the watchman in the building where our exhibit is located. In the end, however, I managed to get away with my loot long before Mr. Andersen arrived to open up the exhibit. As soon as I was safely outside the fair grounds, I headed north, and arrived up here in Cold River toward the end of the morning.

I at once got in touch with Mr. Duffield Watt, and asked him to come around to the dealer's showroom here. By the time he arrived, I had already installed the pump on the rear end of one of the machines which was in stock here. As soon as Mr. Watt saw the complete outfit, he decided that it was exactly what he wanted. I offered to demonstrate it for him, but he said that he would take my word for it that it would perform as advertised. He promptly wrote out his check for the full purchase price of both the tractor and the pump, the dealer gave him a bill of sale, and then one of his mechanics drove the machine off in the direction of the big ditch which he is digging.

Tomorrow morning I will drive my rented truck back to Chicago, where I will await your further instructions. It seems useless for me to go on to Earthworm City, as the meeting which you wired me you wanted me to attend took place at ten o'clock this morning. Besides, there are a lot of things at the fair that I want to see, so I will just stick around there the next few days.

My success in putting over the sale of the tractor and pump to Mr. Duffield Watt naturally fills me with a warm glow of satisfaction. In the first place, I am always particularly happy when I sell a machine which I am so absolutely sure will give complete satisfaction to the purchaser. And, in the second place, it is a real indication of returning prosperity when a man makes up his mind to buy a machine without any long period of negotiation and demonstration, and then pays cash in full. This certainly reenforces my opinion that the depression is over and that all our troubles are at an end at last. And, incidentally, Mr. Watt has stated that if this pump-and-tractor combination works out all right—which, of course, it will—he will buy four more similar outfits.

There is one unfortunate aspect to the situation, however. It seems rather too bad that in order to put over this deal I should have been compelled to demean myself; first, by having to argue with that dumb Andersen down at Chicago, and second, by being compelled to remove by stealth a pump which should have been promptly turned over to me when I first asked for it. For years I have been vainly hoping that sometime the Earthworm Tractor Company might be able to organize itself so that matters of this kind could be handled by somebody who actually understands conditions in the field, rather than by a sales office which is more or less cut off from all actual contact with the customers. I don't want to seem critical or anything like that, but I sometimes have a feeling that it would be a wonderful thing if the office of sales manager were held by a really experienced and practical salesman—such, for instance, as myself.

Most sincerely,
ALEXANDER BOTTS.

OFFICE OF THE PRESIDENT,
EARTHWORM TRACTOR COMPANY
EARTHWORM CITY, ILLINOIS

Monday, July 23, 1934.

Mr. Alexander Botts,
Care Mr. Olaf Andersen,
Earthworm Tractor Exhibit,
Century of Progress Exposition,
Chicago, Illinois.

MY DEAR MR. BOTTS: I have the honor to inform you that the board of directors has appointed you to the position of sales manager of the Earthworm Tractor Company in place of Mr. Gilbert Henderson. I trust that you will send us, at the earliest possible moment, your acceptance of this office.

Cordially yours,

JOHN MONTAGUE,
President Earthworm Tractor
Company.

ALEXANDER BOTTS
SALES PROMOTION REPRESENTATIVE
EARTHWORM TRACTOR COMPANY
CHICAGO, ILLINOIS

Tuesday, July 24, 1934.

Mr. John Montague,
President,
Earthworm Tractor Company,
Earhtworm City, Illinois.

MY DEAR SIR: I have the honor to inform you that I most emphatically refuse your offer of the position of sales manager of the Earthworm Tractor Company. In refusing, I may as well admit perfectly frankly that I would like nothing better than to have the job of sales manager, and I am pretty sure that I would be the best sales manager you ever had. But if you will give the matter a moment's thought, you must understand that my sense of loyalty to my old boss makes it absolutely impossible for me to climb into this office, figuratively speaking, over his dead body.

When I first received your letter, I was at a loss to understand why you should be offering me this promotion so suddenly, and without having given me even a hint of your intentions before-hand. Having thought the matter over, however, I have reached the conclusion that you and the directors of the company must in some way have got hold of the letter which I wrote to Mr. Henderson last Saturday. This letter contained such a clear state-ment of Mr. Henderson's shortcomings—as exemplified in his failure to send me that pump—and it contained such a convinc-ing argument in favor of having as sales manager a really practical man such as myself, that it is no wonder you were stampeded into firing poor old Henderson and offering the job to me.

The whole thing, however, is profoundly disturbing to me. I want to assure you that my letter to Henderson was intended for him alone. All I was doing was merely giving him a well-deserved bawling out. I had no idea that anybody else would see this letter. And I had absolutely no intention of doing anything so base and lowdown as undermining the position of a man who is not only my boss but my friend as well. The old boy has his faults—as no one realizes more clearly than I—but he is, on the whole, a dis-tinctly good egg. He and I have had plenty of fights, in most of which he was in the wrong, but he always treated me absolutely fair and square, and I intend to treat him the same way.

I won't take your old job. And what is more, I won't even work for the company any more, unless you hire back Mr. Henderson at once. If you won't take both of us, you can't have either of us. And you can just take it from me that the poor old Earthworm Tractor Company would be in a sorry way indeed if it were to lose the services of both of us at the same time.

I trust that you will be able to notify me by return mail that this matter has been satisfactorily adjusted.

Yours respectfully, but firmly,

ALEXANDER BOTTS.

———————————

OFFICE OF THE SALES MANAGER
EARTHWORM TRACTOR COMPANY
EARTHWORM CITY, ILLINOIS

Wednesday, July 25, 1934.

Mr. Alexander Botts,
Care Mr. Olaf Andersen,
Earthworm Tractor Exhibit,
Century of Progress Exposition,
Chicago, Illinois.

DEAR BOTTS: Mr. John Montague has turned over to me your letter of yesterday. He claims he can't understand what you are talking about most of the time, and he wants me to answer for him. One reason for his failure to follow your arguments is that neither he nor the directors have seen your previous letter in which you suggested that you would like to be sales manager yourself. Consequently, your theory that this suggestion of yours influenced the directors in choosing you for the office is entirely unintelligible to Mr. Montague. As a matter of fact, the meeting at which you were selected as sales manager took place at ten o'clock on Saturday morning. The letter in which you nominated yourself for this office was written by you on Saturday evening. So it was obviously too late.

I am sorry that you were not present at the meeting on Saturday morning. For several weeks we had been discussing you as a possible candidate for sales manager, but many of the directors were very doubtful. They thought you were inclined to be entirely too wild and that you were hopelessly lacking in intelligence. It was to overcome these objections that I asked you to come to Earthworm City. I had hoped that if you were present, your undeniably pleasing personality might neutralize some of the opposition. And I was much disappointed when you disobeyed my instructions and failed to show up.

When the meeting took place, and you were not there, the task of pleading your cause fell entirely upon me. It turned out to be a rather difficult job. In the first place, I had to concede that most of the objections voiced by the opposition were perfectly true. I had to admit, in all honesty, that when it came to brains and intelligence you are not so very hot, and that there are times when your actions seem to indicate that you have the mind of a child of twelve. I also had to admit that you are inclined to disobey orders, that you are highly erratic, and that there is a wild harum-scarum quality to your mental processes which at times seems to approach very closely to actual insanity.

In spite of all these serious drawbacks, however, I pointed out that you had certain very positive virtues. And when I got onto the subject of these virtues, I was actually surprised, myself, at the number of good qualities you seem to possess. Without stretching the truth in any way, I was able to tell the directors that you are one of the most enthusiastic and energetic salesmen we have ever had. You have complete confidence in yourself and in the Earthworm Tractor. You never know when you are licked, and you always keep going, even in the face of the most appalling difficulties. You seem to have perfect poise at all times. You are friendly and optimistic; you get along with all kinds of people; and when you start talking about tractors, you have a flow of language that is truly overwhelming. You are dependable in the sense that we know you will never lie down on the job. And, most important of all, you pass the pragmatic test—you actually sell tractors.

As soon as I had finished my talk to the directors, they all agreed with me that your high qualities of character and performance were so remarkable and so valuable that they could afford to overlook the regrettable fact that you are slightly dumb all the time and crazy part of the time. They, therefore, voted you in as sales manager. At the same time they approved the rest of our reorganization plan: Mr. John Montague, who is now president, will assume the newly created position of chairman of the board, and I will be promoted to be president of the company.

I want to thank you most sincerely for your friendship, as evidenced by your refusal to accept a promotion which you thought would be at my expense. And I want you to know that I appreciate your loyalty—even though you did not know what you were talking about when you so hastily jumped to the conclusion that I had been fired.

I trust you will wire me at once that you are accepting your new job.

Most sincerely,

GILBERT HENDERSON.

———————

TELEGRAM

CHICAGO ILL JULY 26 1934

GILBERT HENDERSON
EARTHWORM TRACTOR COMPANY
EARTHWORM CITY ILL
CONGRATULATIONS ON YOUR PROMOTION STOP OF COURSE I ACCEPT THE JOB OF SALES MANAGER STOP NOW THAT THE DEPRESSION IS OVER AND NOW THAT YOU AND I ARE STEPPING INTO THESE BETTER JOBS FOR WHICH OUR TALENTS SO WELL QUALIFY US THE FUTURE IS INDEED BRIGHT STOP ADVISE WHEN YOU WANT ME TO COME DOWN AND ASSUME NEW DUTIES

ALEXANDER BOTTS

TELEGRAM
EARTHWORM CITY ILL JULY 26 1934

ALEXANDER BOTTS
CARE OLAF ANDERSEN
EARTHWORM TRACTOR EXHIBIT
CENTURY OF PROGRESS EXPOSITION
CHICAGO ILL
PLEASE REPORT HERE AT ONCE STOP YOUR FIRST
JOB AS SALES MANAGER WILL BE TO TRY TO ADJUST
A LITTLE DIFFICULTY UP AT COLD RIVER WISCON-
SIN STOP DUFFIELD WATT HAS JUST SENT FRANTIC
TELEGRAM SAYING THAT PUMP WONT WORK STOP
WHEN HE FIRST TRIED TO USE IT THERE WAS
A GRINDING CRASH INSIDE AND WHEN HE OPEN-
ED THE GEAR CASE HE FOUND IT WAS FILLED WITH
SPLINTERS OF WOOD STOP I AM DELIGHTED THAT
YOU WILL HAVE TO HANDLE THIS INSTEAD OF ME
STOP THE DEPRESSION MAY BE OVER BUT AS SALES
MANAGER OF THE EARTHWORM TRACTOR COM-
PANY YOUR TROUBLES ARE ONLY BEGINNING TAKE
IT FROM ONE WHO KNOWS
    HENDERSON

Confidential Stuff

OFFICE OF ALEXANDER BOTTS
SALES MANAGER
EARTHWORM TRACTOR COMPANY
EARTHWORM CITY, ILLINOIS

Monday, November 20, 1939.

Mr. Gilbert Henderson,
President Earthworm Tractor Company,
Earthworm Tractor Company Branch Office,
San Francisco, California.

DEAR HENDERSON: I need your help. I have just visited Washington, D.C., in connection with the confidential matter we discussed the last time you were in Earthworm City. I had a long talk with that highly disagreeable, self-important stuffed shirt with the red face and the wart on the side of his nose, whom you will doubtless remember as unpleasantly as I do, and whom I will designate—because of the before-mentioned confidential nature of this matter—merely as General X.

Why they put this superannuated horse cavalryman in a position where he seems to have the final word on equipment for motorized outfits, I do not know. But there he is. And he gets worse all the time. He apparently thinks that the Behemoth Company makes just as good tractors as we do. He says he will consider nothing for the Army but what he calls "tested and tried" commercial models. And he refuses even to look at the new high-speed stuff which our experimental department is now developing.

But I am going to fool him. The old guy is leaving in a few days to spend the winter studying the various artillery outfits in Hawaii. So I am going to ship one of our new specials out there just as soon as it is ready—probably in about a month—and I will instruct our Honolulu representative to force a demonstration on him. If he once sees what we can do, even his obtuse mind cannot help but be impressed.

In the meantime, I want you to contact the guy and give him a sales talk in San Francisco. He will be at the St. Francis Hotel next week. And it is possible he may listen to you more readily than to me, because he is a great respector of rank, and he probably thinks the president of a company is more important and knows more than the sales manager.

I am sorry to be so vague regarding such details as the name of the general and the exact nature of the machine I am going to ship to Honolulu. But you will get the general idea, and I do not want to put too much confidential information in a letter which might fall into the hands of a third person. As you know, the War Department has warned us that we must take unusual precautions to protect our secret plans and designs from the horde of foreign spies which has recently invaded our country.

Very sincerely,
ALEXANDER BOTTS.

TELEGRAM
SAN FRANCISCO CALIF NOVEMBER 22 1939 5 P.M.

ALEXANDER BOTTS SALES MANAGER
EARTHWORM TRACTOR CO
EARTHWORM CITY ILL
THE SUGGESTIONS IN YOUR NOVEMBER TWENTY LETTER ARE NOTED AND I WILL TAKE UP ALL ANGLES WITH YOU ON MY RETURN TO EARTHWORM CITY IN ABOUT SIX WEEKS. IN THE MEANTIME FOR OBVIOUS REASONS I ASK THAT YOU KEEP ALL REFERENCE TO CONFIDENTIAL MATTERS OUT OF THE MAILS
GILBERT HENDERSON
PRESIDENT EARTHWORM TRACTOR CO

OFFICE OF ALEXANDER BOTTS

Monday, December 18, 1939.

Mr. Gilbert Henderson,
San Francisco, California.

DEAR HENDERSON: Since receiving your somewhat brusque telegram, I have not written you at all for almost a month.

Merely keeping still, however, is not the only thing I have been doing. While following your advice—excellent as far as it goes—and observing the well-known military principle of keeping important information away from possible enemies, I have been actively turning my attention to a second, equally well-known principle which you have apparently never even heard of. This second principle requires that we must not, while shutting off the light from others, plunge ourselves into the Stygian darkness of our own smoke screen. In other words, we must have some safe method of transmitting secret information among ourselves.

Having come to the above conclusion soon after receiving your telegram, I promptly appealed to the War Department, and was referred to the Bridgeport Protectotype Corporation, of Bridgeport, Connecticut, from whom I have purchased six of their latest, improved, multiple-cam cipher machines.

These devices are the last word in scientific cryptography. To encipher a message, you pound out the words on a keyboard like a typewriter, and the letters come through completely scrambled up and neatly arranged in groups of five. To decipher, you merely reverse the process. The makers of these machines explain that the basic principle involved in their operation depends on a sequence of alphabetical displacements of varying degree, mechanically produced through the agency of an almost infinite number of minute indentations in the periphery of a series of interchangeable precision-built enciphering cams which are supplied in identical sets for all machines in a group, and are serially numbered, so that a different cam may be used for each message—all of which is supposed to be very simple, but if you can't understand it, don't worry, because I have arranged a setup that is efficient and completely foolproof.

One of the machines has been installed here at the home office, and the others have been sent, with full directions, to our five principal branches. A wire from the San Francisco manager reports that his machine has been placed in charge of a trustworthy employee, and that she has become, after a week of intensive practice, a thoroughly competent operator.

I will therefore bring these remarks to a close, and write out a secret message which will be enciphered by our newly established Department of Cryptography, and enclosed herewith. As soon as you have had the message run through the machine out there, you will be in possession of a bit of confidential news so interesting and important that I am sure you will be both surprised and pleased.

Awaiting your congratulations, I remain,

Your active and resourceful salesman,
ALEXANDER BOTTS.

ENCLOSURE
EARTHWORM TRACTOR COMPANY
EARTHWORM CITY, ILLINOIS
DEPARTMENT OF CRYPTOGRAPHY
MESSAGE NO. 1, CAM NO. 77

DEAR HENDERSON:
OFUTH QSWED MLJKU CVFGR ERDSZ QPGHC GJOLA
SKDJV GUTYW RTFGV IOJKN BHGRT WESDX ZSASQ
KOMHJ DKHFZ ZFJIP NHFES ZBHIY DFRTF CCBHI
MWTSQ ZSEXS KUIRF LXPDF HTYEF XHJBD SPHJE
CBVHT FGRTC DFERS HJUIN MJKIO GHTYR ALGHT
PFPFJ VHRYF GSTEZ CJTHD KKGIY VHRTE AEAIO
HGYTE XFQTW ADSEK FGRPB MNKJY CGRDT FSRQW
DVFGT NMJKI XCSDW QWASZ NMJKU HPAAL VBGIIE
DFRTC HTYGB VFGRT DJIEB PDHVN MZVCN DGAKH

YEURO BGTRE ZGUOP NNFHR GHVIQ FURGE DFTOB
CGYKM NGDEW ALGHB EICMY NFUWJ CFYHL
HNGFW QSDEL HUGWS MQDFL LPFSA CBTPO BFGEW
SRWSZ XCVPD LJKIIJ VBMNS DQYSK XSCEJ RHXOO
BNGLS CVGIQ ZXSKN MWGPD FHTBG MWUFD SHTOI
YUREJ VBAMP XAZMN ZXSQW JKMPO FGRTC DVEFS
HJBUG FKQHG BDFET IYJZX BRTFG CVMPL GFQSW
QGFIB VHGTE CHGYR NSJGE DLJUX KHJRG FGDEQ
XCHOU SCCHU DFTJN MKORD XSQYH BHJTT DFYIK
MHGRD CICHR FVHIO NGREW SUJBSVHTYR NMKOD
FIVBQ STDGE BNHIN BHTYS VHKIK GHEWQ FQJPB
CVFGT NMHYQ XCDFO PLKFW CGRUN BFTED SHUIC
NGYER FYYDU NGRWK ZXSFX BVGHT MNJUI MKWYF
SEXCK JJGHY NGREO POLKI SDWEA GFTDR HRIGY
YGTES VJUON MGUIM GHRYD DFERF GHTVA SJGUE
BVGHT MJKUI VBKJY MBHER DSGTU NGHBU DVEFS
VBGHT NMJKU UYHGB ERDFC WESDX QWASZ RTFGC
MJKUI PHOLM MHUSJ ERDOD CBFGU HGUSM GNRKS
VBGDK BVGHY MHAGE VGFTD NHJYR HSLBC BBAXZ
UYIHJ RXXXX
　　VERY SINCERELY YOURS,
　　ALEXANDER BOTTS.

TELEGRAM
SAN FRANCISCO DEC 20 1939

ALEXANDER BOTTS
EARTHWORM CITY
YOUR SCRAMBLED MESSAGE RECEIVED AM PRETTY
DOUBTFUL ABOUT THIS BUT WILL WITHHOLD FUR-
THER COMMENT UNTIL I GET IT DECIPHERED
　　GILBERT HENDERSON

TELEGRAM
EARTHWORM CITY DEC 27 1939

GILBERT HENDERSON
SAN FRANCISCO
JUST BACK FROM CHRISTMAS HOLIDAY AND FIND
NO NEWS FROM YOU SINCE YOUR WIRE OF A WEEK
AGO PLEASE ADVISE WHETHER ACTION HAS BEEN
TAKEN ON MY IMPORTANT CIPHER MESSAGE OF DE-
CEMBER EIGHTEEN
    ALEXANDER BOTTS

EARTHWORM TRACTOR COMPANY,
BRANCH OFFICE
SAN FRANCISCO

Thursday, December 28, 1939.

Mr. Alexander Botts,
Earthworm City, Illinois.

DEAR BOTTS: Your telegram is here, and I am glad to inform
you that your cipher message is perfectly safe, and will be attended to next week. As this somewhat lengthy delay is a natural
result of imperfections inherent in your cipher system, I am glad
that it has occurred so early in the game. It will show you the
disadvantage of rushing so heedlessly into an experiment which,
to my mind, is distinctly impractical.

The difficulty in the present instance arose because your message arrived just after Miss Priscilla Pratt, our cipher operator, had
left for a two weeks' vacation in Pasadena. The local manager and
I did not want to break in another operator, especially when all
available employees were busy with other tasks.

Besides, it would have been unfair to Miss Pratt to ask her to
come all the way back to San Francisco just to decipher one message. She had postponed her vacation from last summer, and had

especially arranged to have it just at this time, because she is to appear in the Pasadena Tournament of Roses, riding on a float entered by the Santa Clara County Prune Growers' Association. She told us that she is to wear a robe of dark purple, and represent the Queen of the Prunes. And she is so thrilled by the idea that we could not think of disappointing her.

Obviously, there was only one thing for me to do. I locked your message in the office safe, and I will have it deciphered next week when the young lady returns.

Hoping this delay will cause you no inconvenience,

Most sincerely,

GILBERT HENDERSON.

ON BOARD WESTBOUND AIR
LINER NC 13997

Saturday, December 30, 1939.

Mr. Gilbert Henderson,
San Francisco.

DEAR HENDERSON: It is my painful duty to inform you that your failure to cooperate in my carefully worked-out cryptographic plan has plunged the Earthworm Tractor Company into a crisis more appalling than anything I have previously encountered in my entire twenty years in the business. I am now racing westward by plane in a desperate attempt to undo some of the mischief which has resulted from your indifference and inaction. And I have decided to explain the entire situation to you in the hope that you may be able—even at this late hour—to give me a little help. I should have preferred to send this information in a crypto-graphic telegram before I left Earthworm City. But, as long as you will apparently be unable to decipher any messages until the re-turn of your little friend, the Queen of the Prunes, I shall have to hand you the bad news in plain English—hoping and praying that the secret matters I am about to discuss may not be pried open by the evil eyes of foreign agents.

To begin with, I will reveal the information which you so unfortunately failed to get out of my cipher message of December 18. On that day I shipped from Earthworm City, en route to Honolulu, the first of our secret, new, experimental, high-speed, sixteen-ton, heavy-artillery tractors—a truly magnificent machine, powered by a 500 horsepower air-cooled radial airplane motor, protected by seven-eighths-inch, heat-treated, nickel-steel armor plate, equipped with heavy-duty hydraulic bulldozer for emergency road repairing, and accompanied by a 155-millimeter long-rifle cannon mounted on special Earthworm high-speed carriage—the entire outfit being intended to provide the egregious General X with a sensational demonstration of what we can do when we start moving heavy artillery at hitherto unheard-of velocities.

To prevent news of this shipment from leaking out, I loaded the tractor and the gun, secretly and under cover of night, into an end-door automobile boxcar—M.K.T. 337991. After sealing the car, I cleverly contrived to have the shipment billed as two ordinary commercial tractors consigned to our San Francisco branch. I mailed the bill of lading, in the ordinary routine manner, to our office out there; thus completely throwing off the track all snoopers who might be looking for military materiel. And I then requested you, in cipher, to see that the tractor and gun were secretly transferred to a ship and sent on to Honolulu, where I had cryptographically notified our local representative to receive them.

The above precautions—inspired by a letter from the War Department requesting that we exercise great care in protecting military secrets—were admirably conceived and efficiently executed from my end. Their success, however, depended on a certain minimum amount of cooperation from your end.

You may imagine my consternation, therefore, when I received your astonishing letter in this morning's mail and learned for the first time that you had not made so much as a feeble attempt to get even as far as halfway to first base in this affair.

My alarm was increased by a second letter in the morning mail, in which the War Department advised increased precautions because of recently discovered plots by alien espionage agents who have been attempting to steal secret military devices, smuggle them over the Mexican border, and finally ship them across the ocean to certain foreign totalitarian states.

But the final straw was a routine report, also in the morning mail, from the shipping department of our San Francisco branch. This report revealed the hideous fact that M.K.T. Boxcar 337991, instead of going through to San Francisco, had been diverted at Ogden, by request of our San Francisco office, and rerouted to a new destination bearing the strange name of "The Oscar Mroczkowicz Ranch, Oviedo, California."

When I had read this report and had learned, by consulting the map, that Oviedo is in Southern California, right on the Mexican border, I was, to put it mildly, aghast.

At once a flood of ominous questions began welling up in my mind. Who, I asked myself, was this mysterious Mr. Oscar Mroczkowicz, who had apparently acquired a ranch at such a suspiciously strategic point on the border? Was he one of these insidious foreign spies? Had he in some devious manner discovered the true nature of the secret shipment in M.K.T. Boxcar 337991? Had he, himself, inveigled Miss Priscilla Pratt into appearing as the Queen of the Prunes at Pasadena—thus blocking the decipherment of my message? Had he insinuated himself into the confidence of our sales force on the Pacific Coast, pretending that he wanted to buy a couple of tractors for his ranch? And had he then insidiously argued you or somebody else out there into rerouting this particular boxcar? Unfortunately, I did not know.

But one thing was painfully clear and plain. This Mr. Oscar Mroczkowicz was now, or soon would be, in a position where he could, with the greatest ease, smuggle our carefully guarded, secret-model, heavy-artillery tractor across the border, move it by circuitous trails across uninhabited deserts and through lonely mountain passes to some obscure port, and then ship it on an inconspicuous freighter to the shores of a treacherous and malevolent foreign power. In short, one of the most vital secrets of our national defense was in deadly peril. Something had to be done.

At once I sprang to action. Grabbing the telephone, I put in one long-distance call after another; running up an impressive toll bill but accomplishing very little else. Repeated calls to various railroad offices and freight depots all the way from Ogden to Oviedo finally revealed that M.K.T. Boxcar 337991 would probably reach Oviedo tomorrow afternoon. But when I asked that delivery on the car be stopped, I received the idiotic reply that this could not be done unless I produced the bill of lading—which was manifestly impossible over the telephone, even if I had had the bill of lading, which I did not. I explained this to them, over and over, but they paid no attention.

Having failed with the railroad officials, I considered appealing to the police. But this would have revealed our secrets to too many people. So then I tried to call our San Francisco office, and I tried to call you at your hotel, but everybody was away—fiddling like Nero, I suppose, at various pre-New Year's weekend orgies, while I, like Rome, was burning up with futile anger back in Earthworm City.

Finally, I abandoned the telephone in disgust and headed for the airport. I am now halfway to Los Angeles. And when I land there tomorrow morning, I will proceed as fast as possible to Oviedo, where I will take such measures as seem appropriate in view of whatever the situation may turn out to be.

In the meantime, if you have the bill of lading at San Francisco, you may be able to stop delivery on this fateful shipment before it is too late. If not, you will have to gather a force of resolute, trustworthy men, supply them with arms, and fly down to the border. And if I can find some way—legal or illegal, peaceful or violent—to hold things up until you get into action, we may yet thwart our adversaries.

The future is ominously uncertain. But I can assure you of one thing—if that tractor is taken out of this country, it will be over my dead body.

Yours with grim determination,
ALEXANDER BOTTS.

P.S.: I have just landed at L.A., and will mail this at once.

JOE'S DINER, 17 MAIN STREET,
GREASEWOOD VALLEY, CALIFORNIA

January 1, 1940. 5 P.M.

Mr. Gilbert Henderson,
San Francisco.

DEAR HENDERSON: This has been a terrible day. I am so slowed down by mental and physical fatigue, and at the same time so speeded up by emotional excitement, that it is doubtful whether I can write a coherent letter.

But I need your help. So, fortified by five cups of coffee and a large order of hamburg and onions supplied by the excellent chef of Joe's Diner here, I will attempt to give you an account of what has been going on. As I cannot trust you to decipher anything, I shall have to use plain English. Besides, I left the cipher machine back in Earthworm City.

It was a little after sunset last night when I finally arrived at the little village of Oviedo. As the train approached the station I observed, through the car window, a locomotive pulling a single boxcar along a sort of spur or side track which seemed to lead out across the desert. In the dim twilight I was just able to read, on the side of the car, the inscription, "M.K.T. 337991."

With a single mighty spring I shot from my seat, without even stopping to pick up my traveling bag, and landed halfway down the aisle, headed for the car door. A moment later I had leaped from the still-moving train and started running as hard as I could along the side track in pursuit of the boxcar. It was moving too fast for me, however, and in spite of all my efforts it gradually disappeared in the gathering darkness ahead.

Doggedly I followed. After a couple of miles I came to a ten-foot barbed-wire fence, with a closed gate across the track. On the gate was a sign, "Oscar Mroczkowicz Ranch." Inside was a tough-looking guard with an automatic pistol. He told me there was no admittance here for anybody, and pointed to a sign on the fence which read, "Danger. 2100 Volts. Keep Off." But he absolutely refused to give me any further information.

I therefore wished him a pleasant good evening, walked back to town, stole a shovel that somebody had left outside the freight station, and circled around through the desert to a remote section of the fence, where I started digging a passage in the sand under the bottom wire. This job took most of the night, but I finally managed to crawl through. Half an hour later I found the railroad track, evidently a private spur, and followed it till I reached the outskirts of a group of ranch buildings. All was quiet except for a single guard, who was walking a fairly long beat, taking in all of the somewhat scattered buildings.

By this time there was a faint glow in the east—the approaching dawn of the year 1940. But, unlike some other people, I had no time for a New Year's celebration. Waiting until the guard was at the far end of his beat, I crept forward and soon discovered M.K.T. Boxcar 337991 standing at the very end of the track beside a small machinery shed. The end door was open. Cautiously I climbed in, and found myself beside the armored bulk of our mighty sixteen-ton artillery tractor. Then I heard voices. My heart began knocking like a motor with loose connecting rods. Peering out, I saw approaching, through the semidarkness, a dozen or more shadowy forms.

"Yes, sir," said a voice, "I filled up the fuel tank last night, and hitched on the gun. She's all ready to go."

"O.K.," said another voice. "Some of you men bring a few of those timbers over here and lay up a ramp, so we can unload."

By this time the moving shadows—in all probability as ruthless a gang of cutthroats as could be found anywhere—were so close that escape was impossible. There was nothing for me to do but conceal my presence as long as I could. Silently I opened the steel door of the tractor and climbed into the cab. Silently I closed the door and fastened the catches. Then I peered anxiously out through the narrow slits at the front—at the rear—at the sides. I could see nothing.

Nervously I shifted myself around. One of my feet touched the starting button. There was an ear-shattering roar. The five hundred horses in the great motor had come to life.

And at the same moment, in a sudden flash of inspiration, I realized that I was all set to go places. Not only could I bring about my own escape but I could also rescue the tractor.

For the first time this year, I smiled a smile of pure joy and happiness. I set the gears. I opened the throttle. I slammed in the clutch. With a leap like a charging elephant, the huge tractor debouched from the end of the car, dropped four or five feet, and hit the ground with a shock that practically knocked me cold. But the sturdy machine was unharmed. And a few seconds later, when I came to, I found that I was rolling merrily along across the desert. A glance through the slit in the rear of the cab showed me that the big cannon was dutifully following behind.

I shifted into high, speeded the tractor up to about forty miles per hour, turned on the headlights, and began looking for the railroad track, so that I could follow it back to civilization and the protection of the law. But before I found the railroad I came to a deep and, at the moment, completely dry irrigation ditch, with a lot of jagged boulders along the edge.

I stopped. Glancing through the slit in the rear of the cab, I noticed signs of intense activity around the ranch buildings several miles to the rear. A number of automobiles seemed to be setting out in my direction. Then I saw a red flash. A few seconds later there was a bloodcurdling howl, and a violent explosion several hundred yards away from the tractor. It didn't take me long to figure that one out. Those miscreants at the ranch had thought of everything; they had apparently stolen a piece of field artillery somewhere, and they were going into action in a big way.

For a moment I thought of shooting back at them with my own cannon, which was twice as big as theirs. But I had no ammunition. So I decided I had better move along and put as much distance as possible between myself and the enemy artillery. But I did not see how I could get through all those big rocks and across the ditch.

Then I thought of the heavy-duty hydraulic bulldozer on the front of the tractor. At once I lowered the sturdy blade and pushed several cubic yards of desert sand up over and in between the jagged boulders. Then I began skillfully shuttling back and forth, pushing up load after load of sand, building a road across the boulders and partially filling in the ditch. A rotary bulldozer would have thrown the dirt farther and faster. But the plain one did well enough. And after about ten minutes' work I drove across the ditch with the greatest ease.

A short distance beyond, I crashed through a section of the electric fence, setting off an interesting little shower of sparks, but escaping without any damage to myself or the tractor.

In the meantime, the criminals at the ranch had been dropping shells all around me. But they failed to get any direct hits, and the fragments rattled harmlessly off the armor. Even so, the firing was distinctly annoying, so I resumed my speed of forty miles per hour, and before long I was out of range.

It was now broad daylight, and I could see that I had completely lost my way. The railroad and the town of Oviedo were nowhere to be seen. Instead, there loomed up directly ahead of me a rugged and desolate range of high mountains. Too late, I realized that I had come in the wrong direction. But it was now impossible to turn back.

Someday I hope to give you a full account of how I drove that tractor and that gun up the slopes of that awe-inspiring range, winding my way through steep canyons, crashing over crags and ledges, creeping along the edges of dizzy cliffs, and clawing my way up forty-five-degree slopes. Someday I will give you the whole story. But right now I have neither the time nor the energy. Suffice it to say that I finally crossed the ridge. And a short time later, having almost exhausted my fuel supply, I concealed the tractor in a desolate, narrow canyon, placing it so that I could use the bulldozer to roll big rocks down on any of Mr. Mroczkowicz's mugs who might try to follow me.

Then I walked down to this little town of Greasewood Valley. After allaying the suspicions of the natives by telling them I was a lone prospector looking for gold in these here hills, I bought myself some refreshment and started writing this letter. As soon as I have mailed it, I will return to mount guard over my precious machinery.

What I want you to do is organize a relief expedition. You must provide gasoline and oil, and a gang of strong men to carry it up into the mountains. These men should be heavily armed. You must send a boxcar to some lonely point on the railroad. And you must provide a guide who can lay out a route which will enable us to reach the railroad and load the machinery without publicity.

Of course, I could do all these things much more efficiently myself, but I do not dare leave the tractor for more than an hour or two at a time. I will, however, sneak into the town of Greasewood Valley once a day. You can contact me there at Joe's Diner, 17 Main Street. Please hurry. If the criminals from across the mountains get here first, you may find nothing to rescue but the dead body of one who perished fighting for his country.

Your somewhat scared, but ever determined sales manager,

ALEXANDER BOTTS.

MROCZKOWICZ RANCH,
OVIEDO, CALIFORNIA

January 4, 1940.

Mr. Alexander Botts,
Care Joe's Diner,
17 Main Street,
Greasewood Valley, California.

DEAR BOTTS: Your two letters have been forwarded to me here. I highly disapprove of this continuous discussion of confidential matters in plainly written letters. However, you seem to be so completely misinformed about almost everything that I feel compelled to give you the real facts before you engage in any more outlandish exploits. And as long as your cipher scheme has proved so impractical, I will have to use straight English.

It may interest you to know, in the first place, that your plan to ship the new artillery tractor to Honolulu was based on an entirely erroneous assumption. Your friend General X—as you might have known if you had taken the trouble to investigate— changed his plans. Instead of going to Honolulu last month, he came here to Oviedo, where the United States Army has recently purchased a large tract of land known as the Mroczkowicz Ranch, and established thereon a secret and supposedly well-guarded proving ground for mechanized equipment. Mr. Mroczkowicz, the former owner, has nothing more to do with the place. Furthermore, he is not a foreign spy but an honorable, patriotic American citizen who, several years ago, was one of the famous Fighting Irish on the Notre Dame football team.

A week or so ago General X asked me to send to Oviedo a couple of our commercial machines for demonstration purposes. Owing to the inefficient working of your pet cipher scheme, I supposed that M.K.T. Boxcar 337991 contained the machines described in the bill of lading, so it was perfectly natural for me to reroute the car.

Last Saturday I came down here myself to be present at the demonstration. When the car arrived on New Year's Eve, and we discovered that we had one of the new experimental models, the general—nowhere near as dumb as you think—was so interested, and so impatient to see it perform, that he arranged for a demonstration as early as possible the next morning. Thus it came about that he and I were both members of that shadowy group of "cutthroats" which you so dimly discerned in the pale dawn of New Year's Day.

As you have never been lacking in imagination, you can appreciate our surprise and bewilderment when the tractor and the gun apparently unloaded themselves, bursting out of the car, landing on the ground with a terrifying crash, and then rolling off across the desert. As we did not know you were driving, and as your course was perilously close to the international boundary, we had a bad spy scare ourselves. That is why we used everything we had,

119

including an old French seventy-five, in a vain attempt to stop you.

The manner in which you eluded our pursuit prompts me to say a few words about your handling of the tractor. In the past I have had but little opportunity to see you in action, and my knowledge of your driving ability has been largely derived from your own letters, which sometimes, I must admit, have impressed me as being more like fairy tales than factual narratives. Your most recent letter, however, seems, if anything, to understate the facts. So I must apologize for my past skepticism, and offer you my present congratulations. Your performance on Monday was, without exception, the finest piece of rough cross-country tractor driving that I have ever seen.

What you thought was a dry irrigation ditch lined with jagged boulders was really an experimental antitank trench bordered by pointed concrete blocks. This setup was supposed to present an absolutely impassable barrier to all forms of mechanized equipment. So the speed with which you smothered it with sand and then rolled across had the general practically speechless with astonishment.

But later on, as the general, peering through a telescope, followed your course over that appalling mountain range, he regained his voice and pretty near wore himself out complaining that he had found exactly the machine he needed, and here it was, as he supposed, escaping across the border on its way to the laboratories of some foreign power where its secrets could be stolen.

During the succeeding three days, the general's state of mind was rendered even worse by the failure of all pursuing parties to find any trace of the fugitive tractor. And it was not until this morning, when I showed him your letter, that he calmed down sufficiently to tell me that after seeing our tractor in action, he has decided to recommend that the Army place a large order. In view of the general's influence, I consider that this pretty much puts the deal in the bag.

In a few minutes, the general and I are starting by plane for Washington to arrange final details. This means that I cannot take charge of any rescue party. However, we are sending a platoon of cavalry to Greasewood Valley with all necessary supplies. And I will entrust this letter to the platoon leader.

In conclusion, I wish to thank you for staging your remarkable demonstration where I could see it.

Yours with gratitude and admiration,
GILBERT HENDERSON.

P.S.: I still don't like your cipher machines.

Tractors on Parade

EARTHWORM TRACTOR COMPANY
BRANCH OFFICE
GRAYBAR BUILDING—NEW YORK CITY

Saturday, October 3, 1940.

Mr. Alexander Botts,
Sales Manager,
Earthworm Tractor Company,
Earthworm City, Illinois.

DEAR BOTTS: Mr. John Montague, Chairman of our Board of Directors, has written me from St. Petersburg, Florida, that he is very anxious to get hold of a 1904 steam-driven Twenty Ton Model A Earthworm tractor—this being the first track-type machine ever built by the company. If any of these antiques are still in existence, I wish you would do everything you can to acquire one. Mr. Montague is willing to pay up to two thousand dollars, if necessary, but suggests that the price ought to be much lower—especially, if you do not mention his name as the ultimate purchaser.

Why Mr. Montague wants a Model A, I do not know. Possibly, as one of the earliest employees of the company, he may have helped to build it, and may, therefore, have a sentimental interest in it. Or perhaps he may be getting a bit senile.

In any case, Mr. Montague is still a power in the Board of Directors. And, at their meeting on next Friday, October 9, at Earthworm City, he will doubtless have the final word on the proposed pay increase for company executives—which includes you as well as me.

Anything we can do to humor the old gentleman at this time

will not be labor thrown away. A word to the wise is sufficient.

Most sincerely,

GILBERT HENDERSON,
President, Earthworm Tractor
Company.

EARTHWORM TRACTOR COMPANY
EARTHWORM CITY, ILLINOIS
OFFICE OF ALEXANDER BOTTS, SALES MANAGER

Monday afternoon, October 5, 1940.

Mr. Gilbert Henderson,
Earthworm Branch Office,
Graybar Building, New York City.

DEAR HENDERSON: Your letter arrived this morning. And—stimulated by the thought of all the delightful things I can do with the extra pay which you are so artfully dangling before my nose—I have put in an active and successful day at the somewhat unusual (for me) task of attempting to buy a tractor rather than sell one.

My first move was to search the factory—on the chance that we might have a Model A tucked away somewhere. But—although I discovered at least twenty almost prehistoric machines, which must have been taken in trade even before your regime as sales manager, and which are now stored away, forlorn and forgotten, in an old brick building way back at the extreme rear corner of the factory lot—I was unfortunately unable to locate any 1904 Model A Earthworm.

An inspection of the dusty files in the attic of the main building revealed that in 1904 our then small and struggling factory—known at that time as the Farmers' Friend Tractor Company—sold just fifteen Model A machines—all of them here in Illinois. Armed with this information, I started four secretaries telephoning all over the state to various dealers, former dealers, and customers. Most of them had no information of value. But late this afternoon we heard that a Model A had actually been in existence as late as 1930, at which time it was bought for twenty-five dollars by a Mr. Jeremiah Billings, known as "Jerry the Junkman," who lives at the little village of Pineville, Illinois, only twenty miles from Earthworm City.

I at once telephoned Mr. Billings. He said the machine was still in his possession. So I made an appointment to call on him tomorrow morning—at which time I will endeavor to pick up the machine at as low a price as possible. I will inform you as soon as I get possession.

In the meantime, if you are writing to Mr. Montague, you may inform him that the deal is practically in the bag. And you might also drop a few delicate hints about that proposed salary raise—because, if you have made me do all this work for nothing, it will be just too bad.

Cordially yours,

ALEXANDER BOTTS.

EARTHWORM TRACTOR COMPANY
EARTHWORM CITY, ILLINOIS
OFFICE OF ALEXANDER BOTTS, SALES MANAGER
Wednesday, October 7, 1940.

Mr. Gilbert Henderson,
Earthworm Branch Office,
Graybar Building, New York City.

DEAR HENDERSON: It gives me great pain to inform you that this antique tractor deal, instead of being safely in the bag, as I had supposed, has hopped out and is practically gone with the wind. So, if you have not yet written Mr. Montague, you had better hold off. The affair is now in the hands of the lawyers. And you can figure for yourself how much hope there is after I explain what has happened.

Yesterday morning, with two thousand dollars in my pocket, I drove to Pineville and called on Mr. Jeremiah (Jerry the Junkman) Billings at his blacksmith shop and junk emporium on the main street of the village. The shop is a dilapidated wooden structure, and the lot behind it is covered with secondhand automobiles and junk of all descriptions. I found Mr. Billings tapping away at a piece of iron on an anvil—a tall skinny old bird, perhaps seventy years of age, disarmingly shy and retiring, but with a certain air of shrewdness which should have put me on my guard.

After introducing myself, I said briskly, "I should like to look at your Model A Earthworm."

"Wal, I dunno," he said.

Note: The man really does talk like that—using a sort of Uncle Josh, or hick radio-comedian style of dialect. At first I thought it was genuine. But more recently I have come to suspect that it may be merely put on for the purpose of creating an atmosphere of rural innocence and thus making it easier for him to outsmart unsuspecting city slickers like myself.

"Wal, I dunno," he repeated. "The tractors is all out at my farm about a mile east of here."

"Then we'll go out there," I said.

"Wal, I dunno," he said, again. But, after a certain amount of argument, he quenched the piece of hot iron on which he had been working, locked up the shop, and got into my car.

When we reached the farm, he took me into an enormous painted wooden barn—very old and rickety. In one corner there was a small pile of hay, but the rest of the building—instead of being used for animals—was occupied by no less than fifteen weird-looking old tractors. Some of them were early steam jobs. Others were gasoline models of the Taft era. Some had wheels and some had tracks. In the very center of the group stood the clumsy old 1904 Model A Earthworm, apparently in very good mechanical condition, its boiler and smoke stack covered with shiny black enamel and its brass name-plate well polished.

Mr. Billings waved his hand in the general direction of the machinery. "This," he said, proudly, "is my collection."

"What do you mean, collection?" I asked.

"It's like this," he explained. "My regular business is dealing in ordinary junk, but my main interest in life is these rare old tractors. I am a collector—a sort of connoisseur."

"I get you," I said, grasping the idea at once. "You're like an old guy I once knew who had a secondhand furniture store in Chicago. The main shop was cluttered up with nothing but cheap trash, but hidden away in the back room where nobody ever saw it, he had some early American furniture that was really very lovely and very fine."

"That's it exactly," said Mr. Billings, beginning to warm up. "I keep this stuff out here because my regular customers wouldn't appreciate it. They don't even know I've got it. And you are the first person, Mr. Botts, who has seen this collection in over ten years. How do you like it?"

"It's wonderful," I said. "I am particularly impressed with this Model A Earthworm—so much so that I am going to make you an offer. I understand you bought this machine in 1930 for twenty-five dollars, but I am willing to give you a hundred for it—spot cash." I pulled a one-hundred-dollar bill from my pocket and waved it in his face.

Mr. Billings did not react as I had hoped. He merely ceased talking like a dreamy lover of antiques and assumed the air of a Yankee trader. "The machine is not for sale," he said.

"Two hundred dollars," I said, producing another bill from my pocket.

"I told you it's not for sale."

"Three hundred!" I waved a third bill.

"Wait a minute," he said, eyeing me suspiciously, "is there any special reason why you're so het up over buying this particular machine?"

"It's just a sentimental idea," I explained. "As sales manager of the Earthworm Tractor Company, I naturally take an interest in the first model the company ever made."

"In that case, you ought to be willing to pay a whole lot more than three hundred dollars. If you're the sales manager, you've probably got plenty of money."

"How about a thousand dollars?"

"Wal, I dunno—"

"Two thousand," I said, going the whole hog. "But not one cent more." I produced my entire wad of twenty one-hundred-dollar bills, and spread them out before his astonished gaze.

He eyed the money—longingly. He reached out his hand—graspingly. Then he pulled back his hand. His eyes wandered to the big Model A Earthworm. He hesitated.

As I am a very good judge of human nature, I understood at once the conflict that was going on in his mind. As a natural born Yankee trader, he knew he ought to grab the money before I changed my mind. But, as a connoisseur and a really genuine lover of rare old tractors, he couldn't bear to part with this ancient Earthworm.

Finally he shook his head. "I can't do it," he said. "It would be like selling a member of my family—that is, if I had a family, which, being a bachelor, I have not."

"Two thousand dollars is a lot of money," I suggested.

"Yes," he said. "For two thousand dollars I would sell you my blacksmith shop and my whole junk business. But when it comes to genuine antique tractors, I don't sell them, I buy them. The only reason I haven't bought more is that I have run out of money."

"Then you had better take this two thousand," I said. "You could buy a lot of old tractors with that."

"Maybe so—but where could I get anything to compare with this old Earthworm?"

At this point I was struck by a brilliant new idea. I remembered those obsolete tractors in the brick shed at the factory—none of them worth anything as working machines, and having a value of perhaps fifty dollars apiece as scrap. "If you are more interested in old tractors than money," I said, "maybe we could trade. I have some very remarkable relics over at the factory. Some of them are better than anything you've got here."

"I don't believe it."

"All right," I said, "I'll drive you to the factory right now. You can look them over. And you can take your pick of the lot."

"It would just be a waste of time—"

"But won't you even look at them?"

"Wal, I dunno. Maybe, if you would bring them over here, I might give them the once over. And if you've really got anything that is better than the old Earthworm—which I doubt—I might consider making a trade."

"What!" I said. "Me bring all that heavy machinery way over here just to save you a twenty-mile automobile ride?"

"This is all your idea, not mine," he said. "If you want to bring your stuff to me—okay. If not—okay."

That seemed to be his story. And he stuck to it. So, after about ten minutes of futile discussion, I gave up in disgust. Having deposited Mr. Billings at his blacksmith shop in Pineville, I headed back for Earthworm City—resolved to wash my hands of the whole affair. Obviously, there was no sense in wasting my time arguing with this idiotic Jerry the Junkman in a vain attempt to get hold of a superannuated tractor for our senile Chairman, on the mere chance that he might possibly give me a raise in salary. The whole thing was silly.

On the other hand, I had started out to acquire this Model A Earthworm. And when I start something, there is nothing in the world I hate more than to quit and admit that I am licked. Furthermore, if I could put the deal through, and if, because of this, I actually did get this raise in salary, there were certainly a whole lot of very nice things I could do with the extra money. By the time I got to Earthworm City, I had decided to take the mountain (of junk) to Mohammed (the junk man).

I promptly rounded up about twenty-five mechanics from the service department and the repair shop, and we spent the afternoon tuning up those twenty ancient tractors which I had discovered the day before in the old brick storage building near the corner of the back lot.

The machines were in surprisingly good condition. Whoever it was, in the days of long ago, that took these things in trade, must have thoroughly overhauled them with the idea of reselling them. Some of them were so quaintly constructed that it was hard to figure out just how to start and operate them. But our mechanics are the best in the world, and by the end of the afternoon, every last machine had been fueled, oiled, tuned up, and tested on the back lot.

As I tried out one machine after another, I began to feel a growing interest in antique tractors myself. There is a certain magnificence and emotional appeal in these outlandish monstrosities that is hard to explain. At any rate, I got a real thrill out of driving several of the enormous steam-powered jobs—some of which must date back to the days of Grover Cleveland. Never before have I heard such puffing and wheezing and clanking.

I was also much taken by an astonishing creation known as Thompson's Multiplex or Jack-of-All-Trades Tractor, patented in 1908. It is an iron-wheeled gasoline machine completely covered with gadgets and attachments for performing almost all conceivable jobs around a farm—it has retractable plow bottoms and harrow teeth, a mowing-machine cutter-bar, a circular saw on a long arm for cutting wood, a pump and tank for spraying fruit trees, an emery wheel, a rotary post hole digger, and countless other things.

Another machine, known as the "Rolling Drum Tractor" consists of one wheel six feet high and six feet wide, with all the machinery inside. But the one I liked the best is known as the "Gifford Gasoline Mule," of the vintage of 1910. This contraption, believe it or not, is driven by reins, like a horse—the operator being seated on a plow, mowing machine, or other implement hitched to the rear. A pull on the right-hand rein throws out the right-hand steering clutch, causing the machine to go gee. The left-hand rein swings it haw. And pulling both reins all the way back effects a complete whoa. A very simple, neat arrangement and probably a great selling point in the old days when farmers were more used to horses than to machinery.

I was so fascinated by this Gifford Gasoline Mule that I decided I, personally, would drive it to Pineville. And, as my excellent crew of mechanics had no objection to working overtime, we started immediately after supper—thus making the journey by night and avoiding heavy day-time traffic on the road. We made a most interesting parade—a veritable cavalcade of junk. I led the way myself, seated on an old hay-rake, and driving ahead of me the great Gifford Gasoline Mule—temporarily equipped with electric head-lights. Behind me, the other machines wheezed and clattered. And a couple of service trucks brought up the rear in case of breakdowns or accidents. We had no trouble at all, however. We were able to maintain the almost incredible speed of two miles an hour. And, shortly after dawn, we came roaring and banging into Mr. Billing's farmyard.

The old guy rushed out of his house. And, when he saw what we had brought, he was as goggle-eyed as a book collector contemplating the arrival of a whole truckload of Gutenberg bibles. He was so enthusiastic that I thought I had better try to complete the deal before he cooled off.

"You can take your pick," I said, expansively. "I will swap off any one of these beautiful specimens for that old Earthworm."

At once the man's enthusiasm waned. A cold and calculating look came into his eye. "Any one of them!" he said. "I thought you were going to give me the whole shooting match."

"What!" I said. "Give you all twenty of these mechanical masterpieces for one old traveling junk pile?"

"It's not a traveling junk pile," he said. "It's a Model A Earthworm. It's the pearl of my collection. It ought to be worth a hundred of those old wrecks of yours."

"They are not old wrecks," I said. "They are all in good running condition. Maybe I'm a fool to let you have even one of them. I've been thinking it over, and it seems to me there ought to be a market for this sort of stuff."

"You know darn well," he said, "that none of your customers would give you anything for any of them."

"Not my regular customers," I said. "But how about somebody like Henry Ford? They say you can sell him almost anything. And then there are these supply houses in Hollywood that furnish antique gadgetry for costume pictures—"

"You can do as you please," said Mr. Billings, with studied nonchalance. "You heard my offer. It's the whole works or nothing. Take it or leave it."

He started to walk away—thus leaving me in a most distressing quandary. I tried to think fast. I had a feeling that this mug was playing me for a sucker. But, having come so far and done so much work, I could not bear to see the deal fall through. And in the back of my mind were all those visions of the many beautiful things I could do with my extra pay—if I got it.

I ran after Mr. Billings. "All right," I said, "you win."

"I get all twenty machines?"

"Yes."

"All right," said Mr. Billings. "The old Earthworm is yours. But before you leave I'll expect you to put all this other machinery inside the barn."

"Okay," I said.

I summoned my mechanics and we started firing up the old Earthworm. In order to clear a path to the door, we had to move about half of Mr. Billing's tractors outside. But, as they were all in good running condition, this did not take very long. Finally, with a roaring fire and a good head of steam, I opened the throttle and started the old Earthworm rolling. And, as I felt the whole twenty tons of massive stove iron throbbing and heaving under me, I began to feel pretty good. I had saved all of the two thousand dollars. I had swung the deal with a mass of scrap iron worth only a thousand at the most. And I had succeeded in what I had started out to do—the Model A Earthworm was safely in my possession.

But, as it turned out, I was wrong about this. As we came clanking out of the barn, the enormous smoke stack with the flaring spark screen on top hit the top of the doorway. There was a crash. The whole works broke off. The shock gave such a shaking up to the fire in the fire box that a great shower of sparks poured forth. And the next moment the hay in the corner of the barn was blazing merrily.

At once my crew of splendid mechanics sprang to action. Some of them formed a bucket brigade to bring water from the well. Others swarmed over the tractors that remained in the barn, and in a few minutes, by dint of astonishing energy and mechanical skill, managed to get them safely out of the door at the far end. Meanwhile Mr. Billings had telephoned to Pineville, and before long the volunteer fire department and half the population of the village had arrived. But all efforts to stop the flames were in vain. The tractors were all saved; but the barn was lost. Within an hour it was nothing but a pile of ashes.

Somewhat apologetically, I said good-bye to Mr. Billings. "I am sorry this accident occurred," I said. "But now, as there seems to be nothing more I can do, I think I will be heading for Earthworm City with my tractor."

"Oh, no, you don't," he said. "You are the guy that burned this barn down—which leaves me with no place to house my machines. So you've got to rebuild it. And, until the job is done, that tractor is going to stay right here as security."

"The fire was your fault—not mine," I said, "it was you that made that door too low, and then failed to warn me that I would have to unship the smoke stack to get out. And it was you that left that hay lying around so carelessly. Anyway, this tractor is my property. I'm going to take it away. And you can't stop me."

Mr. Billings called to a very tough-looking man in the crowd, and explained the situation. The tough-looking man turned out to be the county sheriff, and a very good friend, apparently, of Mr. Billings.

"Listen, wise guy," the sheriff said to me. "You're not going to take a single tractor away from here. One false move and I clap you in jail for arson."

I could see that the guy meant business. Of course, I had enough husky mechanics to take the tractor anyway. But I am a law-abiding citizen, and I have always made it a rule never to start a riot, especially with officers of the law.

"All right," I said, bitterly. "I'll get my lawyers on this. I'll get a writ of habeas corpus. I'll get that tractor, and I'll sue you besides. I'll show you."

I called my mechanics. We climbed aboard the two service trucks, and headed for Earthworm City.

Since reaching the office, I have conferred with several of our lawyers. But, as usual, they are all talk and no action. The case is perfectly clear, but they insist on fogging it up by quoting incomprehensible statutes, and citing cases like Smith vs. Smith, and

Jones vs. Humperdink, and similar drool. They say they may be able to do something—but it will probably take several weeks.

So now I am trying to think up some plan of my own. So far, I have thought of nothing. But I still have hopes.

Yours in complete disgust,

ALEXANDER BOTTS.

EARTHWORM TRACTOR COMPANY BRANCH OFFICE
WASHINGTON, D.C.

Wednesday, October 7, 1940.

DEAR BOTTS: This will acknowledge your letter of October 5, stating that "the deal is practically, in the bag." As I have been absent from the New York office since yesterday morning, when I was unexpectedly called here to Washington, I have no further news from you, but I naturally assume that the old Model A tractor has now arrived safely at Earthworm City, and that I will have word from you to that effect when I get back to New York tomorrow. Having so efficiently located the machine, you could hardly fail to get possession of it—especially with all of two thousand dollars to work with.

I am especially pleased with your success, because it now appears that the matter is much more important than I had supposed. Mr. Montague has just arrived in Washington, on his way from Florida to Earthworm City for the Directors' meeting day after tomorrow, and he has been telling me exactly why he is so anxious to get a Model A Earthworm.

It seems that several years ago the old gentleman conceived the idea of gathering together, largely for his own amusement, a collection of old tractors—comprising examples of the more important machines of all makes from earliest times down to the present. Fearing that premature publicity might cause owners of old tractors to demand exorbitant prices, and being naturally a pretty closemouthed individual anyway, Mr. Montague decided to operate as quietly as possible. Working through private agents, and without confiding in anyone in the Earthworm organization, he has finally succeeded in accumulating, from junk yards and second-hand machinery dealers all over the country, a collection of rare old models which he fondly believes is the finest thing of its kind in the world. These machines—twenty in all—have been thoroughly overhauled and put in running order, and secretly stored in an old brick building at the extreme rear corner of the factory lot at Earthworm City.

When I told Mr. Montague of your success in locating a Model A, he was as pleased as a small boy at Christmas. "Good old Botts!" he exclaimed, his face fairly beaming with joy. "There is a man that is really efficient! There is a man that gets things done! I shall certainly see that he receives some tangible reward for his handling of this affair."

Mr. Montague then stated that the acquisition of the Model A had brought his collection on to the point where he would like to bring it out and show it off to his friends—especially his colleagues on the Board of Directors.

He expects to arrive by special plane at the Earthworm City Airport at noon on Friday, accompanied by most of the members of the Board. He wants you, therefore, to see that all of his old tractors, including, of course, the newly acquired Model A, are tuned up and put in operating condition so that he can run them around for the edification of all.

I cannot impress you too strongly with the necessity of carrying out Mr. Montague's wishes in this matter. He is tremendously proud of his collection; it is his most prized possession. And he is looking forward with the keenest anticipation to showing it off to the Directors. If you disappoint him, just before the important Board meeting, the results may be most unfortunate.

Very sincerely,

GILBERT HENDERSON.

EARTHWORM TRACTOR COMPANY
EARTHWORM CITY, ILLINOIS
OFFICE OF ALEXANDER BOTTS, SALES MANAGER
Friday, October 9, 1940.

DEAR HENDERSON: Your letter arrived yesterday morning, and I can only say that never before has such devastating news been conveyed in such a blithe spirit and with such complete ignorance of its horrid significance. I am not exaggerating when I tell you that it took the combined efforts of my secretary and three stenographers from the outer office—working with cups of water from the cooler, smelling salts, bicarbonate of soda, and I don't know what else—to keep me from having a complete nervous breakdown right here in the office.

I recognized, of course, that it was Mr. Montague's own fault that his antique collection got traded off to a junk man. He shouldn't have been so secretive and underhanded about his activities, and no reasonable man could possibly blame me for what had happened. But, as a keen student of human nature, I realized, with sickening clarity, that Mr. Montague would probably be very reasonable indeed, and that, instead of an increase in salary, I would be much more apt to get one of those little blue slips stating that the company regrets the necessity of dispensing with my services, etc., etc.

I decided, as soon as I got myself pulled together, that something had to be done, and done quickly, to recover Mr. Montague's tractors from the noisome grip of that wretched junk man. A brief conference with our perennially ineffective lawyers revealed that any sort of legal action would take several weeks. And Mr. Montague was due to arrive the next day. It was obvious, therefore, that I would have to depend on my own efforts alone.

I got in my car and started for Pineville—fully resigned to crawl on my hands and knees, lick Mr. Billings's boots—anything to get Mr. Montague's tractors back. But, as I drove along, my whole mind revolted at this hideous thought. Cringing, and crawling, I told myself, was the sort of thing to which no high-minded salesman such as myself should ever stoop.

And then, in a sudden flash of inspiration, I realized what had been the matter with me all through this affair. I had forgotten to act like a salesman! Deceived by the fact that I was trying to purchase a tractor, I had actually thought of myself as a lousy purchasing agent. I had unconsciously tried to assume the ruthless, cold, codfish-like personality which characterizes so many of the more successful purchasing agents I have met. I had thought only of my own interest. I had haggled, bargained, and attempted in a narrow, grasping and pinch-penny manner to get the better of a tough Yankee trader who could lick me at that game with both hands tied behind his back and his head in a sack. No wonder I had lost my shirt—and Mr. Montague's also.

And all the time I had been wasting my real talents. I had made no use at all of my remarkable ability—as a natural born sales manager—to attack a problem with broad insight, soaring imagination, and the warm human sympathy which is so characteristic of my true nature.

Having realized my mistake, I brought my mind back into its normal channel. And at once the dawn began to break. I started to look at the situation from Mr. Billings's point of view, and I suddenly realized that I rather liked him. I had nothing but admiration for his quaint obsession for old tractors. And I had the deepest sympathy for his predicament in having a wonderful collection and no place to house it. I longed to help him.

I considered the situation from the point of view of Mr. Montague, of the Earthworm Tractor Company, and even myself.

Then I got to meditating on those beautiful old tractors. It came over me that I really liked them—and that almost everybody ought to like them. If I could only have them on exhibition in our new concrete show-room building at the factory, I was sure that they would attract thousands of the nation's most prominent machinery men—many of them prospective purchasers of new equipment. And it was at this point in my meditations that I suddenly conceived the great master-plan that was designed to make everybody happy, and boom the Earthworm Sales Department besides.

At once I stepped on the accelerator, speeded into Pineville, and tackled Mr. Billings at his blacksmith shop with such a warm glow of enthusiasm that nothing could stop me.

"Mr. Billings," I said, with a broad smile, "I am going to do the right thing by you. I am going to let you keep all of the tractors. Furthermore, instead of merely rebuilding your barn, which might burn down again at any time, I am going to provide at once and absolutely free of charge, a magnificent, modern, fire-proof home for your priceless collection—"

"Where?" he interrupted.

"In the beautiful new concrete show-room building at the Earthworm Factory, in which I am going to inaugurate an institution to be known as The Museum of Tractor History. And that is not all. By drawing on our sales promotion account—which is in my sole charge as Sales Manager—I am able to offer you a lifetime job as Curator of the new museum. You will spend the rest of your life living amid your beloved tractors, and explaining their fine points to an admiring public. For this agreeable activity you will receive fifteen hundred dollars a year—which you and I both know is a whole lot more than you can ever get out of your wretched junk and blacksmith business."

"There must be something phony about this," said Mr. Billings. "It sounds too good to be genuine. What sort of strings are attached to the deal?"

"None at all," I said. "All you have to do is sign a contract, which I will prepare later, providing that you leave your collection in the museum during your lifetime, and bequeath it to us when you die."

Mr. Billings furrowed his brow. He tried to make up his mind. At one moment he was the dreamy collector of antiques, tremendously tempted by this offer of a beautiful home for his beloved collection and for himself. The next moment he was the shrewd trader, wondering whether he ought not to gouge something else out of me.

"Wal, I dunno," he said.

This time I was the one that said, "Take it or leave it." This time I was the one that started to walk away. And this time it was old Jerry the Junkman that came running after me.

"I can't quite figure why you're making this offer," he said. "But it will give me a chance to live exactly the sort of life I've always wanted. I accept."

I summoned my mechanics from the factory by telephone. We drove all the tractors of both collections to Earthworm City. And we had them on hand at the airport when Mr. Montague and the Directors alighted from the plane at noon today.

When Mr. Montague discovered that the entire Billings collection had been added to his own, he was overwhelmed. When I told him of the proposed Museum of Tractor History, he was delighted. When I introduced him to Mr. Billings, he was so im-

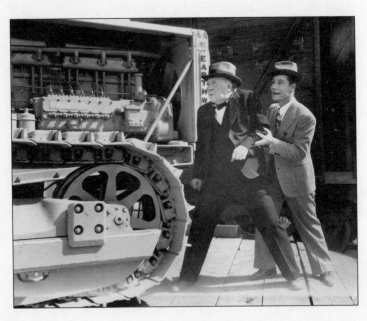

Botts encourages his prospect to get a closer look at the mighty Earthworm tractor in this photograph from the 1936 motion picture. (Wisconsin Center for Film and Theater Research)

pressed by the old junkman's interesting personality and knowledge of antique machinery that he enthusiastically endorsed his lifetime appointment as Curator. And when I privately explained the somewhat ticklish business of Mr. Billings's nominal ownership of the tractors, he proved himself the magnificent old tractor-man I have always considered him—fairly lousy with sweet reasonableness and common sense. "If it pleases Mr. Billings," he said, "it is all right with me—especially as we have actual possession of the stuff."

We then drove the tractors, preceded by a brass band, up Main Street to the factory, with Mr. Montague and Mr. Billings riding on the old 1904 Model A, and tooting the whistle like a couple of kids. Never have I seen two old gentlemen so happy.

And later on, after the Directors' meeting, Mr. Montague told me the pay raise has gone through. You, Henderson, and the rest of the boys get a boost of ten per cent. I get twenty—and maybe I have earned it.

Yours—tired, but not unhappy,
ALEXANDER BOTTS.

Wrong Again, Henderson

TELEGRAM
WASHINGTON, D.C., JULY 30, 1942

CAPT. ALEXANDER BOTTS,
ALASKA HIGHWAY, ARMY HEADQUARTERS,
FORT ST. JOHN, BRITISH COLUMBIA
MY FRIEND GEORGE "SKIPPY" INSKIP, NEWSPAPER
SYNDICATE WRITER, PLANS TO ARRIVE FORT ST.
JOHN NEXT WEEK TO VISIT ALASKA HIGHWAY. I HAVE
TOLD HIM I KNOW YOU WILL BE GLAD TO SHOW HIM
AROUND OVER THE WHOLE PROJECT AND SEE THAT
HE GETS COMPLETE MATERIAL FOR HIS NEWSPAPER
ARTICLES
    GILBERT HENERSON
    PRESIDENT EARTHWORM TRACTOR CO.

DATE: Friday, July 31, 1942
FROM: Captain Alexander Botts,
Former Sales Manager, Earthworm Tractor Company,
Now Chief Deputy Expediter, Alaska Highway Division,
Office for Expediting Construction Equipment and Supplies,
Fort St. John, British Columbia.

TO: Mr. Gilbert Henderson,
President Earthworm Tractor Company,
Earthworm Branch Office,
Washington, D.C.

SUBJECT: All wrong, Henderson

Your wire is here, and you are deeply in error if you think I have any time to waste in showing around any fool reporter. The only basis on which I could even consider it would be in the case you could help me out on my present job, which has kept me busy for weeks writing endless letters and telegrams to Washington in an attempt to get through a large shipment of steel which is urgently needed up at the head of construction in the Rocky Mountains for two two-hundred-foot-span bridges to carry the highway across the Moose River and then back again. This steel was ordered three months ago. One month ago, we heard it was ready to ship. And last week we were informed it would not be shipped at all—it is being diverted to the Pan-American Highway somewhere down near the Panama Canal.

As all my protests so far have been in vain, it occurs to me that you, with all your Washington contacts, might be able to convince the big shots down there that it is absolutely vital for us to have that steel up here. In the past, you have been a good deal of wet smack on jobs like this—especially in the matter of that wire rope I asked for a few weeks ago. But I know you can do this if you try. All that is required is that you make the Washington end of the Office for Expediting Construction Equipment and Supplies send through that bridge steel—they will know what it is.

So now you understand what it will take to get a good break for your newspaper friend. If you will scratch my back with that bridge iron, I will try to play ball with your reporter.

Yours,

ALEXANDER BOTTS.

TELEGRAM

WASHINGTON, D.C., AUG. 3, 1942

CAPT. ALEXANDER BOTTS,
ALASKA HIGHWAY, ARMY HEADQUARTERS,
FORT ST. JOHN, BRITISH COLUMBIA

WAR DEPARTMENT HAS JUST INFORMED ME THAT IN ORDER TO PREVENT VITAL INFORMATION FROM REACHING ENEMY THEY HAVE ENTIRE ALASKA HIGHWAY UNDER STRICT MILITARY CENSORSHIP. ALL REPORTERS BARRED. YOU WILL MAKE SURE, THEREFORE, THAT MR. INSKIP DOES NOT VISIT ANY PART OF PROJECT—OTHERWISE I MIGHT BE IN SERIOUS DIFFICULTUIES FOR MY PART IN HELPING ARRANGE FOR HIM TO GO. HAVE BEEN UNABLE SO FAR TO DO ANYTHING IN RE BRIDGE IRON. LOCAL OECES OFFICIALS POINT OUT OBVIOUS INEFFICIENCY AND LACK OF PLANNING INDICATED BY ARMY REQUEST FOR TWO BRIDGES MERELY TO TAKE ROAD ACROSS RIVER AND THEN BACK AGAIN. WHY NOT JUST STAY ON THE SAME SIDE?

GILBERT HENDERSON

DATE: Thursday, August 6, 1942
FROM: Captain Alexander Botts
TO: Mr. Gilbert Henderson
SUBJECT: Wrong Once More, Henderson

I received your wire and met your friend Skippy Inskip three days ago at Fort St. John, which is the small Canadian hamlet at the southern end of the new highway. And all I can say, Henderson, is that the way you keep changing your mind is almost incredible—especially when you always shift around so as to be all wrong all the time. You were wrong in the first place sending a reporter up here at a time I did not want him. And you were wrong again in demanding that I send him back at the very moment when you were giving me information which convinced me I ought to keep him here and use him.

As soon as I read your statement that the OECES officials accuse the army up here of inefficiency and lack of planning, and that they don't understand why the road has to cross the river twice, I decided that something drastic had to be done.

In the first place, the army up here is highly efficient and plans everything most competently. In the second place, there is ample reason for two river crossings—as will be explained later in this letter. And in the third place, I have sent countless reports to Washington explaining all this in the first place. If all my efforts have so far failed to make even a dent in the ignorance of the officials down there, it will be useless for me to hammer at them any more. And it will probably take more than the mild sort of talk you usually put out to bring real results. So that is where Skippy comes in.

When he arrived last Monday, I at once sized him up as a splendid fellow—young, energetic, full of ideas. I therefore laid all the facts before him, and told him he could do a great service to his country and to the Alaska Highway by writing an article—to be syndicated all over the United States—describing the almost superhuman achievements of the Army Engineers, and showing how their efforts were being sabotaged by the refusal of stupid officials to supply the much needed bridge iron.

"Such an article," I said, "will not only enhance your reputation as a red hot journalist, but will also wake up those torpid OECES officials in Washington—thus making it much easier for Henderson to get some action out of them."

"I would certainly like to write an article like that," he said, "—but only if I can see the road and get my material first hand."

"All right," I said, "I'll take you on a tour of the whole project."

"But how about these rules that Mr. Henderson mentioned barring newspaper men?"

"If mere rules get in our way when we are trying to win the war," I said, "so much the worse for the rules. You can obey the spirit of the law by leaving out everything that might be of value to the enemy. And you will be aiding the war effort by making public information that is sure to stir up favorable action on this bridge iron."

"But this regulation barring newspaper men from the road is an official order, isn't it?"

"I have received no information on the subject through military channels," I said. "Therefore, I am officially ignorant of the whole thing. All I have is mere hearsay evidence supplied by Mr. Henderson, who is nothing but a civilian."

"Maybe they have the order over at Army headquarters. Hadn't you better ask?"

"If I asked, they might tell me. And that would cramp our style."

"But how can you take me along the road, if there is an order against it?"

"Skippy," I said, "are you by chance a mechanic? Do you know anything about the care and operation of tractors?"

"No."

"Never mind. With your quick intellect, and with me to guide you, I think you can get by all right."

"What do you mean?"

"I mean that this censorship order applies only to newspaper men. But a good mechanic would be welcome. Only the other day the Colonel was discussing with me the advisability of bringing up an expert from the Earthworm factory to check over the maintenance of all tractors and make any suggestions for improvement that occurred to him. So all you have to do is visit the project in the guise of a mechanic."

"If it's all right with you, it's all right with me."

"Skippy," I said, "you are a man after my own heart."

We got busy at once. I spent about an hour coaching Skippy on how to be an expert though ignorant—which is not as hard as might be supposed. Then I took him over to Army Headquarters, and introduced him as our new tractor expert to Colonel Kimball, the big boss of the whole southern half of the road. The colonel is such a splendid officer, and has always treated me so well that I could not have brought myself to lie to him. Fortunately, however, he did not ask any embarrassing questions—like "How long has Mr. Inskip been a tractor expert?" So everything went not only very well, but even better than I had hoped. After giving me a mild bawling out for my failure to get any action so far in the matter of the bridge iron, Colonel Kimball thanked me for procuring the services of Mr. Inskip, and invited both of us to fly with him in his private sea plane to a small lake up in the mountains near the head of construction on the road. As this was the exact region I wanted Skippy to see, I gladly accepted for both of us.

An hour later we took off from Charlie Lake, near Fort St. John, and headed north on a delightful trip which provided plenty of thrills and local color for Skippy's article. The weather was perfect, the plane steady and the pilot seemed to know his business. For mile after mile we flew over the ribbon of road winding along through the spruce and poplar forest of the foothills. Then we cut across the Fort Nelson corner and picked up the road again as it headed west, climbed over the first ridge of the Rockies, crossed several small streams, and finally started up the valley of the Caribou River.

"The Caribou is a small stream," explained the colonel. "But even when it becomes swollen by the spring freshets, it will give us no trouble. The slope of the land is so gentle that we have kept the road well above high water, and on one side of the stream all the way."

Even from several thousand feet in the air we could see that this was so. The ribbon of road, cutting through the forest, neither crossed the stream, nor approached very close to it.

Ahead of us loomed the second big range of the Rockies—a rugged mountain wilderness so wild and inaccessible that, before the arrival of the army engineers, it had never been penetrated except by a few lone trappers. Straight in front was Saddle Back Pass—a broad gap covered with a dense growth of spruce and jack pine. As the plane shot through this pass, apparently almost grazing the tops of the tallest trees, we came in sight of a small lake.

"That's Saddle-Back Lake," said the colonel to Skippy. "It's fed by all the drainage from the snow fields in those high mountains to the north. The outlet is at the other end. You'll see it in a minute."

"Look," I said, "There's the road, running along the bank. And there is one of the army camps."

We were flying so low that the brown tents flashed by in no time at all. And before we knew it, the lake was behind us, we were out of the pass, and the ground had dropped away far beneath us.

"There's the outlet," said the colonel. "It's called the Moose River. And that big gash ahead is Moose Canyon. We're going to fly over it to see how the construction work is going, and then come back and land on the lake."

As the plane speeded along, we had a glimpse of the Moose River tumbling down the western slope, and road following along in a wide sweep. Then both road and river entered the depths of Moose Canyon—a great trench perhaps half a mile wide, with perpendicular rock walls at least a thousand feet high. The country on both sides was so rugged and rocky that the canyon was obviously the only possible route for the highway. The river itself occupied only a small part of the width of the canyon floor. The rest was dry land—flat and wooded like the bottom of Yosemite Valley.

"Is this the river," asked Skippy, "where you need the two bridges that Mr. Botts is trying to get the iron for?"

"Yes," said the colonel.

"Why do you need *two* bridges?"

"You'll see in a minute. Notice how the stream hugs the north side—right against the cliff?"

"Yes."

"And there's the road—plenty of room for it on the left bank, between the stream and the canyon wall. It's like that for about five miles. But now look ahead."

In the distance we saw that the stream wandered over to the south side of the canyon. At this point the road crossed the stream on a pontoon bridge that looked like a line of toy boats far beneath us.

"For the next ten miles," said the colonel, "that river hugs the cliff on the south side. We had our choice of crossing over, or blasting the road for ten miles out of the solid rock of the cliff."

The plane sped on. Soon, far below, we saw tractors working

on the last stretch of road. We were over the head of construction.

"What's that thing next to the bank the looks like a raft?" asked Skippy.

"I don't know," said the colonel. "But right beyond it you can see that the river moves over against the north cliff again—which means another crossing—the last one, thank the Lord. Even so, it's a tough problem—because the first bridge is so long it took all our available pontoon material. Probably we'll have to hold up construction while we make a bridge out of some of this local timber. I'll decide after we get down there and look things over."

He spoke to the pilot. The plane stood on its ear in a banked turn, and flew back to the pass. Once more we skimmed the tree tops, then swooped down over Saddle-Back Lake, settled gracefully on the water, and taxied to a beach in front of the camp.

Here the colonel got a jeep, and took us along the road down the western slope, and into the canyon. The river was much wider than it had seemed from the air. We crossed the pontoon bridge. We continued to the end of construction. And here we ran into a sensational development. What we had supposed was a raft turned out to be a recently arrived river barge, propelled by one of our big Earthworm Diesel engines, and carrying a heavy load of fuel oil in metal drums.

This barge had started two months before from the Norman oil fields, almost a thousand miles away on the Mackensie River. The trip was an experiment to see if the oil from these remote wells could be brought to the Alaska Highway by water. Fighting against rapids, rocks, and shoals, the crew had pushed up the Mackensie, the Liard, and finally the Moose River—thus proving that the voyage was possible, but almost too difficult to be practical.

At any rate, they had brought a very welcome cargo of fuel oil for the tractors, and they had also provided a temporary makeshift solution for the bridge problem. The colonel, being a man of action, at once ordered that the barge be used as a ferry boat at this point—thus making it unnecessary to build a wooden bridge.

"However," he pointed out to me, "neither ferry boats, wooden bridges nor pontoon bridges will be any good when the fall rains start and the river rises. We must have that steel so we can put in long spans well above the flood level."

"Colonel Kimball," I said. "I will do everything I can."

"Good," he said. "I am leaving at once on a week's reconnaissance trip out into the wilderness to lay out the course of the road from here on. While I am gone, I would suggest that you leave Mr. Inskip here to look over the tractors, and return to St. John yourself so as to be on hand in case any news about that bridge iron comes in from Washington."

"Yes, sir," I said.

After the colonel left I cautioned Skippy to maintain at all times that expression of owlish wisdom which is characteristic of the expert from the factory. I instructed him to meet all requests for mechanical advice with a dignified statement that he prefers to make no recommendations until he has had time to inspect the job in its entirety. And I explained how he could send his article, when finished, by air mail from Fort Nelson—suggesting, incidentally, that he send a copy to the OECES officials in Washington and thus make sure that they see it.

I then came back to Fort St. John, feeling sure that if Skippy follows my advice, he will get by all right. For the next week I will obey orders and stay here in Fort St. John—well satisfied with myself for the way I have handled things.

Yours,

ALEXANDER BOTTS.

———————

TELEGRAM
WASHINGTON, D.C. AUG. 11, 1942

CAPTAIN ALEXANDER BOTTS,
FORT ST. JOHN, BRITISH COLUMBIA
NEWSPAPER SYNDICATE HAS SUBMITTED INSKIP ARTICLE TO ARMY CENSORS HERE AND THEY HAVE TRIED TO BLAME ME FOR HIS UNAUTHORIZED VISIT

TO HIGHWAY. FINALLY CONVINCED THEM I WAS NOT RESPONSIBLE. I HAVE NOT SEEN ARTICLE, BUT OECES OFFICIALS, AFTER READING COPY SENT TO THEM, ARE SO INCENSED AT WHAT THEY CLAIM IS IMPROPER ATTEMPT TO BRING PRESSURE ON THEM THAT THEY NOW REFUSE TO EVEN CONSIDER SHIPMENT OF BRIDGE IRON. I UNDERSTAND WAR DEPARTMENT HAS WIRED COL KIMBALL TO TAKE SUCH MEASURES IN THIS AFFAIR AS HE DEEMS PROPER. YOUR FAILURE TO FOLLOW MY ADVICE HAS THUS RESULTED IN A SITUATION WHICH COULD HARDLY BE WORSE. WHO IS WRONG NOW?

GILBERT HENDERSON

DATE: Thursday August 13, 1942.
FROM: Captain Alexander Botts
TO: Mr. Gilbert Henderson
SUBJECT: Wrong Again, Henderson

Your wire reached me at Fort St. John two days ago. When I read it, I had a feeling that the main place you were wrong this time was in your statement that the "situation could hardly be worse."

This feeling was prompted by another telegram which had just come in by radio from Captain McGehee, in command of the Advance Earthworm Detachment up at the head of construction in Moose Canyon. McGehee's message read in part as follows: "MR. INSKIP YOUR QUOTE EXPERT UNQUOTE WHILE ATTEMPTING TO REPAIR MOTOR IN BARGE LIT MATCH TO SEE HOW MUCH GASOLINE IN TANK OF STARTING MOTOR AND SET WHOLE BARGE ON FIRE STOP TOTAL LOSS STOP SITUATION SERIOUS NO FERRY BOAT STOP SUBSEQUENT QUESTIONING OF INSKIP REVEALS HE KNOWS NOTHING OF MECHANICS AND MAY BE AXIS SABOTEUR STOP AM HOLDING

HIM UNDER GUARD STOP COLONEL KIMBALL WILL BE HERE THURSDAY REQUEST THAT YOU COME UP AND EXPLAIN YOUR PART IN AFFAIR."

As I have a quick mind, I realized at once that the situation was, on the whole, not so good. Of course no one could blame me because Skippy had attempted a repair job instead of practicing the owlish reserve I had recommended. But I saw that I would have to do some heavy explaining to Colonel Kimball in order to clear things up to the satisfaction of all. As I am a good talker, however, I did not let the difficulty of the job daunt me. And I promptly arranged to take the next plane to Saddle Back Lake.

Before I left, I received a delayed letter from Skippy, written before the unfortunate disaster to the boat. He inclosed a copy of his article. Apparently he had spent a couple of days after I left him in travelling up and down the road, picking up a lot of local color about the three-foot Dolly Varden trout in the mountain streams, the bears that hang around the camps to steal food, and the pet moose at one of the camps with an army dog tag bearing his name—Franklin D. Moosevelt. Skippy also had some swell dope on how the resourceful army mechanics keep the tractors running in spite of shortages of critical parts—welding new teeth onto sprockets, using birch bark for gaskets, old socks for oil-filter elements, and finding a hundred uses for old tin cans, old shoes, and so on.

With his professional nose for news, Skippy had turned up an ancient trapper at the Hudson's Bay Company trading post at Fort Nelson, who claimed he had visited the Moose Canyon region twenty years before, and said there was enough iron ore in Moose Canyon to make a hundred steel bridges. Skippy was inclined to be skeptical about this because the old boy seemed very vague on his geography—claiming that Saddle Back Lake drains eastward into the Caribou River instead of westward into the Moose, as Skippy knew to be a fact.

The main theme of Skippy's article was exactly what I had hoped it would be—that the Army is doing such a swell job up here that the people in Washington ought to send them without question anything they ask for—such, for instance, as the steel for the two Moose River bridges. The article, on the whole, is such a splendid tribute to the men who are doing the work up here that it would be a crime not to publish it.

I imagine, however, that you are getting impatient to hear of my meeting with Colonel Kimball, so that you can gloat over what you think he would probably say to me. For the present, therefore, I will pass over any further discussion of Skippy's article. I will also postpone telling of the interesting plan I worked out on the basis of the information supplied by the ancient trapper at Fort Nelson. And I will get right along to the main event.

It was at about one o'clock in the morning and pitch dark when I arrived at the advance camp. Colonel Kimball had just returned from his reconnaissance trip. He was sitting in his tent consulting his maps by the light of a gasoline lantern. And he asked that Skippy and I be shown in at once.

We entered. At the colonel's invitation, we sat down. Skippy seemed dejected. I, on the other hand, was considerably elated at the thought of the dramatic scene which was about to open.

The colonel was grave. He related Skippy's adventures with the match and the gasoline—substantially as given in Captain McGehee's message to me. He stated that he had received a telegram from Washington, relayed by radio, asking him to handle the matter as he saw fit. And he asked me to give an account of what I knew of the affair.

Sensing that the loyal Skippy had refused to implicate me, I at once set the colonel right on that part of it.

"If anything has gone wrong," I said, "I will assume the blame. I talked Mr. Inskip into coming up here disguised as a tractor expert. I wanted him to beat the censorship, so he could write an article which I hoped would hurry the delivery of that bridge iron."

"And you still think that the article, if published, would have that effect?"

"To be perfectly frank, no. The officials concerned have already seen it, and the effect has been the opposite of what I hoped.

Here is a telegram from Mr. Henderson that you might like to read."

The colonel read it. "The net result of your combined activities," he said, "seems to be that we have now lost all chance of getting that bridge iron—and we have also lost this ferry boat which was so essential in maintaining traffic on the road."

"Oh, there's more to it than that," I said. "Have you seen Skippy's article?"

"No."

I promptly handed over my copy. "If you will read this," I said, "I think I can convince you that Skippy's visit up here has been completely justified."

Being a fair-minded man, and desirous of giving me every chance to present my case, the colonel read the entire article with care.

"It's a good job," he admitted. "There is no reason why it should not be published. It reveals nothing which could be of value to the enemy. And it ought to promote the morale of the men by its recognition of their efforts. However, all this does not excuse Mr. Inskip's unauthorized presence up here, and it does not help us in the present emergency."

"That's what you think," I said. "Apparently you have not given enough attention to the information supplied by that ancient trapper at Fort Nelson."

"If you are referring to the iron ore," said the colonel, "the man is crazy. Does he expect us to set up a blast furnace—haul in coal—establish a steel rolling mill?"

"That's not what I'm talking about. The important part is where he claims that Saddle Back Lake empties into the Caribou River."

"But he's wrong about that. He hasn't been up here for twenty years—he has probably forgotten."

"In twenty years," I said, "a lot can happen—to rivers as well as to men's memories. And I have been working on the theory that the man knew what he was talking about."

"What do you mean?"

"You know that Saddle Back Lake is in a hollow right at the top of the pass?"

"Yes."

"When I got to the lake yesterday morning," I said, "I did a little reconnoitering. And way over on the far side, hidden by a spruce-covered knoll, I found what looked like an old outlet, leading toward the east. It had been blocked by a rock slide that had come down from the mountain—presumably during the past twenty years. So I figured we could clear away the slide, reopen the old channel, and send the water down the Caribou River where it wouldn't do any harm because the road back there is well above any possible high water. Then nothing would come through Moose Canyon here except a little local drainage that wouldn't amount to anything."

"If you think," said the colonel, "that we are going to spend several months moving around a lot of rock on the off chance that we can divert this whole river—"

"You don't have to spend several months," I said. "I borrowed a power shovel from the motor pool yesterday morning and did it in about twelve hours. Come and see."

I grabbed up the lantern, and led him out of the tent and down towards the nearby Moose River. "Never forget," I said, "that when you come to a river and you can't get across, there are always two solutions. You can fool around with such things as boats and bridges—or you can just remove the river."

We reached the bank. We climbed down. We wandered, dry shod, over the rough, slippery stones of what, a few hours before, had been the bottom of the mighty Moose River. In the center we found an insignificant little brook that could be spanned by a simple culvert.

After a long silence, the colonel—fair-minded as always—spoke. "The War Department," he said, "has ordered me to handle your case. You have committed a serious violation of censorship regulations. You ought to be sent to Leavenworth. But Mr. Inskip's article is so good that the Army censorship has decided to release it for publication, provided it has my approval—which I have decided to give. And what you, Captain Botts, have done to this Moose River makes me most reluctant to take any action against you. So my advice is that both you clowns get out of here as fast as you can, and head back for Fort St. John before I change my mind."

So Skippy and I have been returned to Fort St. John, where I have been writing this letter. And now the only thing worrying me is this: How does it happen, Henderson, that, even though you seem to reason things out in a completely logical manner, you always contrive to be all wrong about everything all the time?

Yours,

ALEXANDER BOTTS.

"Keep Moving, Captain Botts!"

EARTHWORM TRACTOR COMPANY
STEVENSVILLE BRANCH
STEVENSVILLE, ILLINOIS

Monday, August 23, 1943.

Mr. Gilbert Henderson,
President,
Earthworm Tractor Company,
Earthworm City, Illinois.

DEAR HENDERSON: Early this morning I arrived here at the recently established Earthworm branch factory, where the Army has assigned me to run some final tests on the new armored tractors and heavy-duty trailers which are now beginning to come off the assembly line. Almost as soon as I entered the factory, however, I ran into a situation so distressing, and so threatening to the success of the whole production program down here, that I have changed my plans so as to devote most of my time to working out a solution of the difficulty. The plan of action which I have laid out will require a lot of work by me. It will also cost you thirty thousand dollars—in view of which I feel that it may be wise for me to explain the whole thing so that you will send along the money without delay.

After checking in at the factory office this morning, I proceeded to the final inspection department to make preliminary arrangements for my tests. Here I ran into old Jim Crocker, whom you will doubtless remember as one of the best of our veteran mechanics. On many a difficult tractor demonstration in the days when I was sales manager, old Jim's skill with motors was the deciding factor which brought success out of threatened disaster. Dependable, competent and hard working, Jim is one of the wheel horses who is so necessary to give stability to the young and inexperienced working force in this new and rapidly expanding plant. Such being the case, it was a distinct shock to hear Jim announce that he was quitting his job.

"What's the matter?" I asked.

"We just decided there is nothing else to do."

"Who is 'we'?"

"About thirty of us—George Miller, Tony Capello, Mike Zippke, Matt Brennan, Henry Smith, Carl Mueller, and a lot more."

"But you are all key men. You can't quit!"

"There's nothing else to do. We have to leave town."

"Why?"

"We're being evicted from our homes. And, on account of the housing shortage, we can't find any other place to live."

"But why should you be evicted? You must have money. Why don't you pay your rent and stick around?"

"It isn't that. They're going to tear down the whole group of thirty houses."

"What!" I said. "Somebody is actually tearing houses down at a time when every inch of space is desperately needed? Is there anything wrong with these houses?"

"No, they are nice little frame dwellings, built about a year ago as a Government housing project right next to the new Army airport on the other side of town. They were all rented to Earthworm tractor men like myself, who came down from Earthworm City to work in the new plant."

"But I still don't understand why they are tearing these houses down."

"Apparently the new airport has turned out to be too small. They find they've got to lengthen the runway. These houses are right in the way. So down they come, and out we go—and back to Earthworm City."

"Couldn't they move the houses to another location?"

"We asked the Colonel at the airport about that. He says at

least half a dozen government agencies have been discussing this for the past three months. They keep passing the buck back and forth. First they decide to move the houses. Then they decide to sell them. Then they go back and decide to move them. But nothing happens. Finally, the Colonel got authority from somebody to throw us out and tear the houses down. He claims the runway has to be lengthened right away, so he's going ahead."

"Somebody ought to stop him," I said. "Isn't the superintendent of the Earthworm factory here doing anything about this?"

"I guess he figures it's not his business. All he is supposed to do is to look after production in the factory."

"He's not looking after production if he lets his best men get away. If he won't do anything, I will. You can tell the whole gang to sit tight and stop worrying. If any of you are thrown out of your homes, it will be over the dead body of Alexander Botts."

A half hour later, I walked in on the Colonel at the air field. After considerable discussion, I suggested that instead of demolishing the houses, he give them to me and let me move them away.

"Okay," said the Colonel. "As far as I am concerned you can do anything you want with them, provided you get them out of the way by Wednesday morning, and provided you will take the responsibility for dealing with any objections that may come from any of the government agencies involved."

"Thank you," I said. "It is a deal."

I spent the rest of the morning interviewing real estate agents, and reconnoitering the entire city and its environs. By noon I had decided that the only feasible site for the thirty houses is a tract of about fifteen acres delightfully situated right next to the new Earthworm factory, with a beautiful view of the foundry, power house and machine shop.

The land is owned by a certain Mr. Bert Scriver. He bought it several months ago for ten thousand dollars. But when I asked him to set a price on it he said he would take thirty thousand dollars, and not one cent less. As I am a good judge of men, I at once sized up this Bert Scriver as the kind of a man that both you and I would much prefer to do business with somebody else. His eye is cold. His hands are prehensile. And his facial expression betokens one who, if he could be there to do it, would steal the last cent from his own widow and orphan children.

Ordinarily, I would refuse to demean myself by associating with such vermin. But we need his land. So I got the disagreeable business over as fast as possible. We drew up a contract of sale between him and the Earthworm Company at his own price of thirty thousand cash. We can take possession as soon as the contract is signed and the money paid. So all you have to do, Henderson, is transfer the money down here and authorize your local treasurer to sign the papers. I will do all the rest. As part of my official testing of the Army tractors and trailers, I will have these machines move the houses. The local Earthworm superintendent has already furnished me with jacks and other tools and some extra help.

Late this afternoon I called on Jim Crocker at his attractive little home, which—like the rest of the thirty houses—is so small, so sturdy, and so compact that moving it will be simplicity itself. When I told Jim and his wife that I was saving their home from destruction, their joy and gratitude were such as would warm the heart of even as cold a businessman as yourself. At once they rushed forth to spread the glad tidings among the people in the other houses. And soon the entire neighborhood was engaged in joyous celebration.

As you can see, my operations down here are of great importance. So you must not delay an instant in sending the thirty thousand dollars—which, under the circumstances, is a very paltry sum indeed. Although Mr. Scriver is skinning us out of about twenty thousand dollars, the net results will be highly favorable. Within a few days, the Earthworm Company will have thirty houses, complete with lots, at a total cost of only a thousand dollars per house, plus a small additional expense for water and sewage connections, street construction and moving. And—more important than mere finances—thirty splendid homes will be saved and many excellent workmen will continue their important work in the Earthworm factory.

I am starting moving operations at once. And I want that money so I can put through the deal with Mr. Scriver before the houses complete their five-mile trip across the city to their new location.

Yours expectantly,

ALEXANDER BOTTS
Captain, U. S. Army Corps of
Engineers, D.O.L.,
Acting Inspector of Armored
Tractors and Heavy-Duty
Trailers at Earthworm-
Stevensville Plant.

EARTHWORM TRACTOR COMPANY
EARTHWORM CITY, ILLINOIS

Tuesday, August 24, 1943.

Captain Alexander Botts,
U.S. Army Corps of Engineers, D.O.L.,
Earthworm-Stevensville Plant,
Stevensville, Illinois.

DEAR BOTTS: Your letter has reached me at a time when I am so swamped with work that it will be impossible for me to give proper consideration to your proposed real estate deal. My first reaction is that it would be unwise for the Earthworm Company to become involved in any housing project. However, it is possible that I may have time to investigate the matter at some time during the next few weeks, and, if so, I shall be glad to communicate with you further.

Yours hastily,

GILBERT HENDERSON,
President, Earthworm Tractor
Company.

EARTHWORM TRACTOR COMPANY
STEVENSVILLE BRANCH
STEVENSVILLE, ILLINOIS

Wednesday evening, August 25, 1943.

DEAR HENDERSON: Your incredibly indifferent response to my earnest appeal for funds arrived this afternoon at the very moment when my need for said funds was so painfully acute that I would have called you at once by long distance except that I feared your hopelessly old-fashioned dislike for talking over the telephone might have caused you so much irritation that you would have turned me down flat, to say nothing of the fact that I myself was so annoyed that I probably could not have explained the situation coherently, which, now that I have completely calmed down, I will do in my usual clear and dispassionate manner, because even if your brain is just a solid mass of nothing, I have got to have that money, and no mistake, and you can't turn me down, especially after all the work I have done.

Probably never before in the history of house moving has a job of this size gotten under way more efficiently and expeditiously. By working Monday night, all day Tuesday, and all Tuesday night, my splendid Army detail managed to get all of those thirty little houses jacked up, and slid onto thirty big trailers, with four more trailers carrying four separate one-car garages, and another loaded down with seven chicken coops—making thirty-five trailers in all. It was a monumental task.

Bright and early this morning the huge convoy got under way. Strung out in an impressive column over half a mile long, the thirty-five beautiful armored Diesel Earthworms, each one with its sturdy bulldozer blade poised gracefully in front, and with its laden trailer behind, moved slowly and majestically into the south end of Stevensville's wide Main Street, which extends for five miles, straight as an arrow, from the airfield, through the center of the business district, and on to the beautiful tract of land which I had arranged to buy from Mr. Scriver.

At first I was considerably worried by a factor which is a little unusual in house-moving technique. Owing to the acute housing shortage, it had been impossible to find any alternative accommodations for the tenants while their homes were being moved. I had therefore been forced to let the people remain in residence. This brought up many problems in connection with cooking, water supply, sanitary arrangements, and so on.

Fortunately, the new Earthworm heavy-duty trailers have all the latest improvements in spring suspension, hydraulic shock-absorbers and pneumatic tires, so that the heaviest loads may be floated along with a smoothness reminiscent of transportation on the old Erie Canal. As an added safeguard, I ordered my tractor drivers to keep the gears in low, and to hold the speed down to one-half mile per hour or less. Before starting, I had of course obtained a permit to move the houses through town, and the Chief of Police had assigned a squad of cops to regulate all traffic on the line of march. At my request, the telephone and electric light companies had furnished linemen to deal with all obstructing overhead wires. And I had appointed good old Jim Crocker—whom I mentioned in my former letter as one of the tenants and also one of our most reliable employees—to serve as chairman of a sort of welfare committee of the householders during the course of the operations.

As a result of all these wise precautions, everything went better than I had dared hope—for a while, at least. Jim and I spent the first few hours hurrying back and forth along the line of march, with eyes, ears and minds on the alert for the first sign of trouble. But there was surprisingly little.

When all the plaster fell off the ceiling of Mike Zippke's dining room, and Mrs. Zippke stuck her head out of the window yelling murder, Jim was right on the job to point out that, after all, this is wartime, and think how much better off she was than people overseas that might have a bomb knock the whole house down. As the lady could think of no adequate reply to this, she shut up.

A little later George Miller's slightly senile Great Uncle Otto, desiring to take a quiet smoke in the sunshine, stepped absent-mindedly out the side door, dropped five feet, and landed in a heap on the pavement. As I was right on the job, however, I was able to pick the old gentleman up, dust him off, and boost him back into the house before he knew what had happened. I then silenced his incipient complaints by handing him an excellent fifteen-cent cigar which I had just purchased for only twenty-six cents.

Several housewives who had carelessly neglected to provide proper supplies for the journey were given jugs of drinking water, groceries, and miscellaneous materials. We even supplied aspirin to one unusually nervous female who was working herself into a sick headache because her best set of dishes had been jarred off the pantry shelf and she foolishly insisted on worrying about what might happen next. And at noon ample box lunches were handed out to the tractor drivers, and to all of the householders who desired them.

Taking it all in all, everything went so smoothly that early in the afternoon I was able to relinquish temporarily all executive details, take my place in an army jeep at the head of the column, and lead our magnificent parade as it entered the central business section of Stevensville.

It was indeed a proud moment for me. Imagine if you can, Henderson, this monstrous cavalcade—thirty-five powerful Earthworm tractors, thirty-five smoothly-running Earthworm heavy-duty trailers, thirty inhabited dwelling houses, four small garages, and seven chicken coops full of chickens—all of them moving majestically along at a speed of one-half mile per hour through the heart of Stevensville, Illinois. Picture to yourself the open-mouthed wonder of the citizenry, the happy frenzy of the small boys, the sharp commands of the traffic cops, the respectful halting of traffic, the roar of the Earthworm tractors, and—last but not least—the quiet dignity of the commander in chief as he rode ahead in his jeep, bowing and smiling to the admiring spectators. Obviously, it was a situation too perfect to endure.

A man rushed out from the crowd. He laid a heavy hand on my shoulder. I turned. Mr. Bert Scriver was leering at me. And, as he walked along beside the slowly-moving jeep, he spoke: "Are you planning to put these houses on my land before you have paid for it?"

"Well," I said, "I had to move the houses away from the airport, and I have to put them somewhere. But you have no cause for worry. The money has been slightly delayed, but I can assure you—"

"You can't put these houses on my land until I get the money."

"But listen—"

"I deal on a strictly cash basis. I don't trust you. I don't trust anybody."

"But I have no other place to put the houses. I've got to put them on your land."

"Yeah? Then read this." He handed me a paper. "It's an injunction, and it says you can't put your houses on my land."

I read the paper. It seemed to say what Mr. Scriver claimed. But, on account of the idiotic legal language, I could not be sure. I jumped out of the jeep, ran into a drug store, called the legal department at the Earthworm plant, and read the thing to one of our attorneys. He said that if I went ahead I might be guilty of contempt of court and in serious trouble.

"But I am an officer of the United States Army," I said, "engaged in a patriotic enterprise."

"That makes no difference," he said.

I went back and argued for fifteen minutes with Mr. Scriver. It did no good. The man's mind seems to be so devious that he thinks everybody else is as much of a crook as he is himself. He actually doubted whether you, Henderson, would come through with the money, and he claimed he was perfectly justified in trying to protect himself from being gypped.

"Very well," I said. "These houses will stay right here until the matter is settled." I sent back along the line of march an order for all the drivers to halt.

The mighty caravan came creaking to a stop. The roar of thirty-five great motors died away. A strange silence settled down. Then a traffic cop rushed up.

"Keep moving, Captain Botts!" he yelled. "Keep moving!"

I tried to tell him that I couldn't. I had no place to take my houses. He called the Chief of Police. I explained the entire situation. The Chief was polite—but firm.

"You got my sympathy, Captain Botts," he said. "You're trying to do a good deed here by moving these houses, and I'm all for you. I'm all against this louse of a Scriver. But the law's on his side. As long as he says no, you can't put your houses on his land. On the other hand, you certainly can't leave them here on the main street."

"It wouldn't be more than a few days—"

"A few days! A few minutes is too much. Listen!"

I listened, and became aware of something which, owing to my preoccupation with the various problems confronting me, I had not previously noted. From all points of the compass came a loud braying of automobile horns. Apparently hundreds of cars, attempting to enter or leave the business district, had become blocked by our line of houses, and the ensuing traffic snarl was getting worse all the time.

"Perhaps I really ought to move these houses," I admitted. "But where can I move them to?"

The Chief began to get a bit impatient. "I don't care where you take them," he said. "But you got to get them off the main stem here, or I'll have to run you in for obstructing traffic."

At this point a couple of other people who had been listening spoke up. One was an officer from the airport. "Don't try to take them back where they came from," he warned. "We've already started to level the ground where they used to stand."

The other man was from the State Highway Commission or something like that. "If you know what's good for you," he said, "you'd better not try to clutter up the roads outside of town."

"And you've got to clear out of here right now," added the Chief of Police. "Come on—get started. And keep moving, Captain Botts!"

"Okay, gentlemen," I replied politely. "I don't know where I'm going, but I'm on my way."

I went back and spoke to the operator of the lead Earthworm tractor. "You will resume your forward progress," I said. "You will get off the main street here, and you will stay off. But you will not go to the tract of land originally designated. Furthermore, you will not go out onto any of the country roads, and you will not return to the airport."

"But where shall I go, then?"

"Whithersoever your fancy directs you. Just avoid the prohibited districts I have mentioned. And—until further notice— keep moving."

I gave similar orders to the rest of the tractor operators. Soon all thirty-five motors roared into action. The mighty cavalcade moved forward and then dispersed as one house after another turned off into the side streets and residence districts of the town. Meanwhile, to avoid any more useless conversations with the Chief of Police, I had quietly withdrawn to my room in the Stevensville Hotel—where I have been writing this letter. I will mail it at once. You will receive it tomorrow morning, at which time all you have to do is wire the treasurer at the plant down here, authorizing him to turn over the thirty thousand dollars to Scriver and close the deal on the land.

So far I have kept out of trouble by following the Chief of Police's orders to the letter. I have moved the houses off Main Street, and I am keeping them moving—even though they are not going anywhere. I plan to put on a new shift of drivers this evening, so I can string out the performance until sometime tomorrow. But you can see that these houses cannot voyage about the town indefinitely. So I need that money, and I need it in a hurry. I am counting on you.

Yours hopefully,
ALEXANDER BOTTS.

TELEGRAM
EARTHWORM CITY, ILL. AUG. 26, 1943

CAPT. ALEXANDER BOTTS,
EARTHWORM TRACTOR COMPANY,
STEVENSVILLE, ILL.
I HAVE REFERRED YOUR REQUEST FOR THIRTY
THOUSAND DOLLARS TO THE EXECUTIVE COMMIT-
TEE OF THE BOARD OF DIRECTORS OF OUR COM-
PANY WHICH IS HOLDING A MEETING HERE TODAY.
   GILBERT HENDERSON

EARTHWORM TRACTOR COMPANY
STEVENSVILLE BRANCH
STEVENSVILLE, ILLINOIS

Thursday evening, August 26, 1944.

Mr. Gilbert Henderson,
President,
Earthworm Tractor Company,
Earthworm City, Illinois.

DEAR HENDERSON: Your telegram, stating that you had weakly passed the buck to the Executive Committee, arrived this morning. And it may interest you to learn that by that time your failure to back me up had produced a crisis so complicated and so devastating that almost anyone except myself would have been completely defeated.

Fortunately, I was at least partially prepared. Having a faint premonition of impending trouble, I had sneaked out of the hotel yesterday evening and spent the night with a friend out in the suburbs. In this way I assured myself a good sleep. And when I returned to the hotel late this morning, I was rested, refreshed, and alert. Even so, I was somewhat appalled at the scene in the hotel lobby.

The whole place swarmed with people—all of them mad as hornets, and all of them looking for me. As it would be impossible for me to repeat the sum total of the angry complaints that poured forth, I will merely mention that the Chief of Police announced that moving the houses all over town was worse than leaving them on Main Street, and if I didn't get them out of town he would have me arrested; the State Highway man said if I even tried to take them out of town he would have me arrested; the Health Commissioner said that if I did not at once correct the shocking sanitary conditions due to the lack of sewage connections to my houses, he would have me arrested; and the colonel from the airport said that if I came near the airport with my houses he would arrest me himself.

Besides these specific threats, there was an endless chorus of complaints, such as:

"Listen, buddy, I'm from the electric light company, and your outfit has knocked down dozens of our lines, and how do you think we can keep ahead of thirty houses moving all over everywhere and nobody knows where any of them are going next?"

"And I'm from the telephone company, and you got to stop knocking over our lines—"

"You got to find our dog—we lost him on Maple Street, and we are now three miles away on Oak Avenue, and how do you think he can find his way back?"

"As a wife and mother, I protest! With this continuous moving, how can my children find their way home from school? How can my husband get home from work? And—good Lord, I just happened to think—how am I going to find my own way home from here?"

"Why don't you tell your tractor drivers to drive more careful? My hen-house sideswiped a tree, and fell off the trailer, and broke open, and the hens are running all over the Third Ward, and you got to come and help me catch them."

And so it went, with everybody yelling louder and louder. The ever-loyal Jim Crocker was doing his best to calm the tumult, but he was helpless. Finally, I started yelling myself; and I yelled so much louder than anybody else that they finally quieted down and listened to what I had to say.

"Ladies and gentlemen," I announced, with an air of complete self-confidence, "I am at this very moment on my way to take such measures as may be required to obviate the difficulties which you have been discussing, and as every one of us is anxious to see this happy result achieved with the greatest possible celerity, I must beg of you, for your own good, to refrain from further fruitless talk and let me proceed at once to the vigorous action which we all so much desire. Thank you."

This little speech was delivered so impressively that my audience was, as it were, nonplussed. I was therefore able to make a dignified exit through the revolving door without any one attempting either to interfere or to follow me—which was just as well, because at the moment I did not have the faintest idea what to do next, and the only "vigorous action" I had in mind was to get out of there before they tore me limb from limb.

As I went scuttling away down the street, I almost ran into a man coming the other way. It was Mr. Bert Scriver, with a smile more disgusting and more triumphant than ever.

"Well, well, Captain Botts!" he remarked. "You're just the man I want to see. I've got everything fixed up. All you have to do is get me another thirty thousand dollars and then you can move the houses onto that land."

"What do you mean—*another* thirty thousand dollars?"

"The first thirty thousand came through about an hour ago. The Executive Committee up at Earthworm City wired an authorization to the Earthworm treasurer down here. So the deal is closed, and the Earthworm Company owns the land."

"Hooray! " I said. "Then I can move the houses out there right away."

"Not so fast, Captain Botts. Before you do any moving, you've got to buy the houses."

"I don't get you."

Mr. Scriver launched into a long explanation. It seems that about a month ago my thirty houses had been transferred to a new Government agency which the general public never heard of, and that this agency had then advertised them for sale by some typically bureaucratic procedure which was perfectly legal but so ineffective that nobody around here knew anything about it— nobody, that is, but Mr. Bert Scriver, who, although he was prac- tically broke at the time, had bid in the houses at the ridiculously low figure of ten thousand dollars, which was supplied by a part- ner whom he had talked into the deal.

By concealing this information while I was moving the houses, Mr. Scriver had deliberately led me into a trap. When he got the thirty grand from the Earthworm Company, he used ten of it to buy out his partner. Thus, having previously held up my house-moving enterprise until he got an exorbitant price for his land, this sneaking viper actually had the effrontery to use the very money I had turned his way to put himself in a position where he could now hold me up for another exorbitant sum. It was the last straw. But I refused to let it break my back. Instead of weakly surrendering, I spoke right up, and denounced the man to his face.

"Surely," I said, "you would not be so unpatriotic as to engage in this low profiteering at the expense of a project which is nec- essary to provide proper housing for men who are engaged in important war work—"

"You're going to buy those houses for thirty thousand, or I won't let you move a single one of them a single inch farther."

"Listen," I said. "That land cost you ten thousand. The houses cost you ten thousand. As a patriotic citizen you ought to sell at cost."

"I suppose," he sneered, "you are trying to tell me I ought to give you the houses, and pay you back ten thousand dollars. Is that your proposition?"

"Exactly," I said. "Do you accept?"

"Certainly not. I want thirty thous—"

"Come with me," I interrupted.

Disregarding his protests, I led him back along the sidewalk and into the lobby of the hotel. The mob was still there. Holding up my hand for silence, I made a little speech.

"Ladies and gentlemen," I said, "I have good news for you. Let me present your fellow-townsman, Mr. Bert Scriver, who owns the thirty houses which have been recently circulating through your fair city. As the owner, he now assumes full responsibility for his property. If you have any complaints, you may start working on him right now."

And I am pleased to report, Henderson, that they started at once, and the way they worked on that poor fish was really something. Apparently the previous complaints, addressed to me, had been somewhat tempered by the feeling that I was at least trying to do the right thing. But Mr. Bert Scriver was known to all as the shifty and unscrupulous character that he is. So they really went to town with him.

All of the accusations which had been previously hurled at me were now repeated with increased bitterness. There were threats of damage suits totalling hundreds of thousands of dollars for mental anguish, loss of hens and dogs, damage to property, malicious mischief, interference with telephone and electric light service, and dozens of other matters. The Health Commissioner said he would bring charges that might result in ten thousand dollars' fine or ten years' imprisonment or both, and the Chief of Police, waving a pair of handcuffs, announced the houses would be moved out of town at once, or else.

By this time Mr. Bert Scriver was pretty well cowed. "All right, Captain Botts," he said, "you can move the houses now, and we'll talk business afterwards."

"First," I said, "I want title to those houses, and ten thousand dollars."

As Mr. Scriver hesitated, good old Jim Crocker raised the cry: "Lynch the bum!" The crowd surged forward, and it took six policemen to hold them. At the door appeared the railroad station agent. "One of them houses," he yelled, "is stalled right on the main line track because the tractor ran out of gas." At this point, the Chief of Police slipped the handcuffs on Mr. Scriver's wrists—which turned out to be the final straw for Mr. Scriver.

Deciding, at long last, to be patriotic, he accepted my proposition—and the rest was more or less routine.

By this evening we had hauled all the houses, including the one from the railroad track, to the new tract of land. Mr. Scriver has signed over the houses to the Earthworm Company. The Earthworm treasurer has his certified check for ten thousand. The Chief of Police has turned Mr. Scriver loose. And all threatened charges and lawsuits have been withdrawn.

So that is all, except that, in closing, I want to congratulate you, Henderson, on having that rare type of personality which enables you to enlist the services of a guy like me to do a good job for you in spite of all your efforts to discourage me.

Yours admiringly,
ALEXANDER BOTTS.

The natural-born salesman even daydreams about Earthworm tractors, as this drawing from the inaugural "Alexander the Great" comic strip illustrates. (University of Vermont Library)

Botts Gets a New Job

CARE OF EARTHWORM TRACTOR AGENCY,
ATLANTA, GEORGIA

Thursday, February 6, 1947.

Mr. Gilbert Henderson,
President,
Earthworm Tractor Company,
Earthworm City, Illinois.

DEAR HENDERSON: I hereby tender my resignation as sales manager of the Earthworm Tractor Company. My reasons are various and cumulative.

Since my discharge from the Army, and since I resumed my former job as sales manager of the company, I have, as you know, been traveling about the country in a salvaged Army plane, visiting our dealers and investigating conditions. Everywhere I have gone, I have heard nothing but complaints—no tractors, no service, no parts, no satisfaction, no co-operation. I have sent you countless letters of protest. I have demanded action. You have replied with weak excuses. You have whined about strikes, shortages and the difficulties of reconversion. From time to time you have urged me to abandon this highly necessary inspection trip; and you have even refused to put me on the pay roll and give me an expense account until I should come in to the factory to be personally installed as sales manager.

So far I have paid my own expenses out of the proceeds of various secondhand-tractor deals. But my money has been running low. The whole situation has been getting so unbearable as to be practically intolerable. And today came the final straw in the form of a letter from Mr. Chester Hamilton, of Kansas City.

You will remember that when I was in Kansas City a short time ago I wrote you about Chester, who is not only the son of one of our most important customers—Mr. George Hamilton—but also one of the finest young men I know. He is a perfect gentleman, a college graduate and a war veteran. He wanted a position through the winter in the bookkeeping department of the Earthworm Tractor Company, so that he could gain some practical experience which would prepare him to handle the accounting and bookkeeping on a large roadbuilding job which his father is starting next summer.

Two weeks ago I sent the young man to you with a letter of introduction. Today, in a letter just received from him, I learn that instead of taking him around to the bookkeeping department and fixing him up with a job, you merely referred him to our general employment office. Apparently this office has been completely reorganized and is now being run by as arrogant a group of crackpots as could be found anywhere outside of Washington, D.C.

Instead of giving Chester the job he wanted, they put him through a "battery of aptitude tests"—whatever that may be. Then they blandly told him he was not fitted to be a bookkeeper. In spite of the fact that there must be dozens of jobs in the bookkeeping department which could be competently filled by anyone with enough brains to graduate from college, they turned him down. So he went back to Kansas City.

The young man is too polite to write me what must be his real opinion. But I am not too polite, Henderson, to write you that I think this is an utterly outrageous way to treat the son of an important customer. It is, as I said before, the last straw. Coming on top of everything else, it is the final grain of salt that causes the solution to reach a point of supersaturation, so that the camel is precipitated to the bottom of the test tube.

In other words, I am through. I have ended my inspection trip. I have sold my plane. I am quitting. I am resigning. But this does not mean you have heard the last of me. I have my plans. I am going to do some undercover investigating. And I will write you as soon as I have anything further to report.

Yours,

ALEXANDER BOTTS,
Former sales manager,
Earthworm Tractor Company.

EARTHWORM TRACTOR COMPANY
EARTHWORM CITY, ILLINOIS
OFFICE OF THE PRESIDENT

Saturday, February 8, 1947.

Mr. Alexander Botts,
Care of Earthworm Tractor Agency,
Atlanta, Georgia.

DEAR BOTTS: You cannot resign. You have not even been hired yet. But we want to hire you. We need your energy and initiative to carry our sales department through this difficult reconversion period. If you will only follow my repeated requests and come in to the factory, I will put you on the pay roll at once. Now that you have got rid of your extravagantly expensive private plane, there should be no difficulty about your expense account. I can promise you my full co-operation in solving the problems mentioned in your letter. In fact, I am already doing everything I can.

Our factory manager tells me that the production of new tractors is gradually rising. The head of our Parts Department assures me that everything possible is being done to co-operate to the fullest extent with everyone concerned, and he further reports that splendid progress has already been made in the implementation of an accelerated program for the more efficient processing and finalizing of parts orders, to the end that we may more effectively expedite the filling of our customers' requirements.

Although I have had no direct word, I am sure your friend Chester Hamilton has received fair treatment. The new director of our Employment Office reports gratifying progress in applying scientific techniques in the analysis of basic individual aptitudes, to the end that they may be integrated to the specific requirements of the various spheres of activity comprised in the totality of our organizational structure.

I am leaving tomorrow for a two weeks' stay in Washington, D.C. I shall be glad to see you there, or, later on, here at the factory.

Most sincerely,

GILBERT HENDERSON,
President, Earthworm Tractor
Company.

EARTHWORM CITY, ILLINOIS

Friday, February 14, 1947.

Mr. Gilbert Henderson,
Earthworm Tractor Agency,
Washington, D.C.

DEAR HENDERSON: Your letter—which arrived just before I left Atlanta—is a splendid example of what I was talking about when I said that the situation has been getting so unbearable as to be practically intolerable. The basic trouble, Henderson, seems to be that you are trying to run this business entirely from the top down.

When I protest about the Parts Department, all you do is consult the slick-talking yes man whom you have mistakenly placed in charge of same. He apparently claims that he is performing miracles with his implementation and processing and finalizing, and he puts out this information in such a jet-propelled fog of high-octane language that he completely conceals the fact that he is falling down on the only thing that matters—shipping the parts.

175

When I ask about the Employment Office, you let yourself become involved in a verbal gas attack dealing with the totality of our organizational structure—and you never find out what is actually happening. This is why I have been forced to take drastic action.

Last week, as you know, I resigned as sales manager. This resignation, of course, is purely temporary; I shall want the job back again just as soon as I complete my present project. In the meantime, I do not want anyone—not even you, Henderson—to know what I am doing. I am not even going to mail this letter to you until the need for secrecy has passed.

It was the day before yesterday that I arrived in Earthworm City in a state of complete incognito. I spent the night at my home on Earthworm Heights. I cautioned my wife and children to keep my arrival a dark secret. Yesterday morning I approached the factory—advancing cautiously behind the cover of a luxuriant beard which I grew in the South Pacific, shaved off on my return, and then grew again because I feel that it gives me such an air of distinction. Instead of going through the front gate, I sidled around the corner and entered the door marked Employment Office. My plan was simple. What I wanted were the true facts about the company's two outstanding sore spots—the Employment Office and the Parts Department. I had therefore decided to enter the Employment Office as an ordinary mug and apply for a job in the Parts Department. By going through the mill, I hoped to get a worm's-eye view of both places.

Note: So far I have progressed no farther than the Employment Office. And what I have found is so much worse than anything I had even dreamed could be possible that I will give you a full account of my almost unbelievable discoveries, so that you will have all the information necessary to act upon my recommendation that the entire personnel of the Employment Office be fired at once for the good of the company.

The first person I met when I entered the door of the Employment Office was the receptionist, who is so courteous and good-looking that you might possibly keep her when you clean out the rest of the gang.

"Good morning," I said. "I want to apply for a job as a sweeper, cleaning out the Parts Department."

Note: I had decided that a job with a broom would be ideal for my purposes. It would provide an opportunity to travel around all over the Parts Department. The work would be light. And it would leave my mind free to observe what was happening, and to meditate thereon.

The receptionist handed me a five-page questionnaire printed in quintuplicate with carbon between the sheets.

"Thank you very much," I said, "but this will not be necessary. All I want is a job with a broom, cleaning out the Parts Department."

"I am sorry," she said, smiling pleasantly, "but the basic questionnaire must be filled out by all applicants for employment."

So I spent a couple of hours filling out little blank spaces with labels such as: Date, Last Name, First Name, Middle Name, Maiden Name, Age, and so on through page after page, giving information on previous employment, social-security status, education, citizenship, and ending up with a request for character and business references, birth certificate, naturalization certificate, Army discharge, if any, and I forget what else.

Since I have been in the Army, filling out idiotic questionnaires is an old story. In the present case, for the purpose of concealing my real identity, I had already chosen a nom de plume. To go with it, I now worked out a complete life history, expressly designed to ward off embarrassing questions and requests for documents. I described myself as Mr. Abner Hopkins, age fifty, born in a wild section of the Ozarks where they had never heard of birth certificates. I further claimed I was unmarried, had no children, and had lived all my life as a sort of hermit farmer in the same remote region. As I had never been employed and had no near neighbors, I could not present any references from anybody or any papers of any kind.

This somewhat flabbergasted the young lady at the desk. But I am a good talker, and I soon convinced her that I simply did not have any documents, and that it was therefore useless for her to demand them. I then asked to be given a broom and shown to the Parts Department. But it was not that easy. I was taken into an inner room with a lot of other applicants. Another smart young lady handed me a book full of little pictures. The title of the book was Mechanical Aptitude Test—Form 37XG.

"Listen, lady," I said. "I don't need to bother with this kid's picture book. All I want is a job cleaning out the Parts Department."

"All applicants for employment are required to take this test," she said.

So I went through the whole book. I looked at all the little pictures of gear wheels and pulleys and little men lifting weights, and I counted hundreds of cubes in pictures. It seemed to me I was getting most of the answers right, but I could not be sure. When I had finished, it was lunchtime.

After a good meal in the factory cafeteria, we were all herded into another room, and handed a paper labeled Basic Vocabulary Test—Form G746.

There were twenty-five words. After each word there were four different meanings. You were supposed to mark the one that came the nearest. The first line read as follows: "Viscous, (a) wicked, (b) sticky, (c) transparent, (d) lively." With my long experience with tractor-cylinder oils, I naturally knew that sticky came the nearest to being right. The rest of the words were familiar for one reason or another. I thought I was doing okay, and I thought I would soon be through this nonsense. But at this point they pulled a dirty one on me.

They brought in another lady teacher, and she ran the papers through a large electric marking machine. This is one of the most appalling devices I have ever seen. Apparently a guy could work for hours on an examination, and then this thing would flunk him in a tenth of a second—which is just what happened to me. The head teacher, after looking over the papers, announced that class was dismissed—all except Mr. Hopkins. I then heard her whisper to the other teacher: "Give this man the extra hard one, Form XX300."

"Hey," I said, speaking up, "all I want is a job cleaning out the Parts Department."

"I am sorry," she said, "but we must ask you to take this extra test." The other girl brought in Form XX300, which had several hundred words of a type which I can only describe as real stinkers.

Normally, I ought to be able to pass any reasonable vocabulary test. After all, I am a master of the English language, with an ability to express myself far beyond the average. This form XX300, however, was definitely out of this world.

Just to make it more bewildering there were a few perfectly ordinary words like horse and cow which would not give anybody any trouble. Then there were double-talk words, which mean something according to the dictionary, but signify nothing when used by businessmen like yourself in such expressions as "the implementation of an accelerated program for the more efficient processing and finalizing of parts orders." Such words, of course, gave me no trouble.

The test was also loaded down with polysyllabic monstrosities such as chimopelagic, atroceruleous, autochthonous, syzygy and dichotomy.

These Greek and Latin derivatives, however, were not the worst. Somebody, with fiendish ingenuity, had run in a lot of good old Anglo-Saxon words like lither, mome, slub, inkle—so short and so simple that everybody ought to understand all of them, except that practically nobody ever heard of any of them. So I presumably flunked this test, although I don't know for sure as yet. By the time I finished, it was five o'clock, the office was closing and they told me to come back the next day.

I spent the evening meditating on such questions as why a sweeper in the Parts Department should be expected to distinguish between a syzygy and a dichotomy. And would it help him in his work if he knew what happened when a lither mome starts to slub an inkle? As the answers eluded me, I finally went to bed.

Bright and early this morning I was back at the Employment

Office—where the procedure at once sank to a new low. Probably you won't believe it, Henderson, but they started me in on a lot of nursery-school games. The teacher brought out a lot of wooden building blocks and had me build a sort of cubistic edifice. To make it worse, the blocks were lopsided, wiggly and defective. The idea was to fit them together as fast as possible.

I had a little bad luck at this point. While bending over the work with intense concentration, I got the end of my beard built into the block structure. A moment later, when I pulled my head back, everything was jerked apart. This caused considerable delay. I was slow in finishing. And the teacher announced that I was very low in structural visualization.

"What," I asked, "is structural visualization?"

"It is much the same as spatial perception," she said.

"Haven't you got a broom test?" I asked. "What I want is a job cleaning out the Parts Department."

By way of reply they gave me a lot of little steel pegs about the size of phonograph needles and had me pick them up with my fingers and fit them, three at a time, in little holes in a board. Then they handed me a pair of tweezers and had me put a lot of other pegs in a lot of other holes in another board. A number of young women applicants for employment took these tests at the same time I did. I noticed that most of them seemed to be doing the job much faster and more skillfully than I was.

At once I began to suspect that these girls were friends of the examiners, and had received unusually easy-to-handle pegs, while I had been stuck with pegs so slippery that nobody could do anything with them. The harder I tried the more elusive they became. Maybe they were magnetized—how do I know? Pretty soon I was chasing them all over the table—getting madder and madder all the time. Then I found myself pursuing them along the floor. The harder I worked the less I accomplished. Finally, just as the bell rang to show that the time was up, I knocked over the table. So I was marked zero on both finger dexterity and tweezer dexterity.

After this I had to check long columns of figures, and I got so mixed up that the teacher said my accounting aptitude was so low as to be practically nonexistent. Next they gave me something called an Occupational Interest and Preference Test, with a lot of questions like whether I would rather spend the evening at a symphony concert, a prize fight, reading a book at home or attending a party.

I can't remember all the other idiocies. There was a Word Association Test which indicated I was either an extrovert or an introvert—I am not sure which. There were psychiatric questions where they wanted to know about headaches, dreams and whether I thought I was usually treated fairly. By this time I had a feeling everybody was treating me unfairly, and I so stated in no uncertain terms—which was probably the wrong answer. And there was also some sort of an Unintelligence Test with questions like, "If the third letter before the fifth letter after M in the alphabet is also the fifth letter after the third letter before M, answer no, but if it is some other letter answer yes."

By the time I had plowed through this, it was lunchtime.

After lunch they photographed me, took my fingerprints and gave me a long physical examination—in which I seemed to do all right. When I got back to the schoolroom where I had taken the mental examinations, I announced, for the hundredth time, "All I want is a job cleaning out the Parts Department."

As usual, however, this did no good. It merely annoyed the lady teachers. And they sent me off—apparently in disgrace—to the office of the principal, a man called Blake.

As soon as I got inside his office, I repeated, for the one hundred and first time, "All I want is a job cleaning out the Parts Department." He started a long discussion to the effect that the tests I had been taking indicated I might be better suited for some other job. So I told him the tests were silly. I pointed out that I knew what I wanted, and he did not. I said I would take a sweeping job or nothing. I further stated, quite frankly, that I intended to write a letter to the president of the company, informing him exactly how the Employment Office was wasting the time, energy and money of both the company and the applicants for employment. The man replied with a lot of arguments to which I naturally paid no attention. After a half hour of completely futile conversation, he threw me out and told me to appear once more at eight in the morning. So I came back home here, where I have been spending most of the evening writing this report.

By this time, Henderson, I sincerely hope I have been able to give you some slight idea of the astonishing way in which the process of hiring a man like myself to sweep out the Parts Department—or a man like young Chester Hamilton to work in the Bookkeeping Department—has been loused up to a point where the luckless applicant is harried for days at a time by being subjected to an incredible series of tests and examinations devised by this group of pseudo-scientists who in some unaccountable manner have insinuated themselves into our previously efficient Earthworm Tractor organization.

Tomorrow I will make a last attempt to get into the Parts Department through the Employment Office. If this effort fails, I will get into the Parts Department some other way. And as soon as I am in possession of all the facts, I will send you a complete report. We can then reorganize the Parts Department and the Employment Office. After this, we can give Chester Hamilton a job in the Bookkeeping Department. And, finally, I will be very glad to grant your request that I resume my old job as sales manager.

Most sincerely,

ALEXANDER BOTTS.

EARTHWORM TRACTOR COMPANY
INTEROFFICE COMMUNICATION
Date: 4 P.M., February 14, 1947
From: GEORGE BLAKE,
      DIRECTOR OF EMPLOYMENT OFFICE,
      EARTHWORM CITY, ILLINOIS
To: GILBERT HENDERSON, PRESIDENT,
      EARTHWORM BRANCH OFFICE,
      WASHINGTON, D.C.
Via: TELETYPE

This is to ask your advice on a very unusual problem.

Yesterday morning a rough-looking character with a heavy beard, giving his name as Abner Hopkins, appeared at the Employment Office and applied for a job cleaning out the Parts Department. Mr. Hopkins could give no references and he had no documentary evidence about himself—a lack which he explained by saying he had spent his entire life in hermitlike seclusion somewhere in the Ozark Mountains.

Mr. Hopkins was given the routine Mechanical Aptitude Test, and passed it reasonably well. In the short vocabulary test, he got all twenty-five words right—which is so unusual that the examiners gave him the most advanced test in their files. This is composed of words so difficult that the average person is not able even to get started on it. To the astonishment of all, the uncouth Mr. Hopkins plowed through this verbal obstacle race like a bulldozer through soft mud. Toward the end he naturally missed a good many words, which had been purposely inserted because they are unknown to over 99 per cent of the adult population. But he ended up with a score considerably higher than anyone who has ever taken this test during the entire existence of our Employment Office.

Following this, the examining staff really went to town on this character. Naturally, they did not want him to waste his talents as a mere sweeper. They gave him a complete battery of tests, a report of which is now on my desk. Some of the more important findings are as follows:

Vocabulary: very high

Personality: extremely extrovert

Habitus: moderately pyknic

Creative imagination: very high

Mechanical comprehension: good

Accounting aptitude: very low (practically nonexistent)

Structural visualization: low

Finger dexterity: very low

Tweezer dexterity: very low

After studying the report on Mr. Hopkins, I had him come to

my office for a personal interview. Unfortunately, he seemed pretty well worn down after two days of tests and examinations. He was in such an irritable frame of mind that it was difficult to carry on a rational conversation with him. I therefore sent him home with the request that he return tomorrow morning. In the meantime I want to get all the information about him I can.

The tests, plus the personal interview, indicate a highly unusual and contradictory personality. Superficially, Mr. Hopkins has many emotional difficulties. He showed great impatience over his inability to handle the little pegs in the finger and tweezer dexterity tests. He announced that he was going to complain to you, Henderson, that our methods are a mere waste of time. He apparently resents being ordered around. With his almost complete lack of accounting ability he would undoubtedly be the type that is always in trouble with an expense account.

Fundamentally, however, he is emotionally mature and well-adjusted—self-reliant, aggressive, optimistic and sociable. Furthermore, he has an unusual power of sticking tenaciously to a single idea. All examiners, including myself, noted the subject's tendency, during the entire testing period, to revert over and over to his basic purpose, expressed in the constantly repeated assertion: "All I want is a job cleaning out the Parts Department."

In analyzing this case, I could not believe that Mr. Hopkins had spent all his life in the remote fastnesses of the Ozarks. And it was completely absurd to think of giving him a job with a broom, cleaning out the Parts Department. The extrovert personality, the low structural visualization and the high creative imagination all indicated that the man ought to make an unusually successful salesman. The astonishing vocabulary indicated a mentality similar to that found in high executives. In other words, the man has a pattern of aptitudes which would admirably qualify him to be sales manager of the company—or even president or chairman of the board.

By the time I had reached this conclusion, I received a special report from our Fingerprint Division, stating that the fingerprints of Mr. Abner Hopkins are identical with a set of prints taken before the war of Mr. Alexander Botts, who was at that time our sales manager. There is thus no doubt that Mr. Hopkins and Mr. Botts are one and the same.

This naturally throws me into a quandary. I am hoping you can help me out. What is Mr. Botts' present status—if any—with this company? Why is Mr. Botts applying for a humble job under an assumed name? And how do you want me to handle this case?

Most sincerely,

GEORGE BLAKE.

EARTHWORM TRACTOR COMPANY
INTEROFFICE COMMUNICATION
Date: 5 P.M., February 14, 1947
From: GILBERT HENDERSON, PRESIDENT,
EARTHWORM BRANCH OFFICE,
WASHINGTON, D.C.
To: GEORGE BLAKE,
DIRECTOR OF EMPLOYMENT OFFICE,
EARTHWORM CITY, ILLINOIS.
Via: TELETYPE

Mr. Botts is still on a leave of absence which was granted him when he entered the armed services. Following his discharge from the Army, he was told that he would be taken back as sales manager as soon as he complied with certain conditions—including a visit to the factory and the disposal of a private airplane. As he has now apparently complied with these conditions, his reinstatement would seem to be in order.

In a recent letter, Mr. Botts bitterly criticized various departments of our company—especially the Employment Office—and threatened to do some "undercover investigating." This undoubtedly explains his present bizarre conduct.

My advice would be that you explain to Mr. Botts the results of your aptitude tests, then offer him the job of sales manager, and see what he says.

Don't worry about any complaints which Mr. Botts may send me. Your estimate of Mr. Botts' aptitudes and personality is so astonishingly accurate that I am more than ever convinced of your usefulness to this company. In two days you have found out almost as much about him as I have discovered in years of close association.

Incidentally, Mr. Botts may withdraw his criticisms of you when he hears your opinion of him—which, on the whole, seems to be most flattering, and the sort of thing most people like to listen to. After all, almost any fortuneteller is a success with his clients as long as he tells them what they want to hear.

Most sincerely,

GILBERT HENDERSON.

EARTHWORM CITY, ILLINOIS

Saturday evening, February 15, 1947.

Mr. Gilbert Henderson,
Earthworm Branch Office,
Washington, D.C.

DEAR HENDERSON: This is an urgent appeal to you to pay absolutely no attention whatsoever to anything I said in the letter which I wrote to you last night, which I did not intend to send you until later, but which got mixed in with some family letters and was erroneously put in the mail this morning. Since I wrote this previous letter, the situation has entirely changed. I arrived at the Employment Office this morning a little late, and ran into young Chester Hamilton coming out of Mr. George Blake's private office. At once he shook hands with the greatest enthusiasm.

"Good morning, Mr. Botts," he exclaimed. "How can I ever thank you for everything you have done for me?"

"I was not aware," I said, "that I had done anything for you that deserved any thanks. I sent you to Mr. Henderson, who sent you to Mr. Blake, who refused to give you a job in the Bookkeeping Department. So you returned to Kansas City—"

"Yes, Mr. Botts. But now I am back again, and Mr. Blake has given me exactly the job I wanted—"

"In the Bookkeeping Department?"

"Oh, no, Mr. Botts. That's the last thing in the world I would want."

"In your letter to me," I said, "you told me very distinctly that you came here and asked for a job in the Bookkeeping Department."

"That is right."

"I don't get it."

"It is like this, Mr. Botts. I asked for a job in the Bookkeeping Department, so I could get some experience. I thought my father needed me as a bookkeeper. But after I had taken a lot of tests, Mr. Blake told me I had no accounting aptitude at all. But he claimed I was exactly fitted for an opening in the Experimental Department. So he offered me the job—which is exactly what I wanted—but I didn't think it was right to take it."

"So what did you do?"

"I went back to Kansas City, and I told my father what Mr. Blake had said, and my father was delighted."

"He was?"

"Yes, he said I had always been so poor at figures that he was pretty much appalled at the thought of having me handle his books, but he was going to give me the job because he thought I had set my heart on it. On the other hand, I knew I was hopeless at figures. But I was going to take the job because I thought father had set his heart on having me do it."

"Well," I said, "you and your father are two of the politest people I ever met. In this case you were too polite."

"Yes, but we found it out before it was too late. So father has hired a real bookkeeper. He feels fine. I have come back here. Mr. Blake has just given me the job in the Experimental Department that I am really fitted for and that I really want. Naturally, I feel wonderful. And that is why I am so grateful to you."

"Oh," I said.

"If it had not been for you, I might never have met Mr. Henderson and been referred to Mr. Blake. And if it had not been for Mr. Blake and his aptitude tests, I might have taken the wrong job and been a square peg in a round hole all my life. So I thank you, Mr. Botts, from the bottom of my heart."

"You're entirely welcome," I said.

He shook hands again and breezed out of the room, leaving me slightly befuddled. A moment later, the receptionist announced that Mr. Blake was ready to see Mr. Abner Hopkins. As I entered Mr. Blake's office I pulled my scattered wits together and greeted the man with a certain new respect.

"Mr. Blake," I said, "I want to be completely fair with you. Yesterday I was somewhat critical of your methods. But this morning, after talking to Mr. Chester Hamilton, I am ready to admit that in some cases it is barely possible that some of your tests may have a certain limited value."

"It is very kind of you to say so," said Mr. Blake. "Please sit down."

I did so. "Yesterday," I said, "when you discussed my own tests I had a feeling that you were talking nonsense, so I paid no attention. This morning, however, if you care to repeat yourself, I shall be glad to listen."

"Very good," said Mr. Blake.

He then gave me a complete explanation of his testing methods—which I will not repeat because it would be too technical for you. The main points, however, are easy to understand. It seems that very early in the testing process the examiners recognized that I was far too gifted to waste on a mere job with a broom. That is why they gave me a complete battery of tests—which proved conclusively that I am ideal material for a high executive position. In the vocabulary test—which all experts agree is far more important than a mere layman such as yourself, Henderson, would suspect—I had a higher score, according to Mr. Blake, than anyone he had ever tested. In the course of further discussion I learned that these tests had been given, as an experiment, to most of the higher Earthworm Tractor executives, including yourself, Henderson. Thus, although Mr. Blake did not say so directly, it became obvious that my superior score made me better fitted for each and every high position in the company than any of the present incumbents—including, of course, yourself.

I had a definite feeling that Mr. Blake would have been glad to certify me for any of these higher jobs, but he felt it would be wiser to pick out some position which he supposed was open. Consequently, he offered me the job of sales manager.

"Mr. Blake," I said, "permit me to congratulate you. You have perhaps made a few minor errors. The ratings you have given me in certain unimportant fields such as accounting and finger dexterity are probably too low. Furthermore, someone has misinformed you concerning the vacancy which you think exists in the position of sales manager. I have reason to know that Mr. Botts' resignation is merely temporary. However, in your handling of the case of young Chester Hamilton, and even more in your recognition of my own high qualifications, you have proved that your testing methods are completely sound. I am happy to accept the position of sales manager, and, in so doing, I am going to make an announcement which will literally stun you with astonishment."

"Really?" said Mr. Blake.

"Yes," I said. "The name Abner Hopkins is merely an alias which I assumed for the purpose of making an undercover investigation of the Employment Office and the Parts Department. As my investigation of the Employment Office is now completed, there is no longer any need for me to conceal my true identity."

I rose from my chair, expanded my chest and threw back my shoulders. "When you gaze on me," I said, "you are gazing on none other than Alexander Botts, sales manager of the Earthworm Tractor Company."

Mr. Blake, to do him justice, managed to conceal his surprise fairly well. I asked him to keep the big news confidential and to certify me as a sweeper in the Parts Department, so that I could go through with my investigation. He agreed.

So I will conclude this letter on a note of complete satisfaction with my achievements. I have successfully settled young Chester Hamilton's affairs. I have proved that the Employment Office is doing a splendid job, so you can now start raising salaries rather than firing everybody. I, myself, am now back on the pay roll as sales manager. And as I consider this position more important than the presidency of the company, you need not worry about me taking your job away from you—even though it has been scientifically proved that I am better fitted for it than you are.

When next you hear from me, I will be cleaning out the Parts Department in a big way.

Yours enthusiastically,

ALEXANDER BOTTS.

Tractor Hoarder

SYDNEY HOTEL,
SYDNEY, MISSOURI

Saturday, June 24, 1950.

Mr. Gilbert Henderson,
President,
Earthworm Tractor Company,
Earthworm City, Illinois.

DEAR HENDERSON: The instant you get this letter, I want you to rush down to the Traffic Department and tell them to ship double-rush, urgent, at once, six 100 H P Earthworm tractors to Mr. Don Hunter here at Sydney, Missouri. This is an emergency. You must act at once. The facts are as follows:

Don Hunter is one of my oldest friends in the construction business. About two weeks ago he ordered six tractors and I promised him that we would ship them within a month. Relying on my promise, Don accepted a rush contract to grade a landing field near here for the United States Air Force. To complete the work on time he absolutely must have these tractors. If the job is delayed, he will have to pay a heavy penalty.

After accepting Don's order, I returned to the factory and told the Traffic Department to put his name at the top of the shipping list. I then left in my recently-purchased station wagon for a vacation in Colorado. Yesterday, on the way back, I stopped off here to make sure Mr. Hunter's tractors had arrived. They had not. I promptly wired the Traffic Department at Earthworm City. They wired back the astounding information that you, Henderson, had personally intervened in this matter and placed Don Hunter's order at the bottom of the shipping list. They added the even more astounding information that they "hoped" to ship Mr. Hunter's tractors in about six months.

Naturally I am loathe to believe that anyone as sensible as you could be guilty of any such idiocy as the Traffic Department implies. Obviously, however, there has been a mistake somewhere. It must be corrected. I cannot come to Earthworm City at present because I am needed here to go over certain technical matters connected with the airport job.

I am therefore appealing to you to see that the six tractors are shipped to Don Hunter at once. He absolutely must have them at the earliest possible moment. I gave him my solemn promise that we would take care of him. My personal honor, and the good reputation of the Earthworm Tractor Company are involved. Do not fail me.

Yours,

ALEXANDER BOTTS,
Sales Manager,
Earthworm Tractor Company.

EARTHWORM TRACTOR COMPANY
EARTHWORM CITY, ILLINOIS
OFFICE OF THE PRESIDENT

Monday, June 26, 1950.

DEAR BOTTS: I am sorry you have been inconvenienced by what seems to me a very reasonable action on my part. About ten days ago the head of the Traffic Department asked my opinion about your request that the Hunter order be placed at the top of the shipping list. He said your action was most irregular. He wondered if he had misunderstood. He tried to check back with you. But you had left on your vacation. He therefore appealed to me.

As you know, it is our policy to be fair and impartial to all customers. I could see no reason why Mr. Hunter, merely because he is a personal friend of yours, should receive special favors. I therefore shifted his name to the bottom of the list where it belonged. The six tractors you had tried to grab for him were shipped to a man whose order had been on file for six months—Mr. Andrew Jackson Paine, of Limestone Bluffs, Missouri.

We cannot grant your request that we fill Mr. Hunter's order at once. Following the recent invasion of South Korea, we have been advised that our entire production of 100 H P Earthworm tractors will probably be required for the armed services. At the request of Washington we have cancelled all civilian orders. A contractor like Mr. Hunter, who is working on a defense project, should apply for a special permit to purchase such tractors as he may need. We have been advised that application blanks for these permits, with forms for supporting affidavits, will be available in a few weeks at a government agency to be designated in the near future.

Most sincerely,

GILBERT HENDERSON.

SYDNEY, MISSOURI

Thursday, June 29, 1950.

DEAR HENDERSON: From your letter I gather that you have meekly accepted the government freeze-up order on tractors, and that you will do nothing to cut through the paper work. I have, therefore, given up all hope of receiving any tractors from the factory at this time. But I am not licked.

I have started to work on the problem from this end. I have already made considerable progress. Before I get through, I will need help from you. And, in order that you may understand what is required, I will explain exactly what I have done so far.

My first move—after receiving your letter early this morning—was to climb into my station wagon and drive to the little town of Limestone Bluffs, which is ten miles away on the bank of the Limestone River. Here I called on Mr. Andrew Jackson Paine— the man to whom you so unfortunately shipped the tractors which ought to have gone to Don Hunter. Mr. Paine seems to be a dealer in supplies and commodities. I found him in a little office at one end of a large warehouse piled high with sacks, boxes and cartons of sugar, coffee, Portland cement and dozens of other materials. Mr. Paine was seated behind a large desk. He was a shrewd-looking, shifty-eyed, rat-like individual. I knew at once I was not going to like him, but I forced myself to greet him as cordially as I could.

"My name is Botts," I said—"representing the Earthworm Tractor Company. I am delighted to meet you. Where are the six tractors we recently sold you?"

Mr. Paine looked at me suspiciously. He said, "The tractors are stored in a machinery shed down by the river—not that it's any of your business."

"Oh, yes it is," I remarked cheerfully. "Those tractors were intended for another customer. They were shipped to you by mistake. But you don't have to worry. I will refund every cent of the $90,000 you have paid for them. And I will see that they are removed and turned over to the rightful owner."

"I am the rightful owner. I paid for them. I am going to keep them."

"You have an important construction job?"

"No. I'm just keeping the tractors for a rise in the market."

"I don't understand."

"I have inside information that a big inflation is coming. Prices will soar. So I have been converting all my money into things. I have gradually been filling this warehouse with supplies and commodities. And now I am branching out into machinery. I'm going to hold those six tractors until I can sell them for two or three times what I paid for them."

"What! You're not going to use them at all? You're just going to hoard them?"

"If you want to call it that," said Mr. Paine. He smiled with smug satisfaction.

For a moment I was speechless. Ordinary hoarders are nothing new. But never before in all my experience had I run across a tractor hoarder. More than ever I realized how right I had been in trying to send these machines to Don Hunter, and how wrong you had been, Henderson, in diverting the shipment to this useless parasite. But I am not one to waste time in vain regrets. I decided to appeal to Mr. Paine's better nature—if any.

"The government," I said, "is asking all good citizens not to be hoarders."

"The government," said Mr. Paine, "is the worst hoarder of all. It buys up potatoes and hoards them till they rot. It keeps millions of powdered eggs in caves in Kansas. It hoards mountains of cotton and wheat and everything else."

"All right," I said. "The government is crazy. But what do you expect? All governments are crazy."

"Not all," he said. "I just read in the paper that the Swiss government has warned its people there may be a war, and it advises everybody to be thrifty and lay in stocks of food and supplies. That's a government I like; it doesn't want to grab everything for itself."

"Don't keep changing the subject," I said. "I'm talking about your six tractors. If you're not going to use them, you ought to sell them to Mr. Hunter."

"Will he pay three or four times the list price?"

"Certainly not."

"Then I'm going to keep them till I can make a big profit."

Clearly it was impossible to appeal to the man's better nature. I decided to try logic. I launched into a fifteen minute lecture on the science of economics—which I will not repeat because you, Henderson, would probably not understand it. Suffice to say that I proved conclusively—by means of a lot of facts and statistics which I made up as I went along—that the country is headed for a period of sharp deflation with such a disastrous drop in prices that in a few months Mr. Paine would be lucky if he could sell his tractors for even half what he had paid for them.

The man was not impressed. He kept insisting he had a private source of information far better than mine. At first he refused to tell me what this was. But I kept needling him with questions. And finally he admitted that he had been consulting some sort of a local soothsayer or self-styled expert in astrology.

"What!" I said. "You actually believe in a charlatan of that kind?"

"He's not a charlatan," said Mr. Paine, "and he has a lot more sense than the half-witted economists and statisticians that you believe in. I know the guy is good. I keep testing him."

"How?"

"Every so often I make him predict things I can check up on—like the weather, and horse races and things like that."

"He actually gets those things right?"

"He has for the past month—ever since I started going to him instead of another man over in Kansas City that used to be good but began getting unreliable. I know how to handle these people. As long as they keep their predictions hitting things on the nose, I stay with them. When they start slipping, I get rid of them."

"It sounds like a good system," I said. "Would you mind if I consulted this expert of yours? I don't seem to be doing so well around here. Maybe I could use some advice myself."

"From the way you have been talking," said Mr. Paine, "you could use plenty of advice—if you have sense enough to take it." He gave me a card with a name and address.

"Thanks," I said, and I wished him a pleasant good morning.

A few minutes later I arrived at a rather shabby house in a back street. There was a sign over the door: "The Mystic Swami of Calcutta."

I rang the bell and was admitted by a timid-looking little man in a flowing robe and a turban. He led me through a dingy reception room whose walls were hung with charts showing such things as the signs of the Zodiac and the measurements of the great pyramid. We entered an inner sanctum with two chairs and a table with a large crystal ball. The Swami started to explain that he would read my future for ten dollars.

"Are you," I asked, "the guy that predicts the future for Mr. Andrew Jackson Paine?"

"He is one of my clients."

"And the old tight-wad pays you only ten dollars a throw?"

"I cannot discuss my client's private affairs—"

"All right, you don't have to." I then got down to business. "I happen to know," I said, "that Mr. Paine has six big Earthworm tractors that you have advised him to hold for a rise in price. If you will reverse yourself, and persuade him to sell those tractors to a man called Don Hunter, over in Sydney, I will pay you a thousand dollars—which judging from the run-down look of this joint, I think you could use." With these words I pulled from my pocket a thousand dollar bill and waved it in his face.

Note: At this point, Henderson, I will have to interrupt my narrative to answer the various questions which are doubtless arising in your skeptical mind. Yes, I actually had with me a thousand dollar bill. It was the last of five similar bills which I received last April as a reward for my part in the apprehension of Professor Van Zandt in the affair of the Geiger counter. Yes, I offered the entire thousand to the Swami. If he could swing the deal it would be worth it, and I have always found I get better results if I pay plenty. No, I do not expect the Earthworm Tractor Company to reimburse me. As you probably remember, this money was set aside for just such an emergency as this.

Naturally I did not want to pay the man in advance. But I had to give him some evidence of my good faith. So I tore the bill in two and handed him half of it. "You get the other half," I said, "if—by the end of next week—you can persuade Paine to sell the six tractors to Hunter."

The Swami eagerly grabbed the torn half of the bill. Then he looked doubtful. He said, "How do I know I can persuade him to sell?"

"You can try," I said. "If you succeed, you get the other half of the bill. If you fail, you hand back the half I have just given you. And you had better not try any funny business, or I'll call in the cops."

The Swami looked alarmed. "You mustn't even think of that," he said. "In the past I've had so much trouble with the police. How I wish I could get into some other business!"

"Why don't you?"

"If I could only get as much as a hundred dollars ahead," he said mournfully, "I'd buy a ticket and I'd go right back to my home town of Calcutta, Maine, where my brother has promised to give me an honest job in his grocery store."

"All you have to do," I said, "is put this deal across and you'll have your hundred and a lot more."

Leaving the little Swami in a state of high excitement, I returned here to the hotel where I have been writing this letter. In a few days I hope to notify you that I have brought about the sale of the six tractors to Don Hunter—thus clearing up the mess which you, Henderson, so unfortunately brought about through your misguided interference in the affairs of the Sales Department.

Most sincerely,
ALEXANDER BOTTS.

EARTHWORM TRACTOR COMPANY
EARTHWORM CITY, ILLINOIS
OFFICE OF THE PRESIDENT

Monday, July 3, 1950.

DEAR BOTTS: Your letter is here. Although I wish you every success in your efforts to persuade Mr. Paine to sell his tractors to Mr. Hunter, I feel it my duty to tell you that I disapprove heartily of your dealing with a fortuneteller of such obviously doubtful reputation. Always remember that you are representing a respectable firm, the Earthworm Tractor Company. Even though you are paying all expenses yourself, I do not like to see you dealing with questionable characters. And please take notice that under no conditions will the Earthworm Tractor Company allow any expense money for soothsayers, fortunetellers, rain makers, witch doctors, necromancers, and similar frauds.

Most sincerely,
GILBERT HENDERSON.

SYDNEY, MISSOURI

Wednesday, July 5, 1950.

DEAR HENDERSON: Thanks for your letter. It has given me a suggestion which will be of tremendous value in coping with an entirely new difficulty which confronted me last night when I paid a visit to the Swami.

The Swami reported that on the previous evening he had advised Paine to sell the tractors. Before acting on this new advice, Paine had demanded what he called a "test prophecy." He had asked the Swami to make a definite prediction as to whether or not it was going to rain on the following Thursday. Naturally, a fortuneteller hates to answer such definite questions; there is too much chance of going wrong. But in this case, Mr. Paine insisted. So the Swami—remembering that this is a season of frequent thunder storms—took a chance and prophesied positively, definitely, and explicitly, that it would rain on Thursday, July 6—which is tomorrow.

This morning dawned bright and fair. The prediction on the radio was for several days of clear weather. I began to worry.

Then your letter arrived. When I read your remarks about "rain makers" and what you call "other frauds," I leaped in the air with joy. Why had I not thought of this myself?

After a few inquiries I drove to Kansas City and hired a private airplane pilot who is in the business of seeding clouds with dry ice or silver iodide or whatever it is they use to cause rain. He will fly over early tomorrow morning, and if he can stir up a shower I have promised him a thousand dollars.

This may seem a little excessive. But, as I have previously stated, I always get better results if I pay plenty. And the situation here is so critical that we cannot afford to take chances. If it rains, Paine will believe the Swami and sell the tractors. If it does not rain, he will not believe the Swami and he will not sell the tractors. And it is so important that we get the proper result that the expenditure of a mere thousand dollars is nothing.

In view of your statement that the Earthworm Tractor Company would not bear the expense of hiring a rain maker, I have decided not to charge this amount to the company. I have a much better idea. As long as I am providing the thousand dollars for the fortuneteller out of my own special funds, and as long as you, Henderson (in view of the fact that you are largely to blame for the unfortunate situation out here) will doubtless want to contribute your fair share, I have decided to let you provide the thousand for the rain maker out of your own income.

Such being the case, I should appreciate it very much if you would wire me the amount as soon as you receive this letter.

Yours expectantly,
ALEXANDER BOTTS.

TELEGRAM
EARTHWORM CITY, ILLINOIS JULY 7, 1950

ALEXANDER BOTTS
SYDNEY HOTEL
SYDNEY, MISSOURI
SHORTLY AFTER RECEIVING YOUR LETTER THIS MORNING MR. HENDERSON WAS TAKEN ILL AND HAD TO GO HOME. HE HAS JUST TELEPHONED ME THAT HE IS MUCH BETTER AND WILL RETURN TO THE OFFICE NEXT WEEK AT WHICH TIME HE WILL ANSWER YOUR LETTER.
    JANE SMATHERS
    SECRETARY TO GILBERT HENDERSON

SYDNEY, MISSOURI

Friday, July 7, 1950.

DEAR HENDERSON: Miss Smathers' telegram is here. I hope that when you receive this letter you will once more be in good health. You will have to be if you are going to stand the strain of reading about the nerve-racking events of yesterday. When I awoke this morning I was delighted to see that the weather was wonderful. The rain was coming down in veritable torrents. I noticed by the calendar that it was Thursday, July 6—the day when The Mystic Swami had prophesied rain. All the time I was eating breakfast I kept congratulating myself for having hired such an effective rain maker. After breakfast I drove through the ever-increasing downpour to Limestone Bluffs. I called on Mr. Paine.

"Mr. Botts," he said, "that Swami is a wonder. At a time when all signs pointed to dry weather, he predicted rain. He was right. And now, when everybody else expects rising prices, he is predicting falling prices. Apparently he knows what he is talking about. So I have decided to sell my tractors. If you will take me to the man who wants to buy them, I will close the deal at once.

For a moment I experienced that exalted ecstasy which always accompanies a final victory over adverse conditions. Unfortunately, the ecstasy lasted only a moment. Then a workman came rushing in with tidings of disaster. "It's the worst rainstorm in years!" he yelled. "The river is rising fast!"

"This town is on a high bluff," I said. "Why worry?"

"The town is all right," said the man. "But Mr. Paine's tractor shed is down beside the river. The water is already level with the floor of the building. And that's not all. They say the big dam up the river has burst. And in about half an hour there will be a rush of water that will wash away the shed and the tractors and everything."

"Is there time to save the tractors?" asked Mr. Paine.

"I don't know," said the man.

"Let's go," Mr. Paine said.

He and his man rushed out—with me right after them. They jumped in Mr. Paine's car. They started off. I jumped in my station wagon. I started off.

I followed them out a road that led along the top of the high river bluff to a wooded area about half a mile outside of town. Here Mr. Paine stopped his car. He and his man got out. I also stopped and got out.

Ahead of us the road led diagonally down the bluff to the flats along the river. Several hundred yards farther on I could see, through the driving rain, a large shed-like building. It was completely surrounded by the rising waters.

Mr. Paine was highly excited. "That's the building where I've got my tractors," he said. "But what can I do? I've got fire insurance—but no flood insurance. I didn't think I needed it. The river has never been so high before. But it's too late now. Or is it?" Suddenly the man seemed to come to a great decision. "If I hurry," he shouted, "I might be able to get some flood insurance even now."

He leaped back into his car. His man followed him. And away they went toward town—leaving me to reflect on the irony of the situation. My thousand dollar rain storm, which had persuaded Mr. Paine to sell his tractors, was now about to wash away those same tractors so that he could not sell them. Under the circumstances most men would have given way to despair. But not Alexander Botts.

Leaving my station wagon parked safely at the top of the bluff, I ran down the road and waded through the flood waters to the tractor shed. I smashed a padlock with a rock and pushed open the big door. In front of me were the six big tractors. The water was only six inches deep. The panic-stricken Mr. Paine had obviously given up hope too soon.

I climbed on the nearest machine and gave a yank to the starting motor. There was fuel in the tanks and oil in the engines. I started the first machine. I ran it outside. I drove it straight up the forty-five degree slope of the bluff. And I parked it in the woods at the top. I came back. I took up the second machine— the third—the fourth—the fifth.

Finally, as I parked the sixth and final tractor in the woods at the top of the bluff, there was a mighty roar. A wall of muddy water, full of wreckage, came swirling down the narrow valley. In no time at all the shed was washed away. But the tractors were safe. I heaved a sigh of relief, and drove back to town—falsely supposing that my troubles were over.

I stopped in at Mr. Paine's office, confidently expecting to put through the tractor sale in short order. Mr. Paine was not there. I went to the fortune telling establishment to see if the Swami had any news. He had none. But before I had been there two minutes, Mr. Andrew Jackson Paine came charging in. Shaking his finger in the Swami's face, he started on a wild tirade.

"You're a swindler!" he yelled. "You've ruined me. The rain that you predicted has washed away my tractors."

"It's not my fault," said the Swami. "I didn't cause the rain. I just predicted it—and I was right."

This made Paine madder than ever. "You said it would rain, but you left out the most important part. You never told me we were going to have a flood. If you didn't know the flood was coming, you are no good as a prophet. And if you knew it was coming, and held out on me, you're a crook. You took my ten dollars under false pretenses."

"I'm sorry—" said the Swami.

Paine kept right on yelling: "If you had told me in time, I could have protected myself. As it was I reached the shed too late to get the tractors out. Then I wasted a lot of time running all over town looking for my insurance agent. When I finally found him he refused to give me flood insurance. Then I tried to drive back to the shed so I could set it on fire and at least get something out of the fire insurance. But I was too late again; the shed and the tractors had washed off down the river. So I have lost $90,000 worth of tractors. And it's all your fault."

"Tractors are pretty rugged machines," said the Swami. "When the water goes down, maybe you'll find they're still there—and in good shape."

"That's right," I said. "And don't forget what you told me. If the tractors are saved you're going to sell them to Mr. Don Hunter."

"Absolutely not!"

"Why not?" I asked.

"In the first place, those tractors are finished—and you know it. In the second place, if they're saved by some miracle, I'm going to hang onto them. As long as this liar here advised me to sell them, I'm going to keep them. I'm going to hold onto them until I'm offered two or three times what I paid for them. That's final."

I could see that the old fool meant every word he said. And I knew that all my carefully laid plans had gone wrong. My solemn promises to Don Hunter were worthless. And I had no idea what—if anything—to do next. I had already tried every possible method of influencing old man Paine. With all my powers of eloquence, I had appealed to his sense of public duty. With logical and convincing arguments based on economics and statistics, I had appealed to his intellect. By enlisting the help of the Swami I had made a powerful appeal to his credulity. Everything had failed. I briefly considered telling him how I had saved his tractors, and appealing to his sense of gratitude. But I knew all too well he would have no sense of gratitude. For a moment I was definitely nonplused.

And then I had one of my brilliant flashes of inspiration. In a sudden rush of understanding, it came over me that the solution to the whole problem was staring me right in the face. Up to this time I had missed it because my own character is so pure, straightforward and honest that it is difficult for me to sympathize with and understand other people who are not as highminded as I am. This explains why I was so slow in coming to the obvious conclusion: The only way to handle Mr. Andrew Jackson Paine would be to appeal exclusively to his lower nature—to his instinct for larceny, his cupidity, his dishonesty, and his desire to cheat his fellow man.

I launched my campaign at once. My first move was to show Mr. Paine that I was on his side. To accomplish this, I turned fiercely upon the poor Swami.

"You have done Mr. Paine a horrible wrong," I snarled. "I demand that you give him back the ten dollars he paid for your lousy weather prediction."

The Swami hesitated. I remembered his fear of the police. "All right, then," I said, "I'll call the cops." I picked up the telephone and started dialing a number.

As I had expected, the Swami went into a panic. He said, "Please, Mr. Botts, don't call the police. I'll give him back his ten dollars."

As the Swami pulled his wallet from his pocket, I reached over and took it. He was too rattled to resist. I opened the wallet and pulled out a ten dollar bill.

"Here you are," I said, handing the bill to Mr. Paine. Then I pulled out the half of the thousand dollar bill which I had previously given the Swami. I put it in my pocket. "Mr. Swami," I said, "you have failed to persuade Mr. Paine to sell his tractors. Thus you have lost your chance to get the thousand dollars. So I am taking back the half which I gave you."

The Swami said nothing. Mr. Paine looked at me suspiciously. At once I opened up on him with the sort of flattery that I knew would soften him up. "I see I can't fool you, Mr. Paine. You're too smart. So I'll tell you the whole story." I then fed him a little fairy tale. I said, "Mr. Hunter was so crazy to buy your tractors that he offered me two thousand dollars if I could swing the deal for him. That's why I offered a thousand dollars to the Swami here if he could persuade you to sell."

Mr. Paine looked horrified. He said, "But that is dishonest!"

"Well," I said, "I got to look out for myself—just like anybody else. And now I have a proposition where we can both come out on top."

"I'm not interested," Mr. Paine said.

"Sure you are," I said. I got him outside where we could talk privately. And I proceeded to outline a plan so low down and contemptible that I was appalled at my own fiendish imagination. Even now, it makes me shudder to think of the menace I would be to society if I ever decided to devote my talents to crime rather than to the honest and worthwhile life of a tractor salesman.

"If we hurry," I said, "we ought to be able to get hold of Hunter before he finds out that your tractors were washed away in the flood. If I keep my mouth shut, there is no reason why you can't sell him all six of them at the full list price of $90,000. We won't take a check. He might stop payment if he found out too much too soon. We'll demand cash."

"How do we know the guy has that much?"

"He's got plenty of credit and plenty of collateral at the bank. They'll give him a loan any time he asks them, and hand out the cash without batting an eye."

"But we can't deliver the tractors."

"We don't have to," I said. "This man Hunter is so crazy to buy those machines that he'll jump at the chance without bothering about any of the usual safeguards. I can draw up a bill of sale that will be ironclad, watertight and lawyer-proof."

"It doesn't sound reasonable to me."

"It doesn't have to be reasonable," I said. "The agreement will state that you give no guarantee or warrant of any kind whatsoever, either expressed or implied. Hunter will have to agree to accept the tractors in whatever condition he may find them. He will have to transport them himself. You take no responsibility in case the tractors are found to be in defective condition mechanically or otherwise. If Hunter refuses to agree to all these terms in writing—we tell him the sale is off."

"Then what?"

"Then he'll come around and sign. He'll hand you the $90,000 cash. And you're all set. I tell you this guy is desperate. He'll agree to anything."

"Then maybe we'd better double the price."

"Listen," I said. "If you go asking for a lot of extra money you may spoil the whole thing. I told Hunter I'd put the deal through at $90,000. So that is all we can ask. Are you with me?"

"Let's go," he said.

For a while the scheme worked very smoothly. We drove over to the town of Sydney. I wrote up the outlandish bill of sale. We took Hunter to the bank. Just as I had expected, the cashier was perfectly willing to make a $90,000 loan. And—even though it was unusual—he agreed to hand it out in cash. Then, just as I thought everything was settled, the cashier made a casual remark which busted everything wide open. "There was a man in here a few minutes ago," he said, "that told me he heard a radio news report about a big flood over at Limestone Bluffs. He said that A. J. Paine's machinery shed was washed away, and six tractors were lost."

Hunter looked at me suspiciously.

I had to say something. I had to say it quick. And I didn't

know what to say. If I explained how I had saved the tractors, Paine would back out of the sale. If I did not explain, Hunter would back out. I could not think of any excuse for sending Paine away so I could talk to Hunter privately. For a moment I was sunk. Then my deep knowledge of human nature came to my rescue. And I knew exactly what to do.

"The report is partly correct," I said. "Mr. Paine's machinery shed was washed away. But I was on hand just before the flood. I drove the tractors up onto high ground. They are safe."

I had told the exact truth, and the effect was just what I had expected. Don Hunter, being an honest man, instinctively assumed that I was honest. He believed me. Mr. Paine, being dishonest, expected me to be just as crooked as he is, and he assumed that I was lying in order to lead our victim into the trap.

The deal went through. Mr. Paine went scuttling away with his $90,000 cash, and we heard later that he had reached the Limestone Bluffs bank and put it into his safe deposit box. In the meantime, Don Hunter and I, with a gang of mechanics, brought the tractors back here to Sydney.

We congratulated ourselves on having given Mr. Paine this wonderful opportunity to put over an honest deal for once in his life. And I changed the thousand dollar bill and gave a hundred dollars to the little Swami so he can go back to Maine and get an honest job in the grocery store.

So everything has worked out beautifully—except for one thing. The rain maker has just called up to report that the storm came up so unexpectedly that he had no time to get his plane off the ground. Thus he had no part in causing the rain and we owe him nothing. This deprives you, Henderson, of the satisfaction you would have had if you had been able to contribute your thousand dollars toward correcting your mistake in sending the tractors to the wrong person. It also deprives you of the part you should have had in this glorious victory over the forces of evil. But don't worry. I will give you a chance some other time.

Most sincerely,
ALEXANDER BOTTS.

Botts and the Impossible Mountain

EARTHWORM TRACTOR COMPANY
EARTHWORM CITY, ILLINOIS
OFFICE OF THE PRESIDENT

Friday, October 16, 1953.

Mr. Alexander Botts,
Sales Manager Earthworm Tractor Company,
Earthworm Tractor Agency,
Midvale, California.

DEAR BOTTS: I have just received an indignant letter from a man by the name of Richard Addison whose address is the Midvale Hotel, Midvale, California. Apparently he wants to buy a tractor. He has asked Joe Bundy, our Midvale dealer, to give him a demonstration. And apparently his idea of a demonstration is some sort of a wild tractor race between an Earthworm and a competing machine across a rugged range of mountains. He says Joe has refused to agree to this, so he is writing me demanding that I either fire Joe or see to it that he conducts his business in such a way as will meet the approval of Mr. Addison.

I understand you will be in Midvale, California, within a few days. I would suggest, therefore, that you call on the irate Mr. Addison and do what you can to smooth him down. Tell him that we cannot put on any such demonstration as he suggests.

Explain to him that the whole idea is out of date. Thirty years ago, when tractors were new, and when the general public had serious doubts as to whether a tractor could keep running all day without blowing up or falling apart, it was sometimes good sales practice to put on a short and dramatic competitive demonstration.

Today, however, a short demonstration means nothing. Any machine can work satisfactorily for several days or even weeks. So our present sales effort must consist in showing the customer that our tractors are so efficiently designed, so honestly built, and so effectively backed up by our Service Department that they give economical and dependable service year in and year out.

Most sincerely,

GILBERT HENDERSON.
President, Earthworm Tractor
Company.

MIDVALE, CALIFORNIA

Monday, October 19, 1953.

DEAR HENDERSON: I arrived this morning in this small but bustling town. I registered at the Midvale Hotel, where I found your letter awaiting me. Right away I called on Mr. Richard Addison. He is elderly but vigorous, and has white whiskers like the picture of Buffalo Bill.

"I am Alexander Botts," I said—"sales manager of the Earthworm Tractor Company. I understand you want to buy a tractor."

"I want to buy at least a dozen tractors," said Mr. Addison, "but I won't spend any money until I know what I'm getting."

"You are absolutely right," I said.

"Of course I am. But this Joe Bundy—this dealer of yours—tells me I'm wrong. I made him a perfectly fair proposition, and he turned it down flat. So I'll have to take my business elsewhere."

"Before you do that, Mr. Addison, I wish you would tell me just what your proposition is."

"I am an old-fashioned businessman, Mr. Botts. I have always made money in old-fashioned ways. And I intend to keep on following old-fashioned principles. Am I right or am I wrong?"

"You are right, Mr. Addison."

"I got my start as a gold miner in Alaska Later I was an earth-moving contractor here in California. After that I promoted various other business enterprises. And recently I have bought some gold-mining properties in the mountains near here. They are small properties, scattered here and there in rough country. So I will need a small fleet of rugged medium-sized tractors that can take light machinery up into the mountains and bring back the gold."

"Mr. Addison," I said, "your worries are over. For the project you have in mind, there is nothing superior to our Model M Earthworm tractor—a rugged, medium-sized, practically indestructible miracle of engineering which can plow through swamps, butt its way through forests, and claw its way over the most rugged mountains."

"That's what you say, Mr. Botts. And that's what your dealer says. But it is also what the salesman for the Rough Rider tractor says about his machine."

"Mr. Addison," I said, "you shock me. I cannot believe that you would actually consider the purchase of a Rough Rider tractor under any circumstances whatever."

"Why not?"

"That is a very delicate question, Mr. Addison. Naturally, I make it a rule never to knock a competitor, but as long as you have brought the matter up, I feel it is my duty to protect your interests by giving you at least a rough idea of the reputation of this tractor among people who know. The Rough Rider Tractor Company is a mere fly-by-night, Johnny-come-lately outfit headed by a group of unethical promoters who are attempting to swindle the gullible public by foisting off upon them a so-called tractor which consists of a lot of second-rate parts and mechanical units recently bought as surplus equipment from the armed forces and hastily thrown together almost without plan or purpose. The result is a mechanical monstrosity which hangs together just long enough for the salesman to collect his money and get out of town, after which it promptly disintegrates."

"That," said Mr. Addison, "is exactly the story that was given me by your dealer, Joe Bundy. Possibly you and Joe are right. But I want proof."

210   "What sort of proof?"

"Always in the past when I have bought tractors I have done so on the basis of a competitive demonstration. That's what I told your dealer. But he gave me a long song and dance about competitive demonstrations being out of date."

"He sounds like Henderson," I said. "Apparently he did not convince you?"

"He certainly did not. I told him I wouldn't even consider his Earthworm unless he would agree to a mountain-climbing speed contest with the Rough Rider."

"Where were you planning to hold this contest?"

Mr. Addison took me to the window and pointed to a lofty mountain range. The lower part was covered with evergreen trees. The upper part was mostly bare rocks. "That is called the Giant Hogback," he said. "On the far side is a little town called Roaring River on a stream of the same name. If you want to drive there in a car, it would take you all day; you have to circle around over several hundred miles of back roads. But there is a mule trail straight over the mountain which is only about five miles long."

"And you want the Earthworm and the Rough Rider to have a race over this mule trail?"

"Exactly. That's the only way I can find out which machine is best at the sort of rough driving I'm going to need in my gold-mining operations."

"Are you going to ride along in one of the machines?"

"No. I have my private plane here. After I start the race, my wife and I will fly over to the small landing field at Roaring River and be on hand for the finish. And I will buy twelve machines of the make that gets there first. The Rough Rider man accepted my proposition right away. Your man refused. He said the whole idea was silly. But I think he's just scared."

"All right," I said. "The Earthworm is hereby entered in this race across the mountain. When do we start?"

"The Rough Rider man says he can be ready day after tomorrow—Wednesday morning."

"What time?"

"Eight o'clock. We'll meet at the paint shop behind the Earthworm agency. That's out at the edge of town, right where the mule trail starts."

"Splendid," I said. "I will be there."

I went over to see Joe Bundy.

"Joe," I said, "I have arranged to put on a demonstration for Mr. Richard Addison. I'm going to race against the Rough Rider tractor across the Giant Hogback."

"Not with one of my tractors, you aren't," said Joe.

"You don't want to make a sale to this guy? His credit is no good?"

"It isn't that, Mr. Botts. I looked him up. His credit is O.K."

"Then what's the matter? Have you ever been over this Giant Hogback mule trail? Is it passable for tractors?"

"I've been over on a mule, Mr. Botts. As far as I know, no tractor has ever done it. If you tried it, you would need a winch to pull yourself up the steeper slopes. And you might need a bulldozer blade to fill in holes and smooth up some of the rough places. Probably you could make it—but you might damage the machine pretty seriously on the rocks, or you might slide off a cliff. It would be a risky business."

"Have you got a Model M Earthworm equipped with a winch and a bulldozer?"

"Yes."

"All right, then; why not be a sport? Why not take a little risk for the sake of making a big sale?"

"If you're so keen on taking a chance, you can assume the risk yourself. All you have to do is sign a paper agreeing to make good any damage and I will turn my Model M Earthworm over to you and let you put on the demonstration yourself."

"It's a deal!" I said. We shook hands on the bargain and I signed an agreement obligating the Earthworm Tractor Company for any loss that Joe might sustain.

This agreement, of course, is a mere formality. I am going to operate the tractor in the demonstration myself. And, with anyone as skillful and as careful as I am in the driver's seat, there is no chance of anything going wrong. I am looking forward with complete confidence to the big event next Wednesday. I cannot lose.

Yours enthusiastically,

ALEXANDER BOTTS.

EARTHWORM TRACTOR COMPANY
EARTHWORM CITY, ILLINOIS
OFFICE OF THE PRESIDENT
                    Wednesday, October 21, 1953.

DEAR BOTTS: This morning I received your letter saying that you were going to disregard my instructions.

This afternoon I received a telegram from Joe Bundy:

BOTTS HAS LOST DEMONSTRATION SEVERAL DIFFERENT WAYS. FIRST HE RAN OVER A PILE OF PAINT CANS AND ALMOST DROWNED OUR CUSTOMERS IN A SHOWER OF MANY COLORED PAINTS. NEXT, HE TOOK EIGHT HOURS TO CROSS MOUNTAIN WHILE ROUGH RIDER MADE IT IN ONLY FIVE. FINALLY, HE LOST THE EARTHWORM TRACTOR IN THE BOTTOM OF ROARING RIVER. RICHARD ADDISON HAS ANNOUNCED HE IS THROUGH WITH EARTHWORM, AND WILL BUY TWELVE ROUGH RIDER TRACTORS. PLEASE SHIP AT ONCE, NO CHARGE, FREIGHT PREPAID, ONE NEW MODEL M EARTHWORM WITH BULLDOZER BLADE AND WINCH TO REPLACE LOST MACHINE.

The above telegram is so astonishing that I will take no action upon it until I receive an explanation from you. And your explanation had better be good. You undertook this demonstration against my instructions. You had no authority to make the Earthworm Company responsible for the loss of this tractor. If we ship a new machine free to Joe Bundy, it will be necessary to deduct from your salary in installments the entire cost, amounting to $8,421.19.

I shall be waiting to hear from you.
                    Most sincerely,
                    GILBERT HENDERSON.

Friday, October 23, 1953.

DEAR HENDERSON: Your letter is here, and I hope you are not taking Joe's somewhat hysterical telegram too seriously. Joe is a good fellow, and the facts as he reported them are entirely correct. However, he gives the impression that I have been pulling off a series of boners out here. And this has led you, Henderson, to make the shocking suggestion that you might actually consider deducting large sums of money from my salary. I hasten, therefore, to assure you that everything I have been doing has been wisely planned and efficiently executed. It is true there have been a few unfortunate mishaps and accidents. But I have thought up an explanation for everything.

As previously reported, I first approached this demonstration with a feeling of complete confidence which lasted until late in the afternoon of Tuesday, the day before the demonstration. Having completed the work of tuning up the Earthworm tractor, I walked over to a garage at the other end of town, where I had been told the Rough Rider tractor was stored. And what I discovered there caused me to do some heavy thinking.

The Rough Rider machine turned out to be even worse than I had expected. The center of gravity is too high. The frame is too light. The entire machine is a traveling junk pile. And it has no winch or bulldozer blade.

While I was looking at the machine, I heard a sudden loud laugh behind me. I turned and found myself confronted by Matt Peabody, a man I had once met back in the summer of 1947, just after he had been fired, for unethical conduct, from the sales department of the Behemoth Tractor Company.

Matt smiled a wide and repulsive smile. He said, "It is a pleasure to meet you here, Mr. Botts. And it will be even more of a pleasure, in the demonstration tomorrow, to show you up for the boob that you are."

"You mean you are in charge of this Rough Rider tractor?"

"Indeed I am," said Matt proudly, "and a remarkable machine it is."

"At least it is unusual," I said coldly. "But do you actually think it has any chance of getting across that mountain tomorrow—let alone doing it faster than the Earthworm?"

"I have no doubts at all," Matt said. "I will be over on the other side of that mountain signing up that guy for twelve Rough Rider tractors before you and your Earthworm are even halfway up this side."

"You are not scaring me a bit," I said. "Good afternoon."

But, as I walked back to the Earthworm Agency, I was definitely worried. A less astute man than myself, of course, would have been greatly encouraged to find himself pitted against such a pathetic machine as the Rough Rider and such a low-grade operator as Matt Peabody. But I am too much a man of the world to be fooled by mere surface manifestations. The more I considered the underlying facts in this case, the more suspicious I became.

Matt Peabody was a little too smug. I knew that Matt was reasonably stupid. But even Matt could not possibly be so stupid as to suppose he could drive that so-called Rough Rider—without any bulldozer blade and without any winch—across that mountain. And yet he appeared supremely confident. Could it be that Matt was meditating some underhanded skulduggery?

I considered Matt's reputation and record. Our competitors in the Behemoth Tractor Company had never been particularly noted for their high ideals and principles. Yet they had fired this guy for what they considered unethical practices. The natural conclusion was that Matt was pretty near as slimy as they come.

Was he, perhaps, planning to sabotage the Earthworm tractor? I resolved to make sure the machine was securely locked up for the night. I also resolved to be on the alert for any dirty work that Matt might try to pull during the contest. But dirty work directed against the Earthworm or myself could hardly be the whole answer. In order to make the sale, Matt had to drive his own tractor up over the top of the mountain—which I was reasonably sure he could not do.

Was he planning to start up the mountain, circle back under cover of the trees, and secretly drive around the mountain? I decided this would be impossible. The distance was too great. Could he secretly load the tractor on a high-speed truck, and haul it around the mountain? No—even that would take too long. Could he load his tractor in an airplane and fly it across the mountain? Again the answer was no. A plane big enough to carry a heavy tractor could not possibly take off from the small-sized airport at Midvale.

The more I pondered the problem, the more baffled I became. I was morally certain that this mug was meditating some form of fraud or chicanery. But I could not even guess what it might be. Finally, about ten o'clock in the evening, I confided the entire matter to my subconscious mind and went to sleep.

It was a wise move. My old subconscious must have been in beautiful shape. The next morning—even before I was completely awake—the answer came to me in a blinding flash of inspiration.

I dressed in a hurry. I ate a hasty breakfast. I rushed over to Joe Bundy's place. I said, "Joe, is there by any chance a railroad across the mountain at Roaring River?"

"Yes," said Joe, "but it's no good to us. If you want to go from here over there by train you would have to travel all over this part of the state and change cars four times. The connections are so poor it would take you about two days."

"I don't want to go over by train," I said. "I just wanted to know whether there was a railroad there. And now I want to use a telephone."

"There's one in my private office."

I went in. I shut the door so Joe could not hear me. After all, there was no point in stirring up Joe until I was sure my hunch was correct. I called the railroad freight agent in the town of Roaring River. I said, "I want some information about that Rough Rider tractor that came in by freight over there last week—or whenever it was."

"You're crazy," said the freight agent. "There hasn't been any tractor of any kind come in here for the past six months."

"I'm sorry," I said. "I must have got the wrong place. Is there any other town near there where this machine might have been delivered?"

"There's a town called Indian Bridge ten miles north of here. There's another town called Red Rock Rapids ten miles south. But who are you anyway?"

"Just a guy that wants some information. Thanks a lot."

I hung up. I called the freight agent at Red Rock Rapids. He didn't know anything about any tractors. I called the agent in Indian Bridge. This time I got the news I had been hoping for.

"There was a Rough Rider tractor came in here about ten days ago," said the agent. "It was consigned to a man called Matthew Peabody. Is that the machine you're talking about?"

"It sure is," I said. "Just where did this guy take the machine?"

"How should I know? What business is it of mine? For that matter, what business is it of yours? Who are you? What is it you want?"

"What I wanted was information," I said, "and you have given it to me."

Again I hung up. I felt pretty good. My hunch had been correct. Obviously Matt Peabody was using two tractors. He was planning to make a brave and convincing start—driving his tractor through the woods up the lower slopes of the mountain. As soon as the going got tough, he would hide the machine in a gully or clump of trees, and climb over the ridge on foot—following a course some distance from the mule path so I would not see him. Then he would pick up the other machine where he had cached it on the other side and emerge from the woods at Roaring River just as if he had actually made the whole trip by tractor. Meanwhile, I would be delayed by having to bulldoze my way through the rough places and pull my tractor up the steep slopes with the winch. Thus, Matt could count on beating me by several hours. It was a slick scheme, but not slick enough.

At first I was going to rush out and denounce the man to Joe and to Mr. Addison and everybody else. Then it occurred to me that a denunciation of a crime before the crime is committed is a little weak. I considered letting the miscreant go through with his nefarious scheme and then revealing the whole thing. But I am not a vindictive man. All I wanted was to win this contest. I never got any pleasure out of humiliating unnecessarily a fellow human being—even if he is such a low character as Matt Peabody.

I decided, therefore, that I would merely take such precautions as would insure a fair contest. I would ask Mr. Addison to copy down the engine number and the chassis number of the Earthworm and the Rough Rider. Mr. Addison would not be likely to refuse this request. Matt could hardly object without arousing suspicion. And once the numbers had been copied, Matt would never dare to show up at the finish with a different machine. His only chance would be to beat me over the mountain fair and square, which would be impossible.

About the time I reached this pleasing conclusion, Joe began yelling that Mr. and Mrs. Addison had arrived, Matt Peabody was driving up in his Rough Rider tractor, and it was time to bring out the Earthworm. I cranked up the machine, drove it out into the yard, and parked behind the Rough Rider, which was standing near the paint shed. Mr. and Mrs. Addison were nearby. Joe and I joined them. Then Matt Peabody walked up. And I was just about to spring my disagreeable little surprise on him by suggesting that we record the numbers on the tractors, when the devious bum got ahead of me by springing the same disagreeable little surprise on me.

"I wish to make a suggestion," said Matt, "which I hope none of you will misinterpret. I am sure that all of us want this to be a completely fair contest. We want to be sure that there is no swapping of tractors—no starting out with one machine and ending up with another. For the protection of everyone concerned, and without implying that anyone is planning anything fraudulent, I would suggest that Mr. Addison copy down the engine and chassis numbers of both machines."

"It sounds silly," said Mr. Addison, "but I can't see that it would do any harm—provided Mr. Botts is agreeable."

"It's perfectly all right with me," I said. I tried to appear nonchalant.

But I will have to admit I was somewhat flabbergasted. While Mr. Addison was copying down the numbers I did some very fast thinking. Was it possible that Matt was actually planning to be completely honest in this contest? I couldn't believe it. I could think of only one way to explain the surprising and disconcerting move on Matt's part. The man had a lot more low cunning than I had supposed. After thinking up this dirty scheme for switching tractors, he had considered the possibility that I might suspect him of this very thing, and ask that the numbers be recorded. To protect himself he could easily have filed off the numbers on one machine and substituted numbers identical with the other.

This was a very clever scheme, and if Matt had been content to leave well enough alone, he might have been all right. But crooks like Matt are always trying to be a little too clever. After arranging for this false proof of his own innocence, he could not resist trying to pile up additional evidence in his favor by throwing suspicion on me. Like the Russians, he was accusing the other fellow of the very crimes that he was planning to commit himself.

And that is where he made his mistake. He aroused my suspicions. He started me thinking. Right away I decided that Matt had fixed the numbers game in his own favor and that I would have to devise some other method to prevent him from starting out with one tractor and ending up with another. Perhaps I could mark up his tractor in some way so it would be completely unlike the other machine. I thought of running into it and denting up the fenders. But Matt could easily dent up the fenders on the other machine.

While I was trying to think of something else, Mr. Addison completed the job of copying the numbers, and yelled for me to drive up abreast of the Rough Rider tractor so we could start the race on even terms. Besides yelling at me, Mr. Addison motioned for me to drive up on the right-hand side of the Rough Rider.

At this moment I noticed a whole row of large cans of paint lined up on the left-hand side of the Rough Rider, between it and the paint shed. Here was the answer to my prayer.

I started my machine. I assumed a facial expression indicating great clumsiness and stupidity. And, instead of turning the machine to the right, I swung toward the left. Above the roar of the motor I could hear everybody yelling at me. I noted that Mr. Addison and his wife were running back and forth in great excitement, pointing at the paint cans and motioning me back. I paid no attention. Calmly, and with a vacant air which gave the impression that I did not realize what I was doing, I drove the big machine over all those paint cans. There were several dozen of them with at least a dozen different colors of paint—all of them brilliant. And the results were extraordinary. As the heavy tractor squashed each can, it split open and the paint spurted forth like water out of a hose. There was a succession of beautifully colored jets of red, orange, yellow, green and blue. At least half of these jets hit the side of the Rough Rider tractor, and by the time I finally stopped, that machine had a paint job the like of which I had never dreamed could exist. It was unique.

While I was admiring this artistic masterpiece, I began to hear some bubbling sort of yells off on the other side. I turned and saw something even more sensational. My paint barrage had been fired in all directions. Mr. and Mrs. Addison had unfortunately happened to be in range.

At once I tried to think of some pleasant little explanation for what had happened. I tried to evolve a series of witty remarks that would cause everyone to regard the situation as a hilarious joke. But there are times when even I cannot think of the exact word to fit the situation. I was speechless.

Mr. and Mrs. Addison, however, were highly articulate. They yelled. They hollered. They waved their arms. They made futile attempts to wipe the paint from their clothes. Obviously, they were in no condition to listen to reason. So I wisely decided to postpone my explanations and excuses. In my long experience in dealing with irate customers, I have found that anger has a tendency to cool down with the passage of time. If I gave Mr. and Mrs. Addison a few hours to think this thing over, I was sure they would be in a more reasonable state of mind.

With this thought, I put the big Earthworm in high and headed for the mountain—pretending that I thought the signal to start had been given. Looking back over my shoulder, I noticed that Joe Bundy and several of his helpers had already started to wipe some of the paint off Mr. and Mrs. Addison. Matt Peabody, after a minute or two of hesitation, apparently decided to join me in the race over the mountain. He came rolling along a hundred yards or so in the rear. But his machine was slower than mine. By the time I entered the woods at the foot of the Giant Hogback, he was a quarter of a mile in the rear. And that is the last I saw of him for many hours.

For most tractor drivers the trip over the Giant Hogback would have been practically impossible. For an expert like me, it was a tough job, but on the whole pretty much routine. At several places I had to set the bulldozer blade at an angle and carve out a roadway around projecting shoulders of the mountain. At other places there were almost perpendicular cliffs which I had to climb on my hands and feet, carrying with me the end of the winch cable, which I would fasten around a large tree or projecting rock. Then I would return to the tractor, start the winch revolving, and let the machine pull itself up backward.

All this was slow work. It took me four hours to reach the top of the ridge. As I started down the other side, a small airplane went by, so low I could see the people inside waving to me. I assumed—correctly, as I learned later—that Joe Bundy had succeeded in cleaning most of the paint off Mr. and Mrs. Addison, and that the three of them were flying over to the town of Roaring River to wait for the finish of the race.

Naturally, I could not tell what Matt Peabody was doing. So I resolved to keep on the alert and be prepared for anything. Unfortunately, what actually happened was so unexpected that I was thrown into what I can only describe as a state of completely disastrous disorganization.

It took me four hours to go down the far side of the mountain. At approximately four o'clock in the afternoon, I emerged from the woods and came rolling merrily into the little town of Roaring River. I went through the public square, and passed the small business district. I approached the railroad tracks along the river bank. I passed the depot. And on the far side I suddenly caught sight of Matt Peabody with his Rough Rider tractor. Also present were Joe Bundy and Mr. and Mrs. Addison. But what gave me the surprise of my life was the condition of the Rough Rider. Its entire right side was splashed with paint. Needless to say, I could hardly believe my eyes. So far, in this affair, I had run into nothing but bad luck. And now that I was suddenly presented with this incredible piece of good luck, I was so nonplused that I more or less forgot what I was doing, and where I was going. This, as it turned out, was unfortunate.

While I was gawking in wide-eyed wonder at the scene before me, my own Earthworm tractor rolled on across the railroad tracks and down the river bank, carrying me with it. We landed in the water with a tremendous plop. The Earthworm disappeared beneath the waves, and I found myself swimming in the turbulent waters. I struck out bravely for shore, but the current was too strong. I was swept a hundred yards downstream. And I finally landed on the opposite bank.

At once I rushed back to a point opposite the depot and began frantically waving my arms and yelling for somebody to come and get me. Joe Bundy finally sent a car. As the nearest bridge was ten miles away, it took quite a while. And it was during this interval that Joe sent you that unfortunate telegram. I don't want you to hold this against Joe. He is a good man. He means well. But he just does not have the mental ability to size up an unusual situation the way I can.

As soon as I got back where I could talk to Mr. Addison and take charge, I straightened everything out so easily that I almost hate to mention it because you will think I am boasting.

However, to keep the record straight, I am pleased to report that the Earthworm tractor in the river was easily rescued. We managed to get a hook on the end of a wire rope fastened around the draw bar, and the engineer of a switch engine obligingly pulled the machine up on the bank, where a crew of local garage mechanics cleaned out the water and soon had the machine running as good as new. Mr. and Mrs. Addison, just as I expected, had considerably calmed down since the paint incident. Fortunately they had not yet signed up to buy any Rough Rider tractors. And soon they were completely fascinated by what I told them about the strange activities of Matt Peabody and his Rough Rider tractor.

I set forth my theory—as I have previously explained it to you, Henderson—about how Matt had used two tractors with identical numbers. I pointed out that Mr. Addison had definite proof that I had driven the Earthworm across the mountain; he had seen me at the top. But Matt Peabody had quite obviously never even been near the top.

"You have a plausible-sounding theory there, Mr. Botts," said Matt, "but it's going to be pretty hard for you to prove it."

"That is something that had been worrying me," I said. "I was afraid I would have to hire a large gang of men to beat through the woods on the other side of the ridge and try to find where you had hidden that other tractor. I might have been forced to waste a lot of time trying to locate the place where you bought the paint that you smeared on this machine to make it look like the other one. I might have had to waste a lot of Mr. Addison's time checking with freight agents to prove that you received two tractors, one at Midvale and the other on this side of the mountain. Fortunately, however, you have saved me the trouble. At Midvale I slopped a lot of paint on the left-hand side of your tractor. Over here, you were in such a hurry that you slopped paint on the right-hand side of this other tractor."

I turned to Mr. and Mrs. Addison and asked, "Am I right or am I wrong?"

They thought back. They compared notes. Finally they said "You are right."

"Very good," I said. "The rest will be very simple. Matt Peabody will take his tractor and get out of here. The rest of us will fly back to Midvale. Joe Bundy will prepare an order for twelve Earthworms. Mr. Addison will sign it, and I will write everything to Mr. Henderson, who will be both surprised and pleased."

So Matt did, and we did, and Joe Bundy did, and Mr. Addison did, and now that I have made my report I hope that you Henderson, will react as predicted.

Yours proudly,
ALEXANDER BOTTS.

Botts and the Fire Bug

HAPPY ISLAND HOTEL
HAPPY ISLAND, FLORIDA

Tuesday, February 23, 1954.

Mr. Gilbert Henderson
President Earthworm Tractor Company
Jupiter Island, Florida.

DEAR HENDERSON: I don't want to interfere with your vacation over on the east coast. However, a very serious situation has arisen here on the west coast. And want to give you the straight dope before you hear any rumors or round-about stories which may give you a false idea of what has been going on.

This morning I called on our dealer in Tampa and found him sunk in gloom.

"I am feeling very bad," he said. "Last week a man named Benjamin Bunker, down south of Sarasota, signed an order for over two hundred thousand dollars worth of Earthworm equipment."

"Is that bad?" I asked.

"Wait till you hear the rest. This man Bunker has a lot of money—made it in Wall Street or somewhere—and he has bought an island with a small hotel on it. He calls it Happy Island, and he plans to develop it in a really big way—spending money like water."

"Trying to show a loss on his income tax return?"

"I don't know about that. But he plans to put in a modern motel, and a lot of luxury cabins, with extensive water supply and sewage systems. He plans a swimming pool, an eighteen hole golf course, a drive-in theater, and a causeway to connect the island with the mainland. All this means a lot of earth moving. Mr. Bunker has had no experience with such things, but he has decided—instead of hiring a contractor—to handle the job himself so everything will be done exactly the way he wants it."

"But why are you feeling so gloomy?"

"Just before you came in," he said, in a voice trembling with emotion, "Mr. Bunker called by telephone and told me to hold up the entire order indefinitely."

"What's the matter?"

"It seems a man named Orville Griggs, a salesman for the Goliath tractor dealer here in Tampa, has arrived on the scene and persuaded Mr. Bunker to hold everything until he sees a demonstration of Goliath tractors and equipment."

"All right," I said, "we'll make it a competitive demonstration. And the Earthworm will prove so superior that the Goliath man won't have a chance."

"That's what you think, Mr. Botts. But I am not so sure. Last week this Orville Griggs put on a one-day competitive demonstration against our local man over at Orlando. And he stole the sale right away from us."

"He must be quite a salesman."

"He is, Mr. Botts. He used to be a barker for a carnival. Later he sold sports cars and expensive motor boats. He has been working for the Goliath dealer only a couple of weeks. He doesn't know too much about tractors. But he certainly has a terrific sales talk."

"I don't see how mere sales talk would convince anybody if there is a competitive demonstration. If the Earthworm and the Goliath are working side by side, almost anybody could recognize the superiority of the Earthworm—provided he knew anything at all about tractors."

"That's just it, Mr. Botts. This customer at Orlando—like Mr. Bunker down at Happy Island—never owned a tractor before. He had no way to check up on Mr. Griggs' extravagant claims for the Goliath and his slanderous belittling of the Earthworm. To a person who is unfamiliar with tractors, one machine looks much like another, except that the Goliath is painted a silly two-tone blue, has an elaborate enameled trademark stuck on the radiator header, and is thus more impressive to the uninitiated."

"I see what you mean," I said. "The Goliath has a fancy paint job. It is built well enough to last through a one-day demonstration. Also, the price is lower. So the poor ignorant customer buys it. And a few months later, when a sturdy Earthworm would just be properly broken in, the Goliath starts going to pieces, and the customer realizes—too late—that he has been stuck."

"Exactly, Mr. Botts. At this very moment I have on my own back lot here a Goliath machine which I recently took in trade. It has been run for only six months. But already the tracks, the sprockets and the truck rollers are almost completely worn out. When you try to run it, the bearings thump and bang, the pistons slap, the gears howl, and great clouds of blue smoke pour from the exhaust."

"I know," I said sadly. "In my travels around the country I have run into all too many of these wretched Goliath contraptions. And I share your concern over this Bunker deal. It would, of course, be too bad for you and for the Earthworm Company to lose this two-hundred-thousand-dollar order. But a far more important consideration is our duty—as reputable tractor men—to protect Mr. Benjamin Bunker from the fraudulent machinations of Mr. Orville Griggs, and to make sure that Mr. Bunker does not spend a large sum of money for a lot of so-called machinery which will soon degenerate into a pathetic mass of dilapidated stove iron and miscellaneous scrap."

"You are perfectly right, Mr. Botts. I'm going down to see Mr. Bunker as soon as I can. I have several appointments today and tomorrow that will be hard to get out of—"

"You have no cause for worry," I interrupted. "As of this moment I am taking charge of the entire situation. I am leaving at once for Happy Island. And you may stay here to take care of your other business affairs, serene in the knowledge that the handling of the Bunker deal is in the best possible hands."

With a cordial handshake and a cheery goodbye I strode from

the room, climbed into my car and headed south around Tampa Bay. Late this afternoon I drove across an ancient wooden bridge—about a hundred yards long—which spans the channel between the mainland and Happy Island. I left my car in a parking lot which contained several dozen other cars. As I approached the attractive hotel I passed a number of men strolling around with name cards pinned on their lapels. Apparently a convention of some kind was going on.

When I entered the hotel lobby I noticed two men seated on a davenport facing a large picture window. One of them, a rather slick-looking specimen, had a briefcase bearing the words GOLIATH TRACTOR COMPANY. I assumed—rightly, as I found out later—that he was Mr. Orville Griggs. The other man—who turned out to be Mr. Benjamin Bunker—was a large, distinguished-looking gentleman with handsome grey hair. As I came up behind the two men I could not help overhearing their conversation.

"That old wooden bridge," said Mr. Bunker, "is getting pretty rickety. It won't last much longer. Of course I could rebuild it right where it is—over the open water at this end of the island. But a causeway would be better. And the best place for it would be the far end of the island, which is separated from the mainland by that mangrove swamp over there." He pointed out the window.

Mr. Griggs spoke up: "You are perfectly right, Mr. Bunker. And the best way to build that causeway is by using Goliath machinery—not Earthworm."

Following this statement, Mr. Griggs—much to my astonishment—launched into a smooth and plausible harangue that followed word-for-word a sales talk which I myself wrote several years ago for the use of our own salesmen against just such competitors as the Goliath tractor. Mr. Griggs had quite obviously stolen one of our Earthworm sales manuals containing this speech and he was now using it against me by merely switching the names of the tractors.

"Of course," he said, "I never knock a competitor. I am happy to concede that the Earthworm resembles the Goliath in that it has an engine, a transmission, and a pair of crawler tracks. But honesty compels me to point out that the resemblance is purely superficial. Where the Goliath uses high-grade triple-heat-treated alloy-steel forgings of tremendous strength and toughness, the Earthworm employs mere stove-iron castings so full of sand, gas bubbles, blow holes and other flaws, that they tend to break up, disintegrate and fall apart in a mere matter of weeks or even days. While the gears in the Goliath transmission are machined and polished with a precision that is almost incredible—"

"You told me all that this morning," said Mr. Bunker. "You don't have to repeat it. I have already telephoned the Earthworm dealer to hold up my order."

At this point I must admit I was a bit non-plussed. From the sample I had heard, I was convinced that Mr. Griggs had already used against me practically all of the arguments I had intended to use against him. These arguments, when employed by me in extolling the superiority of the Earthworm, are of course the very essence of truth. As distorted and perverted by Mr. Griggs, however, they were a mere tissue of lies and falsehoods. But they were so cleverly set forth (ironically enough in my own words) that Mr. Bunker had obviously been impressed. In short, Mr. Griggs had beaten me to it. He had stolen my own best sales talk. And if I now tried to use it, I would only make myself ridiculous. It would sound to Mr. Bunker as if I were merely parroting Mr. Griggs in a futile and stupid attempt to twist his own arguments against him.

While I was weakly wondering what to do next, Mr. Griggs resumed the conversation.... "I will ask our Tampa dealer to send me a Goliath tractor with a wheel scraper and a competent operator. They should be here tomorrow or next day, and I will then give you a sensational demonstration of causeway building."

"Tomorrow or next day will be too soon," said Mr. Bunker. "I don't want you to build that causeway until I have plenty of time to watch you. Right now the season is at its peak. I'm having one convention after another. I'm so busy running the hotel that I won't have time for anything else for several weeks. I ought not even to be sitting here now talking to you. Can't you put off your demonstration until some time next month?"

Here I decided to interrupt. "Good afternoon, gentlemen," I said. "I am Alexander Botts, Sales Manager of the Earthworm Tractor Company. I could not help overhearing part of your conversation. If you are going to have a demonstration of the Goliath tractor, I would suggest that you have a demonstration of the Earthworm at the same time. I am particularly anxious, Mr. Bunker, to have you see the new Earthworm forged steel torque eliminator. There is nothing like it on any other tractor."

"On the contrary," said Mr. Griggs, "the new Goliath torque eliminator is so far ahead of the Earthworm that there is no comparison. Our torque eliminator is so new that probably Mr. Botts has never even heard of it."

"What's it like?" I asked.

"It is so new, Mr. Botts, that I have not yet had time to study it. But I will know all about it by the time we put on our demonstration."

I noticed that Mr. Bunker was listening with grave interest—just as if we were talking sense. "What sort of an octane selector do you have?" I asked.

"The finest there is," said Mr. Griggs.

Note. I had introduced this discussion of torque eliminators and octane selectors for the purpose of finding out how much Mr. Bunker and Mr. Griggs really know about machinery. The way they both apparently accepted without question the existence of these purely imaginary features convinced me that neither one of them knows anything practical about either the construction or the operation of tractors. In addition, I was now convinced that Mr. Griggs is a monumental and egregious liar. All this to some extent explained the effectiveness of Mr. Griggs' sales talk. We all know to what heights of eloquence a salesman can rise when he is hampered neither by facts nor information. And the eloquence is doubly convincing when the prospective purchaser is equally ignorant. Having sized up Mr. Bunker and Mr. Griggs in this keenly analytical manner, I was now ready to make a definite proposition.

"Mr. Bunker," I said, "if you are going to have a competitive Earthworm–Goliath demonstration, I hope you will have it right away. This would be better for me, because I would like to clean up this deal before next week when I have to leave for the north. And it would also be better for you, Mr. Bunker."

"How so?"

"I do not think it is safe, Mr. Bunker, for you to depend any longer on that rickety wooden bridge which seems to be the only way of driving over here to the island. It may collapse and fall into the water at any moment. Furthermore, the timbers look as if they had been treated with some preservative like oil or creosote. This has undoubtedly made the bridge highly inflammable. It might easily catch fire from a carelessly thrown match or cigarette and be completely destroyed. Without that bridge, your hotel business would be in a bad way, wouldn't it?"

"It sure would," said Mr. Bunker.

"Then you ought to build your new causeway at once."

"That bridge has been there a good many years," said Mr. Bunker. "I think I can risk it for a few weeks more."

Naturally I was disappointed. But I don't like to argue with a customer. So I merely said, "It has been nice meeting you, Mr. Bunker. Any time you want a demonstration just notify the Earthworm dealer in Tampa. He will send down the necessary equipment. I'll try to be here myself, but I can't be sure. I am now leaving for Tampa. Goodbye and good luck."

"Goodbye and thanks for coming," said Mr. Bunker.

Mr. Griggs smiled a rather smug smile but said nothing.

I returned to the parking lot. As I climbed into my car, I noticed Mr. Griggs walking down to a small casino on the shore where they apparently serve cocktails and light meals. It looked as if he might be planning to stay on at the island. If so, he would bear watching. I decided to change my plans.

I removed my suitcase from the luggage compartment and walked up to the hotel. I slipped the room clerk a ten dollar bill and asked that I be given a room next to Mr. Griggs. The clerk was happy to oblige.

"Don't tell him I'm here," I said. "Don't tell anybody. I want this to be a surprise."

"Yes, sir," said the clerk.

By the time I was installed in my room—which is on the second floor—it was six o'clock. I ordered my dinner sent up. And after eating it I started writing this report—using a pencil, rather than my portable typewriter, so as not to make a lot of noise which might disturb guests in adjoining rooms.

And this consideration for the rights of others has brought me some very interesting results. At about eight o'clock, just as I finished writing the previous paragraph, I heard someone entering the next room. Then, through the thin partition, I heard the voice of Mr. Orville Griggs. He was speaking in tones that were perfectly clear in the dead silence which then prevailed, but which would have been completely inaudible if I had been clattering away on my typewriter.

It is not my practice, of course, to eavesdrop on other people's conversations. But in this case I could not help overhearing. And what I heard was most illuminating. Mr. Griggs was putting through a long distance call to the Goliath tractor dealer in Tampa.

"Is that you, George?" he said. "Well, this is Orville Griggs. I'm at Happy Island. I have a swell chance to get ahead of the Earthworm people and put on a demonstration of causeway-building for Mr. Bunker. But I've got to hurry. I want you to send down a 15 ton Goliath tractor and a wheel scraper right away. And send a good operator. You can't get hold of anybody tonight? All right, have him start first thing in the morning. I'll be expecting the machinery and the operator by the middle of tomorrow afternoon."

Following this conversation I heard the door of the adjoining room open and close. I opened my own door a crack, and saw Mr. Griggs disappearing down the hall. Cautiously, I followed. He descended the stairs, slipped out a side door, and walked down the road toward the wooden bridge. As it was a reasonably dark evening, with a brisk wind rustling through the palm trees, I was able to sneak along a few hundred feet behind Mr. Griggs without being either seen or heard.

I watched his shadowy figure as he ducked into a clump of

bushes and then emerged with two five-gallon cans. After pouring the contents of one can on the wooden floor of the bridge, he disappeared underneath the structure with the other can. A couple of minutes later he came out and started hurrying back toward the hotel. I shrank back behind a tree to let him pass, and then cautiously approached the bridge to see what he had been doing. Just as I reached it, there was a sudden burst of flame, and almost at once the entire structure was burning furiously.

I rushed toward the hotel yelling: "Fire!" The guests started pouring from the front door. A fire hose was run out from the hotel, but it was too short. A bucket brigade was formed, and soon a fire engine arrived on the mainland at the far end of the bridge.

But it was too late. The fire, fanned by the wind, had too much of a head start. And in a surprisingly short time the ancient bridge was a total loss.

As we struggled back into the hotel lobby, Mr. Orville Griggs made a sudden and dramatic appearance. Addressing Mr. Bunker and the assembled guests and members of the hotel staff, he spoke as follows:

"I have good news for you. None of you are going to be marooned here with your cars. Nor will it be necessary for you to risk your valuable machines by attempting to ferry them to the mainland on dangerously-improvised barges, rafts or makeshift ferry boats. I have just been talking by long distance telephone to the Goliath tractor dealer in Tampa. He is sending us a demonstration Goliath tractor equipped with a wheel scraper. This incredibly efficient machinery will arrive tomorrow afternoon and start work at once. By the end of the next day we will have a solid causeway of ample width leading from the island across the mangrove swamp to the mainland. It will then be possible for guests to arrive and depart with their cars. And it will be possible for Mr. Bunker to bring in his supplies and transact his business in a normal manner."

These remarks were greeted by hearty cheers from the audience, and Mr. Bunker rushed forward to congratulate the smug-smiling Mr. Griggs.

All this time I had been lurking inconspicuously in the rear of the crowd—biding my time. Obviously, Mr, Griggs had not noticed me, and supposed that I was miles away. This meant that he had a very disagreeable surprise in store.

I waited until Mr. Griggs retired to his room. I then knocked on his door. When he opened it, I stepped inside and closed the door behind me. I fixed him with a stern and hostile glance, pointed an accusing finger directly in his face, and spoke in severe and impressive tones. "Mr. Griggs," I said, "your crimes have been discovered, your misdeeds have been found out, your devious deceptions have been unmasked, and retribution is at hand!"

For a moment Mr. Griggs was speechless with astonishment. His face—either actually or in my imagination—turned pale. And when he finally spoke it was in weak and trembling tones.

"I thought you had gone back to Tampa," he said.

"I changed my mind," I said. "I decided to keep an eye on you. And it's a good thing I did."

"I don't know what you're talking about, Mr. Botts."

"Oh, yes, you do. I have definite evidence that you set fire to the bridge. You burned it down on purpose."

"You're crazy," he said. "Why would I do a thing like that?"

"The motive," I said, "is obvious. You thought I had gone back to Tampa. You thought you had the field to yourself—for the time being. So you decided to demonstrate your miserable Goliath, and put over a sale before I found out what was going on."

"What's that got to do with burning down the bridge?"

"You know just as well as I do, Mrs, Griggs. In the first place, you wanted to create a disaster so you could rescue Mr. Bunker and thus gain his undying gratitude. In the second place, you wanted to set up a situation where Mr. Bunker would let you put on your demonstration in a hurry—without waiting till I could get here with an Earthworm."

"It's a very pretty story, Mr. Botts. But nobody would believe it. You have no proof."

"I have plenty of proof, Mr. Griggs. I occupy the room next to yours. I heard you telephone to Tampa and order a tractor and scraper sent down here. And you did this before the bridge burned—not after. This proves you had everything planned ahead of time. And that's not all. I followed you down to the bridge. I saw you set it on fire."

"You can't prove it," said Mr. Griggs weakly. "You can't even prove that you were down at the bridge."

"I can prove it very easily, Mr. Griggs. I was the man that discovered the fire. I spread the alarm. At least half a dozen of the hotel guests can testify under oath that they saw me running from the bridge toward the hotel shouting 'Fire!' So you see, Mr. Griggs, I've got you right where I want you. I have enough evidence to convict you of the crime of arson and send you to jail for many years."

"You mean you're going to call in the police?"

"That all depends on you," I said. "If you get away from here and stay away, I'll keep quiet. Otherwise, I'll tell my whole story to Mr. Bunker and to the police. Think it over."

For me this was definitely the high point of the evening. The only trouble was that it did not last. After a short period of hesitation and confusion, Mr. Griggs pulled himself together so rapidly, and came back with such a surprising show of resourcefulness and low cunning that I was the one who began to be confused and uncertain.

"Mr. Botts," he said, "you have built up such a plausible case here that I think I will have to borrow it and use it against you— just the way I have sometimes borrowed some of your best sales talks."

"What do you mean?" I asked.

Mr. Griggs smiled an evil smile. "I am going to accuse you of exactly what you have just accused me of doing. I am going to use a lot of the same details. I might even claim I heard you telephoning for an Earthworm tractor before the fire. And then I can add enough more to my story so that I will have a much better case against you than you could ever hope to have against me."

"But that's impossible," I said. "It was you that burned the bridge down—not me."

"That's your story. But you can't back it up. You can't bring in a single witness who saw me go down to the bridge or come back. But suppose I accuse you of burning the bridge? You told me yourself that there are at least half a dozen people who can swear they saw you running away from the scene of the crime. So I would have a much better case than you, Mr. Botts."

"But you can't do this to me," I said.

"Why not? And that isn't all. It was you—not me—who put up a big argument this afternoon begging Mr. Bunker to have a demonstration right away. It was you—not me—that suggested the bridge might burn down. After I have reminded Mr. Bunker of all this I can explain how you, Mr. Botts, obviously wanted to create a disaster so you could rescue Mr. Bunker and gain his gratitude. I could also explain how you wanted to set up a situation where Mr. Bunker would let you put on your demonstration in a hurry."

"This is absurd!" I said. "You can't possibly be planning to accuse me of a crime that you know very well you committed yourself!"

"That all depends on you," he said. "If you get away from here and stay away, I'll keep quiet. Otherwise, I'll tell my whole story to Mr. Bunker and to the police. Think it over."

For me this was definitely the low point of the evening. And the more I considered the situation, the more I came to realize that Mr. Griggs had me. At the moment I could not think of any way to come back at him with any show of resourcefulness or low cunning.

"Very good, Mr. Griggs," I said, "I will get away from here first thing in the morning—or even sooner. Goodbye."

I came back here to my room where I have been working on this report. I have given you a full account of the situation, partly—as I explained in the beginning—to let you have the straight story before you hear any inaccurate rumors—and partly to clarify the situation in my own mind.

I am happy to report that I have now reached a few tentative conclusions. In my estimation—and I am a good judge of men—Mr. Griggs is a very reckless character. If I make any move to influence Mr. Bunker, or even if I fail to leave this place by to-morrow morning, I am certain that Mr. Griggs will accuse me of burning down the bridge. In that case I would be compelled—in my own defense—to accuse him of the same crime. Presumably neither of us would have enough evidence to prove anything, and the situation would degenerate into such a vulgar mud-slinging contest that the gentlemanly Mr. Bunker would be completely disgusted and would refuse to buy either an Earthworm or a Goliath.

I have decided, therefore, to leave here first thing in the morning and go back to Tampa. In the meantime I will try to plan my next move. What I really need is a victory so sensational and so complete that Mr. Bunker will be convinced beyond any possible shadow of a doubt that Alexander Botts and the Earthworm are on the side of the angels and that Mr. Orville Griggs represents nothing but the powers of darkness.

At the moment I do not have the faintest idea how I can accomplish this happy result. So I will assign the problem to my subconscious mind, and turn in for a good night's sleep, hoping that in the morning I may have some bright new ideas.

If you want to get in touch with me, you may address me in care of our Tampa dealer.

Yours optimistically,
ALEXANDER BOTTS.

TELEGRAM
JUPITER ISLAND, FLA. THUR., FEB. 25, 1954

ALEXANDER BOTTS
EARTHWORM TRACTOR AGENCY
TAMPA, FLA.
AM AMAZED AT YOUR MEEK SURRENDER TO GRIGGS, AND YOUR IGNOMINIOUS RETREAT FROM HAPPY ISLAND. YOU ARE HEREBY DIRECTED TO RETURN AT ONCE AND MAKE A VIGOROUS AND WHOLE-HEARTED ATTEMPT TO REGAIN WHAT YOU HAVE LOST, AND PUT OVER THIS IMPORTANT SALE FOR

EARTHWORM. WHAT IS THE MATTER WITH YOU?
HAVE YOU LOST YOUR OLD-TIME COURAGE AND
INITIATIVE?
GILBERT HENDERSON
PRESIDENT EARTHWORM TRACTOR CO.

TAMPA, FLORIDA

Friday, February 26, 1954.

DEAR HENDERSON: Your wire has arrived, and I am disappointed at your misinterpretation of my report. My surrender to Griggs was not meek—it was crafty and deceptive. And my retreat from Happy Island was strategic—not ignominious. When I told you that I was consigning all problems to my subconscious mind, you should have known I was almost certain to come up with an adequate solution by morning.

As a matter of fact, I did much better than that. After only about an hour of sleep, I suddenly awoke with a group of ideas—so brilliant and so promising that I went into action at once. The methods I chose to employ, however, were slightly devious. Although amply justified by the circumstances, they were, in fact, so underhanded that it is doubtful whether they would be approved by anyone with such a matter-of-fact and unimaginative a mind as yours, Henderson. This would be especially true if you are still in as critical and fault-finding a mood as you were when you wrote that telegram.

Such being the case, I will spare your feelings by omitting some of my more crafty and clever preparations, and merely state that my first move, after waking up in the middle of the night, was to get dressed, pack my suitcase, descend to the lobby, and hire a bell boy to row me over to the mainland—where I mailed my previous report to you and then registered at a small hotel not far from the mangrove swamp where Mr. Bunker planned to locate his causeway.

At once I put in a telephone call to the Goliath tractor dealer in Tampa. As I am very clever at imitating other people's voices, I was able to convince him that I was Mr. Orville Griggs, that the demonstration was off, and that he was not to send down any machinery. I then called the Earthworm dealer in Tampa and outlined to him the slightly devious plans which I have mentioned previously.

I then turned in for a good sleep. The next day I had my meals sent up, and sat around, observing what went on out in the mangrove swamp, and awaiting developments.

On Thursday afternoon—yesterday—I finally emerged, and walked down to the edge of the swamp where I found Mr. Bunker leaning against a palm tree and contemplating the landscape.

"Well, well, Mr. Botts," he said. "Where have you been all this time?"

"I've been looking for an Earthworm tractor and scraper," I said, slightly distorting the facts. "Our dealer shipped them from Tampa yesterday so I could use them to demonstrate in competition with the Goliath, but they seem to be lost somewhere between Tampa and here."

"Even if you had been on hand," said Mr. Bunker, "it would have done you no good. The Goliath demonstration tractor arrived yesterday. It has just finished the causeway. And it has done such a magnificent job that I have decided to buy an entire fleet of Goliath equipment. Here comes the machine now."

From out of the swamp there emerged a large and impressive tractor, slightly smeared with mud, but gleaming proudly with its coat of brilliant two-tone blue, and displaying the flamboyant Goliath trademark on its radiator. In the driver's seat was a young and skillful operator. Beside him sat Mr. Orville Griggs. As the tractor stopped in front of us, Mr. Griggs leaped to the ground, gave me a suspicious glance, and then spoke to Mr. Bunker.

"How do you like it?" he asked.

Mr. Bunker grasped him enthusiastically by the hand. "I congratulate you!" he said. Then, pointing to the tractor, he announced, "That is the kind of machine I am going to buy."

Mr. Griggs smiled triumphantly. "This particular machine is a demonstrator," he said. "It will be returned to our dealer. But within one week I will deliver to you an entire fleet of beautiful brand-new Goliaths."

Note: This was the moment for which I had been preparing. As long as I could not convict Mr. Griggs of the crime which he had actually committed, I had decided it would do just as well to rig up some evidence that would prove him guilty of an entirely different crime which he had nothing to do with at all. And the fact that both Mr. Bunker and Mr. Griggs are completely ignorant of tractors made this absurdly easy for an expert like myself.

I stepped forward and addressed Mr. Bunker in a quiet and almost apologetic tone of voice. "I hate to interrupt you," I said. "And I hate to bring you bad news. But I feel it is my duty to warn you that you may be making a serious mistake in buying machinery from Mr. Griggs here."

"Mistake? How could I make a mistake in buying any such wonderful machine as this?"

"The machine seems to be all right," I said. "What I am talking about is Mr. Griggs. He is not the kind of man you ought to do business with. He is dishonest. He is a crook."

Mr. Griggs reacted exactly as I expected. "I am not a crook!" he yelled. "I didn't do it. It was Mr. Botts that did it."

"Did what?" asked Mr. Bunker.

"Burned down that bridge," said Mr. Griggs.

"Wait a minute," I said. "I'm not talking about the bridge. I'm talking about this tractor here. And I accuse you, Mr. Griggs, of dishonestly and deceptively putting on a demonstration with a special high-grade machine. On the strength of this demonstration you were hoping to persuade Mr. Bunker to sign a large order and then you were going to ship him a lot of entirely different, low-grade, Goliath tractors."

"You're crazy," said Mr. Griggs. "How can this machine be any better than the machines we would ship Mr. Bunker? All Goliath tractors are made in the same factory. They are all the same quality."

"Sure they are," I said. "But this is not a Goliath. It's an Earthworm." I climbed up onto the machine (which our Tampa dealer, following my instructions, had painted blue and shipped down the day before). I tore off the big Goliath trademark (which our dealer had fastened on) revealing the word Earthworm, cast in the metal of the radiator header.

"You see what I mean," I said. "Mr. Griggs has actually had the effrontery to disguise this Earthworm—"

"I did not!" said Mr. Griggs. "Where's that operator? He can tell you I don't know anything about it."

The operator had disappeared. (Presumably, following my instructions, he was on his way back to his regular job at the Earthworm Agency in Tampa.) At this point, our Tampa dealer arrived and introduced himself.

"That's my tractor," he said. "Somebody stole it yesterday morning, and painted it blue and brought it down here."

"I did not!" shouted Mr. Griggs. "I never stole it! I never painted it blue! I don't know anything about it! I thought it was a Goliath all the time!"

"Mr. Griggs," said Mr. Bunker, "you can't expect me to believe that any tractor salesman would be so ignorant that he couldn't tell the difference between his own machine and another make— regardless of paint and trademarks. You are obviously a fraud, Mr. Griggs. You and I are through."

"And that's not all," said our dealer. "If you are not out of town within one hour, Mr. Griggs, I will call the cops and have you arrested."

Mr. Griggs protested. He shouted. He whined. He even repeated his story that I had burned down the bridge. But by this time he was so thoroughly discredited that Mr. Bunker paid no attention to him. And finally he gave up, drove his car across the new causeway and disappeared. Soon after, the dealer and I drove back to Tampa—where I have been writing this report and where the dealer has been working on the details of a greatly enlarged Earthworm order which Mr. Bunker has already signed.

Cordially,

ALEXANDER BOTTS.

Botts and the Daredevil Driver

EARTHWORM TRACTOR COMPANY
EARTHWORM CITY, ILLINOIS
OFFICE OF GILBERT HENDERSON, PRESIDENT

Friday, January 31, 1958.

Mr. Alexander Botts,
Sales Manager,
Earthworm Tractor Co.
Earthworm Tractor Agency,
San Angelo, California.

DEAR BOTTS: I need your help. While you are in San Angelo, I want you to call on Mrs. Hortense Pettibone, president of the Pettibone Manufacturing Company, and persuade her to sign the enclosed contract. This is a matter of vital importance to our company. The facts follow.

You are, of course, aware that we have recently shipped to a number of our dealers advance pilot models of Earthworm tractors equipped with our recently developed system of electric finger-tip controls. You have received complete descriptions of these controls, and you have been advised that our production department has promised an ample supply in the very near future.

It now appears that a serious bottleneck has developed. The new controls require a very special type of patented small-size planetary gears made only by the Pettibone Manufacturing Company of San Angelo. We had understood that we could acquire exclusive rights for these gears. But last week Mrs. Hortense Pettibone, who has recently inherited control of the company from her late husband, wrote me an angry letter accusing the Earthworm Company of being dishonest and untrustworthy, and threatening not only to break off relations with us but also to sign an exclusive contract with our competitors, the Behemoth Tractor Company, who are also developing a system of finger-tip controls in direct imitation of our own.

Nobody here at the factory has any idea as to what may be the cause for Mrs. Pettibone's astonishing outburst. But we all agree that if she carries out her threats it will give the Behemoth Company a considerable advantage over us.

Under the circumstances, I feel that a personal interview with Mrs. Pettibone is indicated. The chief engineer of the testing division of our experimental department, Mr. Cornelius Northcraft, who has been working on these controls, plans to fly out to San Angelo within a few days. When he arrives, I want the two of you to call on Mrs. Pettibone and make every effort to persuade her to sign the contract—which gives us exclusive rights to the special gears for five years. Mr. Northcraft is not much of a public-relations man, but I want him with you to discuss any technical points that may come up.

With all best wishes,

Most sincerely,

GILBERT HENDERSON.

SAN ANGELO, CALIFORNIA

Monday, February 3, 1958.

DEAR HENDERSON: Ever since I arrived in town this morning I have been so busy I have hardly had time to read my mail or catch my breath. When I called on Ted Smith, our local dealer, I found him in a state of such complete despair that I had to bend every effort to cheer him up.

"What seems to be the trouble?" I asked.

He took me over to the window of his office, and we looked out. On his lot were parked dozens of Earthworm tractors, scrapers, graders and even power shovels.

"From your reports," I said, "I had gathered you have a big inventory—mostly equipment you had to repossess."

"That's right, Mr. Botts. Two thirds of what you see there is what I had to take back from a contractor who went busted. From this distance it looks like new, but that's just because I've put it in shape and painted it up."

"It is always distressing," I said, "to have to repossess stuff. But there is no sense in crying over milk that has spilled over the dam. You'll just have to sell this equipment to somebody else. Do you have any good prospects?"

"Yes, Mr. Botts. One of our local contractors, Joe Parker, has just bid in a big irrigation-ditch job. He will need to buy a lot of machinery. But he doesn't want what I've got here."

"Why not?"

"He was in here yesterday, Mr. Botts. He said the Behemoth tractor dealer had been after him and had promised to demonstrate for him day after tomorrow a Behemoth tractor equipped with their new finger-tip controls. This sounds so good to him that he has practically decided to give the business to Behemoth."

"Listen," I said, "the new Earthworm system of finger-tip controls is so far superior to Behemoth that there is no comparison. Several weeks ago we shipped you a pilot model, and we sent you a booklet explaining everything. Has this stuff arrived?"

"Yes. I have the machine. I have the booklet. And I have located a young man right in town here who says he has recently worked for the Earthworm Tractor Company at Earthworm City. He understands about these new controls, and he has offered to give a demonstration. But all this will do me no good."

"No good!" I said. "This is the answer to your problems. All you have to do is demonstrate this new machine to your friend Joe Parker. He will at once recognize the superiority of our carefully engineered finger-tip controls over the hastily thrown-together Behemoth imitations. And he will buy Earthworms."

"Yes, he'll buy a lot of brand-new Earthworms, which will be fine for the Earthworm Company, but it won't help me in selling all this equipment I have on hand. You have no consideration for us dealers. You ought to let us get rid of our old stock before you make it obsolete by coming out with fancy improvements."

"Ted," I said, "have you read the booklet we sent you—the one that tells all about these new controls?"

"I haven't had time."

"That's no excuse," I said. "All communications from the Earthworm Tractor Company are important. You should read them the instant you receive them. And I have news for you. On page 27 you will find a statement explaining how these new controls can be installed, at a very reasonable cost, on our older machines."

"Say! Maybe you've got something."

"Of course I have. And we had better get busy right away. Where can I find this contractor, Joe Parker?"

"He's probably in his office, two blocks down the street."

"All right," I said, "I'll call on him right away and arrange for a demonstration. In the meantime, you had better get after that operator. Have him give the new tractor a workout and tune it up."

I walked down the street, called on Mr. Joe Parker and gave him such a lucid and fascinating description of our fingertip controls that he became definitely interested. He said he would be delighted to attend a demonstration on Wednesday morning.

When I got back to Ted Smith's establishment I noticed a young man with red hair climbing into the driver's seat of one of the tractors parked outside Ted's office window. I recongnized at once that this was the machine with the new controls.

"I suppose," I said to him, "that you are the operator who has been hired for the demonstration day after tomorrow?"

"Yes," he said. "I was just trying to figure out how these controls work."

"You mean you've never driven one of these machines before?"

"Oh, I've driven plenty of tractors. And when I was working for the Earthworm Company somebody explained about the new finger-tip controls. So, even though I have never actually driven one of these things, I know enough to get by."

"Wait a minute," I said. "Maybe you'd better not drive that machine."

"I don't know who you are," he said, "but I'm not working for you. I was hired by Mr. Smith, and he told me to warm up this tractor. So that's what I'm going to do. I just love to drive tractors. I love to do stunts with them. Stick around and I'll make your hair stand on end."

He stepped on the starter and pushed a few of the little control levers. The big machine went roaring off across the lot, made a quick hairpin turn and came back so fast I had to duck around a corner of the building to keep from getting run over. The next time I looked, the machine had just climbed over a pile of timbers and started a series of wild loops and turns. The young man was having trouble with the controls. He yanked the levers this way and that, but only succeeded in heading for the big plate-glass window of Ted Smith's showroom. With a final frantic heave he pulled out by the roots the whole bracket with all the little levers. This broke several of the cable connections and stopped the engine. The tractor hit the plate-glass window with a mighty crash and stopped with its front end about two feet inside the showroom.

Ted Smith and several of his mechanics came rushing out just as I yelled at the operator, "You are fired!"

He got down off the tractor. "It was not my fault," he said. "How can I steer the machine when those controls are so weak that they just fall apart?"

"You are fired," I repeated. "I ought to call a cop and have you put in jail. But I haven't time to bother with you. So you can just get out of here and never come back. We'll send you a bill for the repairs later on." I turned to Ted Smith. "Do you agree with me?" I asked.

"Absolutely," he said.

The young man departed. We examined the machine. Ted Smith's chief mechanic assured us he could reconnect the cables and fasten the bracket back in place within a couple of hours. I suggested that he build up the bracket and its fastenings with his arc-welding set, so that it would be strong enough to withstand almost any kind of jerk or shock. The chief mechanic agreed to do this. Ted picked up the telephone to order a new pane of glass, and I came back to the hotel here.

After a hearty lunch, I have been spending the afternoon writing this report. Ted has just telephoned that the tractor is in perfect running order once more, so I can look forward to day-after-tomorrow's demonstration with the greatest confidence.

Incidentally, the situation is so favorable that I almost have a feeling it cannot last.

Yours,

ALEXANDER BOTTS.

P.S. Later. I regret to report that truer words were never written than the last line of my letter. Just after signing my name, I happened to put my hand in my pocket and found a number of letters which Ted Smith had handed me upon my arrival in his office, but which I had been too busy to open. One of these letters was from you, including the gear contract, and requesting me to call on Mrs. Hortense Pettibone.

I got busy at once. I found Mrs. Pettibone at her home. She turned out to be an elderly lady, possibly as much as eighty years old, but very energetic, hale and hearty. She is just the kind of person I know how to handle, provided I have half a chance. In this case, however, I had practically no chance at all. As soon as she heard I was from the Earthworm Tractor Company she launched into a veritable tirade of abuse, repeating the remarks you quoted in your letter and adding many more. When I refused to fight back and merely listened with patience and sympathy, she gradually quieted down and finally asked if I had anything to say for myself.

"If you'll start at the beginning and tell me all the facts in this case," I said, "perhaps we can accomplish something constructive."

"All right, Mr. Botts. I have a grandson whose name is Roscoe Pettibone. He has recently completed two years' service in the Army, and he was very much disappointed because he was assigned to the infantry. What he is really interested in is machinery—especially tractors."

"Very commendable, indeed," I said.

"Exactly, Mr. Botts. He came home several weeks ago and then left for Earthworm City to apply for a position."

"Was he successful?"

"Yes—or so he supposed. That was before he found out that the Earthworm Company is controlled by a lot of liars."

"Exactly what happened?"

"He was hired by a smooth-talking character who bore the title of assistant sales manager. It seems the sales manager himself was off on a trip somewhere."

"Go on."

"So the assistant sales manager took on Roscoe as a trainee, and he made all kinds of rosy promises. Roscoe was to work in various departments of the company so as to learn the business. As he learned, he would be gradually promoted in the sales department until he reached a position of real importance with a salary in keeping with his very real abilities. I hope you realize, Mr. Botts, that my grandson is an unusually capable young man."

"I am sure of it, Mrs. Pettibone."

"Roscoe's first assignment with the Earthworm Company was on the demonstration farm. This is a place where they take prospective purchasers and distinguished guests to let them see Earthworm tractors and other equipment actually working. Roscoe was given a job driving a tractor, and he was very happy. He just loves to drive tractors, and he is very good at it. He drives with a great deal of style and dash. There is nothing wrong with that, is there?"

"Certainly not," I said. "I always like to see an operator with style and dash."

"They don't seem to appreciate it at Earthworm City, Mr.

Botts. After only three days, that assistant sales manager went back on his solemn promises and for no reason at all ordered my grandson to get out."

"He fired him? And gave no reason?"

"He gave no reason that made any sense. It is true that Roscoe had run into a little bad luck. In his efforts to put on as good a demonstration as possible and show off the tractor to greatest advantage, he had perhaps driven a little too fast and a little too close to some of the other equipment. He sideswiped a couple of other tractors and a blade grader. On the third day he knocked out a supporting post from under some bleachers which happened to be occupied at the time by a delegation from the British Embassy in Washington. The bleachers came down, but fortunately nobody was hurt. It really was nothing at all, but that assistant sales manager used it as an excuse to get rid of my grandson. So now you can see why I have lost all confidence in the Earthworm Tractor Company."

"I sympathize with your point of view," I said. "On behalf of the Earthworm Company I apologize. A great wrong has been done your grandson. As sales manager of the Earthworm Tractor Company I am overruling my assistant and hiring back your grandson."

"And I suppose you want me to agree to furnish my gears exclusively to the Earthworm Company?"

"If your grandson works for Earthworm, you wouldn't want to sell your gears to Behemoth, would you?"

"But how do I know you won't fire my grandson again?"

"Please believe me, Mrs. Pettibone. I would never even dream of firing your grandson."

The door opened and in came the same redheaded young man who, earlier in the day, had driven the tractor through the plate-glass window. "Hello, grandmother," he said. "I've decided to leave for Chicago in a few days to apply for a job with the Behemoth Company."

"This man here," said Mrs. Pettibone, "says you can have your job with the Earthworm Company back again if you want it."

"Not a chance," he said. "I wouldn't work for Earthworm

again if they came crawling to me on their bended knees. I've just had another fight with them."

"What do you mean?"

"The Earthworm dealer here in town offered me a job driving one of his tractors in a demonstration. So I went around this morning, and I hadn't been there ten minutes before some guy from the factory arrived and fired me."

Roscoe took a long look at me. "And here," he said, "is the man that fired me!"

I will have to admit that for once in my life I was momentarily speechless. Mrs. Pettibone glared at me. "Mr. Botts," she said, "is this true? Did you fire my grandson this morning?"

"I guess maybe I did."

"And that's not all," said the young man. "He insulted me. He threatened to call a cop and have me put in jail."

"I see," said Mrs. Pettibone grimly.

"I can explain the whole thing," I said.

"I do not wish to discuss the matter," said Mrs. Pettibone. "I am through forever with you, Mr. Botts, and with the Earthworm Tractor Company. You will get out of here at once, or I will call my butler and have you ejected."

Being a very good judge of people, especially hot-tempered old ladies, I realized that Mrs. Pettibone was in no mood to listen to explanations, no matter how reasonable. I decided to depart as pleasantly as possible, thus paving the way for further discussion at a more auspicious time.

"Well, Mrs. Pettibone," I said, "it has been nice meeting you. I only hope you have enjoyed our little chat as much as I have."

In closing I will admit that I have no idea what my next move will be. Consequently, following my usual habit when confronted with a difficult problem, I will consign the entire matter to my subconscious mind, and after a good night's sleep I am almost certain that I shall think of something interesting.

With all good wishes,

Most sincerely,

ALEXANDER BOTTS.

TELEGRAM
EARTHWORM CITY, ILL., FEB. 5, 1958

ALEXANDER BOTTS, SAN ANGELO, CALIF.
YOUR LETTER RECEIVED. ANY ATTEMPT ON YOUR PART TO NEGOTIATE FURTHER WITH MRS. PETTIBONE WILL OBVIOUSLY MAKE MATTERS WORSE. CORNELIUS NORTHCRAFT OF THE TESTING DIVISION OF OUR EXPERIMENTAL DEPARTMENT PLANS TO ARRIVE IN SAN ANGELO SOMETIME TO-DAY. LET HIM HANDLE EVERYTHING.

GILBERT HENDERSON

SAN ANGELO, CALIFORNIA
Wednesday evening, February 5, 1958.

DEAR HENDERSON: You will probably remember that when I mailed you my report last Monday evening I was planning to refer to my subconscious mind the various problems which confronted me, hoping that after a good night's sleep I would awake with a complete solution for everything. Strangely enough, when I awoke on Tuesday morning I was completely uninspired. I had no solution for anything. I therefore spent most of Tuesday in a state of meditation, and early in the evening I had the sudden inspiration I had been waiting for.

I called young Roscoe Pettibone on the telephone. "I have been told," I said, "that you are planning to go to Chicago to apply for a position with the Behemoth Tractor Company. I thought you might like to know that a Behemoth tractor salesman has arrived in town with one of his machines, which he plans to demonstrate tomorrow. If you get in touch with this salesman and assist him in the demonstration, he might put in a good word for you with the home office."

"Thank you," said young Roscoe. "Who is speaking, please?"

I mumbled a few syllables so indistinctly that he could not understand and then hung up.

The next morning—today—Mr. Cornelius Northcraft, the engineer from the testing division of our experimental department, arrived. I at once explained to him that in order to persuade Mrs. Pettibone to sign the contract it might be necessary to give her grandson a job with the Earthworm Company. "I tried to hire him myself," I said, "but for some reason he had taken such a strong dislike to me that he refused. That means you will probably have to hire him in your testing division."

Unfortunately, as you remarked in your letter, Mr. Cornelius Northcraft is not much of a public-relations man. He is one of those austere scientists with a one-track mind who are so wrapped up in the narrow, material aspects of their work that they have no understanding of the larger, human aspects of the business.

"The Earthworm Tractor Company," he said, "employs me for one purpose and one alone—to run the testing division as efficiently and effectively as possible. I never hire an assistant until I have made a thorough investigation to determine whether he has the necessary engineering or mechanical qualifications. It is almost an insult for you to suggest that I hire a completely unknown young man merely to curry favor with his grandmother."

"But we have to have those gears. You know that."

"Certainly," he said. "But we should handle things in a reasonable manner. We should explain to Mrs. Pettibone that there is no logical connection between the contract for the gears and a job for her grandson. As soon as she understands this, we can talk business in a rational manner."

"Maybe so," I said. "But right now it is time for that demonstration."

We called at Ted Smith's office, where he handed me your telegram. Then we all went to the vacant lot next to Joe Parker's office. One of Ted's regular mechanics was on hand to drive the Earthworm with the finger-tip controls. Also on hand was the Behemoth man with his tractor equipped with its own finger-tip controls. Assisting the Behemoth man was Roscoe Pettibone. Seated in a car parked at one end of the lot was Mrs. Hortense Pettibone, who had evidently come to observe and admire her beloved grandson. There was also a small group of spectators.

The Earthworm went through its paces first. Ted Smith's steady and reliable mechanic drove the big machine here and there, pulling various pieces of heavy equipment and demonstrating the beautiful action of the finger-tip controls.

Then it was time for the Behemoth to show what it could do—and to provide a crucial test for my plans. So far, everything had gone well. Young Roscoe had followed my suggestion and was actually on hand, and I was reasonably certain about what would happen next. I have often noticed that Behemoth salesmen are great blabbermouths. In order to distract the attention of a possible buyer from the obvious defects of their machines, they keep up a continuous flow of boastful and misleading sales talk. In this case I had every reason to suppose, therefore, that the Behemoth man would stick close to Joe Parker and let Roscoe do the driving.

I was right. The salesman started his harangue, Roscoe climbed into the Behemoth and the critical moment had arrived. As you know, I am a very good judge of character. I had sized up young Roscoe as an undisciplined thrill seeker—the type of witless wonder who never learns from experience. Would he justify my faith in him? For a long moment I held my breath.

Then I breathed a sigh of relief. With a whoop of delight he opened her up and went charging across the lot, knocking over a fuel pump, narrowly missing a half dozen spectators and plowing full speed into a pile of empty oil drums. When he emerged on the far side of the pile, he was almost on top of a stack of drain tile. He gave a mighty heave on the controls and managed to miss the tile. But the Behemoth finger-tip controls were mounted on a bracket obviously copied from the Earthworm. This bracket broke off, the cables came out by the roots and the tractor stopped.

Roscoe was running true to form. But this time it was the Behemoth salesman who blew up. "Look what you did, you idiot! You jackass! You stupid oaf! Get out of here! You're fired!"

Roscoe came back with his familiar excuses. "It was not my fault," he said. "Those controls are so weak that they just fell apart for no reason at all."

At this point I addressed a few words to Roscoe, making sure that Joe Parker heard what I said. "Young man," I said, "you are perfectly right. The Behemoth is obviously a poorly constructed machine. The Earthworm controls would never come apart like that."

By this time Roscoe was mad at everybody. "You're a liar," he said. "The Earthworm controls are no good either."

Before anyone could stop him, he came over and jumped on the Earthworm tractor, placed his hand against the control bracket and shoved with all his strength. Nothing happened. He jumped down, picked up a length of drain tile, jumped back on the tractor and made a swing like Babe Ruth hitting a home run. The drain tile shattered against the bracket—but the bracket held firm.

By this time Mrs. Hortense Pettibone had joined our little group. She was telling the Behemoth salesman what she thought of him.

"How dare you insult my grandson?" she said. "I demand an apology."

"If that's your grandson," said the Behemoth man, "I still say he's an idiot and a jackass and a stupid oaf. I will not apologize—and he is still fired. Nobody would hire a nitwit like that."

"That is not true," said Mrs. Pettibone. "Another company has recently offered him a very fine position. He turned this down because he thought the Behemoth Company would treat him better. But after this disgraceful episode he may change his mind." She turned to her grandson. "I want you to come home with me," she said, "so that we can discuss your future plans."

As Mrs. Pettibone and Roscoe drove away, I realized that the time had come for me to act—and act fast. Leaving Ted Smith to follow up our advantage with Joe Parker—which soon resulted in a splendid sale—I started an even more important talk with Mr. Northcraft.

"Mr. Northcraft," I said, "for a long time I have admired the unusually competent engineers you have in your testing division."

"Thank you," he said.

"And I have also admired your remarkably skillful mechanics and operators. Nowhere else in the world could anyone find a group of men who handle machinery so deftly, so skillfully, so carefully and so safely."

"I am glad you appreciate my men. I am very proud of them."

"And you have a right to be," I said. "I was wondering if you would have any objection if I were to make a slight suggestion—in a constructive spirit, of course."

"Certainly not," he said.

"It is a pleasure," I said, "to deal with a man who is obviously so broad-minded." I then went on to tell him how Ted Smith had hired a young operator and how this operator had ripped the Earthworm controls out by the roots. I explained that it was this same young operator whom we had just seen tearing the Behemoth controls to pieces, but failing to damage the Earthworm controls.

"The reason the Earthworm controls stood up so well," I said, "is that Ted Smith's chief mechanic reinforced the control bracket and thus corrected the weakness it possessed when it left the factory."

"I cannot understand," said Mr. Northcraft, "why this weakness failed to show up in our very exhaustive tests."

"Were these tests conducted by your unusually high-grade mechanics?"

"Certainly."

"Maybe that's the trouble," I said. "A high-grade mechanic usually has a feeling of deep affection for a piece of machinery. He cannot bring himself to abuse it."

"Wait a minute," said Mr. Northcraft. "What you have just told me has suggested an idea. It occurs to me that we have been using high-grade mechanics to test our tractors on the assumption that these machines would always be handled by the same sort of skilled personnel. Then when the machines get out in the field they have to withstand a great deal of abuse from ignorant yokels like the young man we have just been watching."

"Your mind works so fast," I said, "that it's hard for me to keep up with you. But I think you really have an idea there."

"Of course I have an idea. What we need in the testing division is at least one poor operator."

"You mean a sort of careless, accident-prone, wild and woolly individual?"

"That's right."

"Where," I asked, "do you suppose we could find such a character?"

Mr. Northcraft pondered. Then his face lit up with a sudden inspiration. "I've got it!" he said. "I've got it!"

"What?" I said.

"I'm going to hire that young operator. Do you know his name? Do you know how to get hold of him?"

"Certainly," I said.

We called on Mrs. Pettibone and her grandson. She was now so mad at the Behemoth man that she had forgotten to be mad at me. Mr. Northcraft offered Roscoe a job in the testing division. He accepted. Mrs. Pettibone signed the contract giving us exclusive rights to the gears for five years. She was still so suspicious, though, that she put in a clause by which the contract would become null and void if the company at any time terminated the employment of her grandson.

As we walked out, Mr. Northcraft said, "This Roscoe Pettibone must be the same young man you were talking about earlier this morning. You didn't persuade me to hire him just to get on the good side of his grandmother, did you?"

"How could you think that?" I said. "Hiring Roscoe was your idea, not mine."

"Probably you're right," he said.

So you see, Henderson, I am obeying your orders, gladly and willingly. I am letting Mr. Cornelius Northcraft handle everything, including young Roscoe.

Your grateful sales manager,

ALEXANDER BOTTS.

Alexander Botts and his lovely companion bid farewell to the throngs of Earthworm tractor fans everywhere in this promotional movie still from 1936.